Islam and Education
Conflict and Conformity in Pakistan's Madrassahs

Islam and Education
Conflict and Conformity in Pakistan's Madrassahs

SALEEM H. ALI

OXFORD
UNIVERSITY PRESS

Great Clarendon Street, Oxford OX2 6DP

Oxford University Press is a department of the University of Oxford.
It furthers the University's objective of excellence in research, scholarship,
and education by publishing worldwide in

Oxford New York

Auckland Cape Town Dar es Salaam Hong Kong Karachi
Kuala Lumpur Madrid Melbourne Mexico City Nairobi
New Delhi Shanghai Taipei Toronto

with offices in

Argentina Austria Brazil Chile Czech Republic France Greece
Guatemala Hungary Italy Japan Poland Portugal Singapore
South Korea Switzerland Turkey Ukraine Vietnam

Oxford is a registered trade mark of Oxford University Press
in the UK and in certain other countries

© Oxford University Press 2009

The moral rights of the author have been asserted

First published 2009

All rights reserved. No part of this publication may be reproduced, translated,
stored in a retrieval system, or transmitted, in any form or by any means,
without the prior permission in writing of Oxford University Press.
Enquiries concerning reproduction should be sent to
Oxford University Press at the address below.

This book is sold subject to the condition that it shall not, by way
of trade or otherwise, be lent, re-sold, hired out or otherwise circulated
without the publisher's prior consent in any form of binding or cover
other than that in which it is published and without a similar condition
including this condition being imposed on the subsequent purchaser.

ISBN 978-0-19-547672-9

Typeset in Times
Printed in Pakistan by
Kagzi Printers, Karachi.
Published by
Ameena Saiyid, Oxford University Press
No. 38, Sector 15, Korangi Industrial Area, PO Box 8214
Karachi-74900, Pakistan.

For Maria,
For her tireless efforts to educate by example of personal piety

* * * * *

Education is not the filling of a pail but the lighting of a fire.
William Butler Yeats

Education is the ability to listen to almost anything without losing your temper or self-confidence.
Robert Frost

The deeds of any one of you will not save you (alone)...always adopt a middle, moderate and regular course whereby you will attain your target of Paradise.
Prophet Muhammad (PBUH)*

---

*Hadith narrated by Abu Huraira, *Sahih Bukhari, Kitab Ar-Riqaq* (Book 76), Chapter 18, Hadith, no. 470. (Translation by Muhammad Muhsin Khan, Muslim World League, 1980).

CONTENTS

Preface ix
Acknowledgements xiv

1. The Dynamics of Education and Conflict — 1
2. The Madrassah Phenomenon: Origin and Context — 13
3. Empirical Case Analyses: Ahmedpur East and Islamabad Capital Territory — 44
4. Madrassahs and Violence: Is there a Connection? — 68
5. Funding of Islamic Education — 91
6. Madrassahs and Modernity: The Role of Government and other Stakeholders in Conflict Prevention — 104
7. Education, Development and Conflict Prevention: The Role of Foreign Powers — 130
8. Ways to Reconcile Traditional Education with Modernity — 152

Epilogue: Beyond the Red Mosque — 172

Appendices — 181
  1. Data from 1994 Study
  2. Dars-e-Nizami Curriculum of Madrassahs (books and dates of publication under major categories of curriculum)
  3. Administrative Units in Punjab and Rationale for Delineation (particularly of Dera Nawab/Mehrab Wala)
  4. Madrassah Reform Strategy and Budget from the Government of Pakistan
  5. List of Qualitative Interviews Conducted

Bibliography — 197
Index — 207

PREFACE

Islamic educational institutions have come under intense public scrutiny in recent years because of their perceived linkage to militancy. However, much of the research thus far has relied upon anecdotal accounts and investigative journalism. In particular, Pakistani madrassahs (or seminaries) have been the focus of much media coverage. My initial aim in this book was to provide an empirically grounded analysis of madrassahs in Pakistan, thereby informing the larger discussion concerning the role of Islamic education in conflict causality. However, I soon realized that the lessons of Pakistan find connections with experiences among Muslim populations worldwide and it would be worthwhile to go beyond the kernel case and also draw broader historical and political lessons.

As with many social science research endeavours, I began this study as an inductive case analysis of a relatively small geographic region. Given my training in environmental planning and conflict resolution, I was particularly intrigued by the location of Islamabad's main Islamic schools within the 'greenbelt' zones that were otherwise prohibited from infrastructure development. As I looked deeper into the matter, what became apparent was that politics and international conflicts had played an important role in the decisions that led to these structures being situated in environmental conservation zones.

The objectives of the empirical study that initiated this book were three-fold:

1) To document the demographic characteristics of areas in rural and urban Pakistan where madrassahs are prevalent using geographic information systems, thereby providing some context to the rise of this phenomenon.
2) Use the data gathered to address the following research question: what are the linkages between madrassahs and regional conflict, based on the recruitment and career placement dynamics of madrassah graduates?

3) Inform the public debate in Muslim and non-Muslim countries on educational reform initiatives based on a systematic, rather than a symptomatic understanding of the phenomenon.

PREVIOUS DATA GATHERING BY RESEARCHERS IN PRESENT STUDY

The field research team leader for the Pakistani study was, Syed Tauqir Hussain Shah who had authored a study in 1994 as a member of the Pakistani civil service on the rise of madrassahs in Ahmedpur district. He subsequently was a Watson Scholar at Brown University and continued with this research as part of his research programme. This is where I was teaching a class on conflict resolution and met Tauqir and decided to collaborate with him on a larger study. We had access to data sources within the government and the madrassah establishment based on our familiarity with the region that would be very difficult for most expatriate scholars to obtain.

Ahmedpur East subdistrict is in the province of Punjab in Pakistan, a region that has gained notoriety for being a hub of sectarian violence. One of the recently banned religious organizations *Jaish-e-Muhammad* (Army of the Prophet) has its headquarter and a major following in the area. The area is also regarded as a strong-hold of another banned organization *Sipah-e-Sahaba* (Army of Companions of the Prophet). These organizations had very close institutional linkages with the Taliban government in Afghanistan (Rashid, 2000). Workers of these organizations have been charged with targeted violence against western targets in Pakistan after the fall of Taliban. Key members of Jaish-e-Muhammad have been charged with the murder of *Wall Street Journal* reporter Daniel Pearl. The role of terrorist mastermind Ahmed Omar Saeed Shaikh in this tragic case also motivated me to write this book for a larger audience since the question of education has figured prominently in his criminal profile. Frequently the role of Omar Shaikh as a well-educated individual who had gone astray was used by terrorism analysts to dismiss the salience of Islamic education in violence. During my high school years at Aitchison College in Lahore Pakistan, I had known Omar Shaikh before his move towards jihadism. While there is no doubt that Omar Shaikh received a Western education, the culture of Islamist militancy that led him astray was nurtured by systemic roots which had profound connections to institutions of learning and processing information within Muslim societies. A nuanced analysis of the matter was thus in order, starting with a specific case study of a region and building upon that to synthesize historical and sociological arguments.

The growth of madrassahs has also been hypothesized to be a result of deeply embedded poverty in Pakistani society and a breakdown of state services in rural areas. In order to test this hypothesis, a specific analysis was made of madrassahs in Pakistan's capital Islamabad in comparison to data from Ahmedpur. Unlike Ahmedpur, Islamabad is an urban centre and relatively prosperous and rich in terms of economic opportunities and social services like health, education and employment. Yet, madrassahs are also found here and are flourishing.

Islamabad was chosen as the urban case region for studying madrassahs because of the relatively high income and literacy of the area in comparison to Ahmedpur and the influence of immigrants from the Northern tribal areas. Furthermore, Islamabad is the capital and will most likely be the first area where government reforms will be implemented. A sub-division (basic administrative unit in Pakistan) such as Ahmedpur, on average, has a population of approximately one million. Islamabad also has a population of about a million people. We can safely regard the two areas in which the study was conducted as representative samples of rural-urban dynamics.

METHODS AND ANALYTICAL APPROACH

Considering the complexity of the issue, multiple research methodologies were employed to achieve the research and policy objectives of the project.

a) Geographical Information System (GIS) Based Analysis

The geographic location of madrassahs in each of the two study regions were mapped using *ESRI-Arc* software. Data on household income, literacy, environmental factors (agricultural productivity, access to water and food), were overlaid onto the madrassah data set for demographic comparison and to establish any spatial clustering trends.

b) Survey/Primary Data Collection

Primary data collection by establishment surveys of all madrassahs in the two geographical regions–Ahmedpur and Islamabad were carried out. Two groups of field workers/interns collected the data, on a pre-designed form. The field workers were trained in a workshop in order to ensure integrity and uniformity of data. All survey data was collected using interview transcription to avoid comprehension error in linguistically diverse areas.

c) Interviews with other Stakeholders

Structured and semi-structured interviews were held with the following stakeholders: managers and teachers at madrassahs and schools; leaders and officials of local government; alumni of madrassahs and notable donors from the community; senior government officials dealing with the issue at the Federal and Provincial level, in the Ministry of Interior, Home, Education and Religious Affairs; members of the newly established Pakistan Madrassah Education Board and law-enforcement officials who have records of any complaints of sectarian violence from madrassahs. Special arrangements were made for anonymous interviews with the Criminal Investigation Department and Crises Management Cell (departments responsible for anti-terrorism operation) to determine any direct linkages between madrassah graduates and terrorist/criminal activity. (A list of interviews conducted is given in Appendix 5.)

d) Focus Group Discussions

Once data was compiled and analyzed, focus group discussions were held, with leading religious leaders, government functionaries and officials of law enforcement agencies in order to revalidate the findings. The hypothesis that madrassahs are filling the void created by a poor delivery of education and social services has not been addressed in any previous analysis. This important proposition has been further tested through in-depth oral histories and feedback in focus group sessions.

This study acknowledges and respects that madrassahs are a vital institution in Islam and, indeed, in many cases even non-Muslims have sent children to madrassahs because of their high quality of education (such as those in West Bengal, India). However, Pakistani madrassahs have endured much interference from various sources that have led to certain differences in operational style and function as compared to their historical predecessors. Hence a study of their potential linkage to conflict is in order.

I would also like to stress that focusing on madrassah reform does not preclude reform of government and private schools in Pakistan as well. Educational reform as a whole is essential in Pakistan, as in most developing countries. However, prioritizing madrassah reform due to its potential linkage to sectarian violence should be considered.

THE PANORAMIC PURPOSE

The ultimate aim of this study is to prevent the escalation of existing regional conflicts as well as the perceived conflict between Islam and the West, while providing guidance to policy makers regarding their attempts to reform educational institutions. In his recent book Identity and Violence, Amartya Sen (2006) proposes ways of reinterpreting our identities by synthesizing themes of our common humanity. While perhaps too optimistic about human cooperative impulse, Sen suggests that self-denial and discipline might be reconciled between cultures and challenges the notion that the West has been the originator of the so-called 'liberal' values. While in many of my writings I have been critical of contemporary Muslim practices, I do not feel obliged to disavow Islamic traditions or practice as a necessary prerequisite for being an 'educated' individual. For this, I was once accused by a devoutly secular friend of 'running with the hares while hunting with the hounds.' If being conciliatory towards age-old belief systems, and willing to embrace multiple identities is tantamount to being on both ends of the food chain, I am content with my ambivalence. Nevertheless, there is a need to make tough policy choices as we negotiate the limits of tolerance in education throughout this manuscript.

This book will hopefully bring integrative and analytical clarity to the issue of Islamic education–moving away from both the propagandist negative accounts about madrassahs as well as the naively positive accounts that downplay the impact of traditional education on Islamic societies.

ACKNOWLEDGEMENTS

I would like to thank the United States Institute of Peace for funding this research and providing my team complete independence in conducting our work. Due to the political sensitivity of this topic, especially in the Muslim world, it is important to stress that there was absolutely no influence exercised by any US government institution regarding the findings of this study and the book manuscript.

The field team leader in Pakistan Dr Syed Tauqir Hussain Shah deserves foremost gratitude since he managed most of the fieldwork. Dr Shah had the cooperation of numerous governmental and nongovernmental agencies that was essential to the success of our work. The staff and leadership at the various madrassahs and mosques across Pakistan that allowed us access for interviews and survey collection made the study possible and we owe our deepest appreciation to them. Barrister Zafarullah, a madrassah graduate and now a practicing attorney in Islamabad, and Dr Anis Ahmad of the *Rifaa Academy* in Islamabad were particularly helpful in arranging some of these interviews. Special thanks for research assistance provided by Ms Marriam Khan and Mr Khurram Malghani, who also managed the web site for the project. Family support is always essential for such efforts. My mother, Dr Parveen S. Ali, provided substantive comments on the draft and I benefited greatly from her deep knowledge of Islamic tradition and her own experiences as an educator in Pakistan. My sisters, Farzana and Irfana have both been educators in Canada and Pakistan, respectively, and cheered me along the way.

This book is dedicated to my wife Maria, who embodies the challenges and rewards of educating our children to embrace positive human conformity while resisting cultural dilution.

1

THE DYNAMICS OF EDUCATION AND CONFLICT

The educational process in all its forms has generally been regarded as a means of human development from a primitive self-serving existence to one that is focused on collective achievement and the betterment of society. However, this positive assumption about education has been challenged time and again through history as well as through empirical analysis of societal behaviour. Before embarking on a detailed study of Islamic education and conflict, it is important to first evaluate the overall connections, if any, between educational processes in general and conflict. Such a deductive start to this study is aimed at clarifying key causal pathways and keeping at bay preconceived notions about conflict that are so tempting to ponder. Various social scientists and development practitioners have struggled with a useful definition of education. For the purposes of metrics, the United Nations tends to use literacy as a very rough corollary for educational potential while recognizing that this is a very crude and insufficient, perhaps, even misleading metric.

Since this study is interested in ascertaining the linkage between education and conflict, perhaps the most suitable field of inquiry to define educational achievement comes from contemporary psychological research. Most psychologists would agree that educational achievement entails appreciating the consequences of learning and making choices after critical evaluation of options and limitations. Educational achievement also means inculcating a search for truth and developing a curiosity to test beliefs. The ability to learn from personal experiences and life skills are also part of an educational mandate (Life Learning, 2003).

While education has played an essential role in transferring knowledge about natural processes and human ingenuity, thereby leading to improved quality of life indicators in the long-run, its short-term role in conflict development or reduction is less clear. In order to understand any linkage between education and conflict, let us consider some hypotheses that could potentially link these two phenomena.

KNOWLEDGE ACQUISITION AS A MEANS TO AN END?

Educational institutions have certainly played a valuable instrumental role in career development for communities. Utilitarian motives behind educational achievement are the most prevalent in developing countries where education is considered the surest path to economic success. It is thus particularly interesting to consider that religious movements have often dismissed such economic motives in educational achievement. Rather, education is considered a means of understanding scripture in many religious traditions and adherence to worldly strands of knowledge has been generally considered a derivative product of such matters.

The Islamic concept of education also has a holistic vision that is termed *tarbiya* in Arabic and encompasses both substantive learning (*ta'lim*) and also ethical conduct that leads to piety (*ta'dib*). There is an implicit goal of *tarbiya* to achieve success in this world as well as the hereafter.[1] Traditional notions of Islamic education have made a distinction between knowledge of faith and knowledge of the world which has also been institutionalized in different educational aims. Seminaries are means to educate the religious scholars while worldly schools can train other professionals. The question of employability with a limited curriculum is also dismissed by some Islamic scholars on account of a strong fatalistic theology that proclaims that providing livelihoods (*rizq*) is the domain of God. For example, one notable Pakistani scholar Maulana Muhammad Taqi Usmani responded to a query about livelihoods of graduates from religious schools as follows: 'The Creator of the world gives daily bread to dogs, donkeys and swine, so why won't he do the same to those who uphold his religion. So seminaries need not worry about the employment problems of their students.'[2]

Nevertheless, governments are still concerned about livelihood issues and in most countries standardized tests are a means by which all students are evaluated and schools licensed accordingly. However, in some cases, governments may instead address employment concerns by lowering standards for unconventional educational institutions in order to ensure that their graduates can pursue career paths with the mainstream. In Pakistan, the employability of graduates from religious schools prompted the government during President Zia-ul-Haq in the early eighties to equate degrees from religious schools to mainstream institutions without requiring the former to meet the testing standards or curricular framework. Thus educational institutions can be politicized in the context of development and livelihoods justification without appropriate quality control.

Apart from the utilitarian ends of schools, there is also the larger issue of societal cohesion that educational institutions are expected to instill. An appreciation at some level of universal norms of human rights that transcend cultural relativism is now gaining increasing acceptance in many Western countries. Gender equality and the protection of children's rights are perhaps the most fundamental of such global norms that are now trumping cultural exceptionalism. There are other lifestyle characteristics such as homosexuality that are often relegated to the level of 'tolerance' in contemporary educational discourse. Religious organizations are often most strident in advocating independence in their views on such matters and not forcing respect. There has been considerable debate on this matter, particularly between educational sociologists. In responding to the work of J.M. Halstead (2004), who presents a more conservative view on the limits of sex education, Michael S. Merry (2005) asks the question 'should educators accommodate intolerance?' For the purposes of this study, the answer to this question will be dependent on whether such intolerance is linked to active conflict. If the practice in question is not likely to cause any empirically observed social disruption, then the tone of intolerance needs to be considered more acutely to gauge if there is any potential that intolerance about particular groups may lead to conflict.[3] Intervention to prevent prejudicial learning may then be in order. A value-based debate of this kind can only be resolved if certain key assumptions about individual choice versus societal good are addressed through collective learning which includes the acquisition of holistic knowledge but also a wider appreciation for alternative perspectives.

CRITICAL REASONING AND CONFLICT: AN IBERIAN PARABLE

Despite its disciplinary merits, religious education has an inherent propensity to reduce critical thinking since there is a predisposition to ideological beliefs that often discourage questioning of Divine plans. While such tendencies have been moderated at times and science has been allowed to flourish under moderate religious rule, the underlying tension between questioning the unquestionable remains.

Contemporary Muslims usually point to the golden age in Iberia when critical reasoning and scholarship flourished under Muslim rule. They often remind critical Jewish friends of how rabbis and scholars such as Maimonides flourished under Muslim rule. The irony of Iberian Islam is that the tolerance for which the Moors are celebrated today by even the most radical Muslims, was the cause of many schisms in Islam. The egalitarian Muslim rulers of Spain were constantly threatened by militant jihadist forces, which ultimately prevailed in the form of the Al Muwahhid dynasty. Once the Al Muwahhid rulers took control of Cordoba from their more tolerant Umayyad predecessors, Maimonides and his family were given the dire choice of either converting to Islam, being killed or exile. They decided on exile in Morocco.

The Umayyads had been more tolerant and willing to encourage pluralistic expression and education perhaps because of their own dark experiences with fanaticism when the victorious Abassid caliph had killed most of their forefathers in Damascus and moved the caliphate to Baghdad in AD 750. Abd-ar-Rahman, the only surviving prince, had escaped to Spain to establish what became the Muslim caliphate in Iberia based on conquests by Tariq-bin-Ziad and Musa bin Nusair a few decades earlier.

The ruins of the fabled city of Madinat-uz-Zehra—built by Abd-ar-Rahman III, also tell a tale of the tension between the forces of dogmatic belief and critical and artistic creativity within Islam. The city took 40 years to build and at the time of its completion was considered the most splendid in Europe. It included some 400 buildings—inns, schools and workshops, even a zoo. However, the extravagant splendor of this marvelous complex was short lived. In the year 1010 invading forces destroyed and burnt it to the ground. In this case the invaders were Berber Kharijite Muslims.[4]

While King Ferdinand and Queen Isabella, the Christian conquerors of Granada, at least maintained the buildings and gardens of the Alhambra upon conquest, the Berbers completely destroyed Madinat-uz-Zehra. For the next 900 years the ruins remained unexplored. The Cordoban dynasties that built Madinat-uz-Zehra were moderate, tolerant Muslims who encouraged disagreement and critical thought. The fanatics equated the Umayyad tolerance with waywardness that had to be stopped. Many Christian rulers too succumbed to the same purist urge. This led to an almost complete ethnocide of Muslims and Jews on the Iberian Peninsula. The power of divisive dogma is potently exemplified by this parable, but not confined to it. Numerous other examples of dogma stifling critical reasoning can be found in many ideologically-driven communities.

Perhaps the most stark modern-day reminder of an absolutist educational institution that was established to quash critical reasoning was the 'University of Dawah (evangelism) and Jihad' established by Professor Abdurrab Rasul Sayyaf in Peshawar, Pakistan during the mid-eighties (Weaver, 1998). Since 2001, the founder of this tell-tale 'university' that produced terrorists such as Ramzi Yousef has since gone back to Afghanistan and is among the rival warlords vying for supremacy with the Karzai government. The cooptation of the formal educational paradigm of a 'university' is particularly interesting in this case. Similarly, we may find that the stifling of critical reasoning and agenda-driven education can be found in many names and brands and careful extrication of the institution is essential for evaluating its merits. It should be noted here that like Christianity, Islam is a strongly evangelical religion. Even the more enlightened institutions of higher learning such as the Islamic University of Islamabad which have courses as far a field as global trade and environmental law have a 'Da'wah Academy'. This should itself not be a cause for concern, since Islam ordains that there must be 'no compulsion in religion',[5] except when other competitive forces of evangelism are stifled in countries like Saudi Arabia.

In such a vacuum of critical reasoning, the most insidious intervention that can occur is the proliferation of spurious conspiracy theories that masquerade as fact. During the Spanish inquisitions, rumour-mongering and selective anecdotal information was used to falsely incriminate people believed to be harming Christian values. Following the First World War, Germans were questing for answers to why such a war happened and found sanctuary in simplistic explanations being offered. Similarly, in Islamic societies as well, stories of conspiratorial designs by non-Muslims are frequently applied to vilify countries and communities. The psychology of conspiracy theory formation suggests that under conditions where critical thinking skills are poorly developed, communities find simple solutions to complex problems most reassuring.

The power of prejudicial rumours within an educational context cannot be underestimated. For example, the 1968 Kerner Commission on Civil Disorders in the United States estimated that half of all violent race riots during the 1960s were caused or exacerbated by rumours. In recent years the power of rumours within an educational context has gained much greater traction. Peter Knight has observed in his notable work *Conspiracy Nation* (2002, p. 7) that conspiratorial narratives are often framed against globalization and reflect 'the far more scary anxiety that we can no longer tell the difference between Them and Us.' Mistrust as a precursor to conflict can thus remain tacit and an isolated incident can trigger this repertoire of misinformation leading to violence. It is interesting to note that modern educational systems and a culture of questioning that is the hallmark of good science can also be the progenitor of conspiratorial behaviour. Cognitive relativism emanating from good scientific inquiry can thus be misappropriated by the conspiracy theorist as a license for creating alternative and often false narratives. As noted by Fine et al (2005, p. 256), religious groups might often be suited to resist rumour since the 'political plausibility' of any argument is filtered by belief, revelation and scriptural authority. However, they go on to note that 'rumour is often embedded within social institutions,' particularly educational and religious in character. Therefore, if the institution itself begins to espouse such ideologically-driven conspiracy narratives, the credibility factor for the community of practitioners or believers is much higher. The impact of the rumour is thus far more acute in those religious institutions that do not foster a civic culture of critical reasoning.

EDUCATION, SOCIAL NORMS AND COOPERATIVE BEHAVIOUR

Education as a social phenomenon has an ever-expansive definition since any human experience can be claimed to have some level of cognitive impression and learning value. Civil activism is thus believed to have educational merit and has been used at times to trivialize formal education. For example, even the Gandhian approach to education has been described by Lavanam (2005) as: 'There is education in experimentation, there is education in fighting injustice, there is education in preparing an individual to be a better individual and a society to be a better society.'[6] However, the value of formal education and understanding objective reality cannot be underestimated. Often in the context of such formal education, one can find means of curbing deviant behaviour and fostering cooperation between communities. It is important, however, to remember the distinction between formal education and regimented education. The ability to have critical thinking skills is central to a constructive formal education.

There is growing empirical evidence that effective intervention in early educational programmes can also reduce aggression and conflict from endogenous and exogenous sources. Thus a child who may have some predisposition to aggression due to genetic factors or environmental challenges at home (such as aggressive parenting), may also benefit from specific conflict mitigation programmes. In a recent study of classroom-based cognitive behavioural intervention Daunic et al. (2006) tested the ability of such programmes in Florida to: a) increase students' knowledge of social problem-solving strategies and b) improve ratings of student aggression and anger/expression control. The six-step training programme was found to have significant positive impact in both these categories.

The quality of education in the earliest years can thus have a strong influence on the ability of students to manage their anger impulses that are likely to be more pronounced in conflict zones. Children in the Middle East and other high stress environments are thus in even greater need of such programmes. In cases where they might be deprived of such efforts or get negative reinforcement through provocative indoctrination, the impact on conflict escalation can be profound. At the same time, appropriate educational intervention in even the most horrendous conflicts can play an important role in peace-building.

At the heart of such efforts is a genuine peace education curriculum that is culturally appropriate but embraces the universal principles of human justice. UNICEF has defined peace education as follows:

> The process of promoting the knowledge, skills, attitudes and values needed to bring about behaviour changes that will enable children, youth and adults to prevent conflict and violence, both overt and structural; to resolve conflict

peacefully; and to create the conditions conducive to peace whether at an intrapersonal, interpersonal, inter-group, national or international level.[7]

The development of a peace education programme in Sierra Leonne following the civil war in 2004 illustrates the speed with which communities can move towards reconciliation. It is interesting to note that Sierra Leonne has also been linked to various Islamist networks by some investigative journalists (Farah, 2004) and thus provides an added connection for the purposes of this study. Following the war, the largest peace-keeping force in the country following the conflict has also been from Pakistan and there has been considerable cultural exchange between the two countries as a result of their presence. The lessons gained from the peace education programme in Sierra Leonne are thus particularly instructive. Religion was a salient part of the conflict resolution pedagogy in this case and Muslims and Christians worked together to use theology as a means of peace-building (Bretherton et al, 2006).

Contact theory provides some insights on how school settings can be ideal places for approaching intractable conflicts and entrenched prejudices (Allport, 1954). The power of formal education fused with constructive contact techniques in peace-building is exemplified by an educational activist project in the town of Acre, a city with a mixed demographic of Arabs and Jews in Israel. The five-year programme was based on four key themes:

a) Cooperation—maximizing gains for both communities
b) Investigation—relevant moral inquiry of social problems
c) Literacy—respect and empowerment of subordinate groups through information exchange
d) Community—creating a spirit of holistic democratic coexistence

Each of these themes constitutes the acronym CILC, which was how the programme was commonly known in the region. The CILC model emphasized working within and across schools bringing Arab and Jewish educators together for training at all levels. This was followed by very detailed curricular review and amendments where needed. Parents were also engaged as part of the process to ensure that the educational process did not change direction beyond school. In her detailed evaluation of the programme, (Hertz-Lazarowitz, 2004) found that the programme had profound positive impacts on mutual respect and peace-building. Even after the start of the second *intifada*, the principals from Arab and Jewish schools continued to meet. While relations were severely impacted by external political factors, there was an indelible impression that effective peace education made on the community.[8] Through the course of this book we will see how such programmes may be transferable and the impediments to their implementation in some contexts.

SOCIAL MOVEMENTS AND VARIETIES OF EDUCATIONAL INSTITUTIONS

The use of educational institutions for political ends is a well-established tradition across cultures and societies. Exemplified recently by anti-war activism at universities in the West as well as the rise of Marxist movements in schools in South America or the Ayatollah ascendancy at Tehran University, institutions of learning are often places of revolution. Ideas invigorate young minds to action but Alexander Pope's prescient observation of 'a little learning being a dangerous thing'[9] is just as true today. While the independence of educational institutions must be maintained, some level of quality assurance and critical reasoning is also essential to ensure that captive audiences of students are not manipulated. This matter acquires particular potency in American higher education under the life-long tenure system for faculty. There are times when universities are accused of being too insular and professors for not venturing beyond the ivory tower before tenure but perhaps being too adventurous and confrontational after tenure is granted. The relationship between activism and academia is thus quite frayed even within Western institutions (Croteau et al eds., 2005).

The responsibility of educators to inform without provoking societal conflict is also gaining further attention as demonstrated by the case of Colorado Professor Ward Churchill in 2006. His use of defamatory rhetoric towards US soldiers sparked outrage in conservative media outlets and led the university to consider revoking his tenure.[10] In other cases, high school teachers and professors who have certain political views about the Middle East are now profiled as being biased by organizations such as 'Campus Watch'.[11] Interestingly enough, many Muslim students feel that American academia is wary of Islamic learning and even Muslim professors who teach politically sympathetic views on the Middle East are theologically secular. They are quick to compare this phenomenon to scholars of other faiths who might be more publicly faithful. In a recent article in a national Islamic publication, a graduate student from Georgetown University describes the situation as follows:

> Muslim professors can be identified as progressives in that they want to radically change Islam in favour of a 'modern Islam' that is compatible with Western liberalism. Among such professors are expatriates who have particular grudges against their home countries. These trends have led Muslim students to be disillusioned..... and led to the rise of alternative forms of Islamic education that are independent of the university. Muslim students flock to 'deen intensives'; enroll in online courses; attend weekend classes; and occasionally travel overseas to study with traditional scholars (Mirza, 2005, p. 38).

The trend described here is beginning to change as a new generation of Muslim academics reaches the shores of tenure-track positions. Of particular note are UCLA law professor Khaled Abou El Fadl, and Wisconsin law professor Asifa Quraishi who make no apologies for being practicing Muslims while teaching about Islam. However, their task has not been easy as innuendoes have still been hurled against them.[12]

Just as professors may be accused of detachment on the one hand and activism on the other, students are often accused of being too apathetic about the world around them and not being sensitive to global change. In an editorial published in *The Harvard Crimson* in 2004, titled 'Activism in Academia' the staff of this venerable student paper commented that 'the most oft-touted allegations against our generation is that it reeks of apathy. And while we can speak of admirable instances where students at the College defied that accusation, it's certainly true that student activism on some issues—could be stepped up. Students at Harvard must remember that to complain of the status quo is not enough; they must be active in order to effect change.' This feeling is increasingly being echoed by students across the world and has been culminating in events such as The World Social Forum. Regrettably many of these forums have been co-opted by anarchist forces and US-bashing ideologies that detract from any particular problem-solving.

Similar to other social movements, religious motivation has often been linked to violence as well as peace building. Like any powerful human phenomenon, religion can be wielded to either end and has tremendous potential to instill pugnacity as well as cooperation. There are some remarkable stories to be told of graduates of Islamic schools that have been able to bridge their education with Western traditions. Consider the case of Bahtiar Effendy (2003), who started his formal schooling in the Pesantren Pabelan in central Java, Indonesia in the early 1960s. While at this Islamic boarding school, he received an American Field Service scholarship and attended Columbia Falls High School in Montana. Subsequently, he returned to Jakarta for his college degree and then went back to the States for his doctorate at Ohio State University. Following his doctoral degree, Dr Effendi returned to his homeland and joined the faculty of the Islamic State University in Jakarta. Such interactions, while rare, are possible between educational traditions and deserve more careful study and analysis.

This book attempts to consider varieties of educational traditions within Islam and their adaptive strengths and weaknesses within a changing world. What, if any, are the peculiarities of Islamic education that lead commentators to make linkages to political conflict? How might we explain the spectrum of schools that produce culturally distinct but functional members of modern society in some cases while producing dogmatic clerics in others? Are their systemic factors that go beyond individualized variables, such as personality type or access to resources, that need to be considered? The next chapter begins to answer these questions by first considering the most inescapable variables of historical influence from within Islamic tradition as well as external geopolitical pressures.

NOTES

1. Scholar of Egyptian educational reform Timothy Mitchell (1991) has argued that religious disciplines were historically taught as a craft; and also that the use of the term *tarbiya* for human nurture is a neologism in the modern period.
2. Muhammad Taqi Usmani, 2005. *Fazilat-ilm-o-Ulama*. Delhi Farid Book Depot, 1999. Translation quoted by Yoginder Sikand (2005), p. 167.
3. In January 2007, the hiring of notable Muslim feminism scholar and lesbian rights activist Ghazala Anwar to assume the position of dean in the International Islamic University in Islamabad, Pakistan caused much dissent within the student community. The higher education commission initially supported her and in her response to a critical newspaper article Dr Anwar responded with a larger mission

of her willingness to accept this position and move to Pakistan from her permanent academic position in New Zealand as follows: 'This controversy provides us with an opportunity to exercise our conflict resolution skills, to develop rules by which we can discuss and disagree about topics that might be sensitive or volatile, and to resolve the issue in a manner that our relationships are enhanced.' *The News* (Islamabad), 2 February 2007. However, soon thereafter, the student protests became so vitriolic that the HEC withdrew support and Dr Anwar was forced to return to New Zealand.

4. The term 'Kharijite' is used to describe the first fanatical sect of Islam that emerged during the time of the Caliph Ali (the Prophet's cousin and son-in-law). The major schism in Islam between Shia and Sunni occurred over disagreement regarding dynastic succession (preferred by the Shias) to a meritocracy favoured by the dominant Sunni movement. During a battle between Ali and his meritocratic challenger Muaawiya in 656, an arbitration was decided upon which displeased the more puritanical elements in the population. They felt that no compromise was allowable in Islam on matters of principle and sided against both Ali and Muaawiya—hence they were given the name 'Kharijites' (which comes from the Arabic word 'Al-khwaraj, meaning 'those who leave or disagree').

5. The famous Arabic phrase taken from the Qura'an Chapter 2, verse 256: *'La ikraha fi-din.'*

6. Lavanam's talk on All India Radio, Vijayawada on 3 October 2005 at 8.15 p.m.

7. UNICEF Peace education site: www.unicef.org/programme/education/peace_ed.htm

8. A similar programme in which I was involved as co-director in 2004 and 2005 was to use environmental issues as a peace building tool between Middle Eastern populations. The programme was hosted in Toledo, Spain for six weeks in the summer as a symbolic gesture to show that coexistence had historically occurred here between all three Abrahamic faiths. The parent organization of this effort, The University of the Middle East Project continues to operate teacher education institutes for high school instructors from the region. Details at: http://www.ume.org

9. From Alexander Pope's *Essay on Criticism,* published in 1711.

10. The issue of the derogatory comments about soldiers was deemed to be protected under constitutional freedom of speech but the inquiry regarding Churchill was expanded to include allegations of misuse of tribal affiliation and plagiarism. The inquiry has not resulted in any tangible adverse effect on Churchill's career.

11. A project of the Middle East Forum, the campus watch website, provides provocative quotations from university faculty, particularly those condemning Israel. http://www.campus-watch.org

12. Khaled Abou El Fadl is also a member of the US commission on international religious freedom. Interestingly enough, as a practicing Muslim he comes under fire by organizations such as Campus Watch for being a 'stealth Islamist' while also receiving death threats from militant Muslims for his criticism of Wahabbism and the Iranian regime.

2
THE MADRASSAH PHENOMENON: ORIGIN AND CONTEXT

The proliferation of madrassahs or Islamic schools[1] in much of the Muslim World has been noted with particular consternation following the terrorist attacks of 11 September 2001. The perceived linkage between radical Islamic education and militant behaviour against Western interests, has led development agencies and governments to focus their resources on educational reform.

However, there is scant empirical research grounded in rigorous social science on the socio-environmental roots of this phenomenon and its consequences. While the topic has received widespread media coverage and has been discussed within the broader context of radical Islamization, the research has generally been predicated on observational accounts and anecdotes, that range from strongly positive to vehemently negative. Akbar S. Ahmad (2002) regards madrassahs to be a 'cheaper, more accessible and more Islamic alternative to education.' Singer (2002) calls them a 'displacement of the public education system.' Jeffrey Goldberg (2000), even before 9/11/2001, terms them as means of 'education of the holy warrior.' Andre Coulson (2003) refers to madrassahs as 'weapons of mass instruction.' Most consequentially, the 9/11 Commission refers to madrassahs as 'incubators of violent extremism.'

Recently there have also been revisionist accounts of madrassah prevalence that question the sensationalism of some media reports. In an opinion article for the *New York Times* (14 June 2005), Peter Bergen and Swati Pandey have referred to concern over madrassahs as a 'myth'. This assertion is based on a study on the background of seventy-five terrorists behind major attacks on Western targets and concluded that only nine attended madrassahs. Similarly, ethnoconflict psychologist Marc Sageman (2004) suggests that the roots of conflict are not to be found in madrassahs since only 17 per cent of his study sample of terrorists had madrassah linkage. Focusing particularly on Pakistan, Zahab and Roy (2004) suggest that the same conclusion but incriminate the government in distorting education through state-run schools and curricula, (which were revised in late 2006 to respond to such critiques). The travel-writer and historian William Dalrymple (2005) has also taken exception to sensationalism about madrassahs and provided a more humane and nuanced account of madrassahs in South Asia, particularly those in India that have been far more moderate. However, none of these studies focus on sectarian violence nor the linkage to regional conflicts, a differentiation that this study attempts to make. Furthermore, this study has a more expansive view of education that can be incubated in schools or madrassahs but pervades popular culture more widely.

With regard to madrassahs in Pakistan, of particular note has been a controversial study prepared with World Bank funding that questioned the need for such anxiety over madrassahs by providing data that suggested their limited prevalence within the larger context of Pakistani schooling (Andrabi et al, 2005). This study contends that much of the information in reports and government documents, including the 9/11 Commission report of the US government, have largely predicated their estimate of madrassah enrollment on anecdotal accounts. In particular, the study targets the work of the International Crisis Group–ICG (2004) for perpetuating an error in calculation of madrassah percentage.[2] While there was indeed a decimal calculation error in the ICG report, the World Bank study misses the major point that the exact number of madrassahs might not necessarily be consequential in terms of conflict linkages. Tahir Andrabi, the lead author of the World Bank study himself noted that the colonial revolutionary T.E. Lawrence had once spoken of the power of a few committed revolutionaries in Arabia as follows: 'give me 1 per cent of the population and I will give you a revolution.'[3] Nevertheless, I am not suggesting that madrassahs are necessarily revolutionary organizations but that research in this regard should not solely focus on their absolute numbers but on their sociopolitical context. It is, nevertheless, worth noting that official estimates of madrassah numbers have fluctuated dramatically.

Unlike the World Bank study that relied on Pakistan household census data and conducted some of its own household surveys to ascertain from families where they were sending their children for schooling, our study team relied on exhaustive establishment surveys of each madrassah in Ahmedpur and Islamabad. We thus got firsthand information from the schools themselves about enrollment, funding sources and connections with sectarian activity. The usual critique of establishment surveys in this context can be that schools might not provide accurate information about enrolment for strategic purposes of either gaining more government funding or diminishing scale to avoid political suspicion. However, we relied on local staff from villages in the area to conduct the surveys and to provide quality assurance. We also supplemented our quantitative analysis with detailed interviews at the local and regional level with clerics, government officials, madrassah students, researchers from academia, journalists, and representatives from non-governmental organizations. Our aim is to provide an integrative, nuanced and prescriptive analysis that can have greater policy relevance and applicability.

DEFINITIONS

The word 'madrassah' is derived from an Arabic word *darsun* meaning lesson. In contemporary Arabic, the word 'madrassah' means 'centre of learning' (the Arabic plural form is 'madaaris', but for the sake of clarity we will use the English equivalent plural form 'madrassahs' in this manuscript).[4] The Arabic word madrassah generally has two meanings: in its more everyday usage, it means school; and in its secondary meaning, it is an educational institution offering instruction in Islamic subjects including the Qur'an, the sayings of the Prophet Muhammad (PBUH), jurisprudence and law. Madrassahs are in some ways analogous to a seminary in Christian tradition.

Madrassahs generally provide free religious education, boarding and lodging and are in many contemporary cases patronized by low-income families. However, some rich and middle class families also send their children to madrassahs for Qur'anic lessons and memorization where they are usually day students. A madrassah student learns how to read, memorize and recite the Qur'an properly. Madrassahs issue certificates of various levels. A primary or part-time religious school and one focused primarily on Qur'anic recitation and memorization is often referred to as a *Maktab* (derived from the Arabic word for books *kuttab*),[5] and an integrated school with various levels is simply called a *Madrassah*. While the distinction between a maktab and a madrassah may be important in some contexts—often both are affiliated with mosques and religious institutions and may share teachers. What is also significant is that many madrassahs are residential and often these institutions play a more significant role in shaping the personality of students. Our study thus tries to differentiate between residential and non-residential madrassahs where possible. There are of course many regional variations on these differences such as the *Msid* and *Kuttab* Qur'anic schools in Morocco and Northern Africa (Boyle, 2004).

To address the problem of a lack of schools in every village, the government in the mid 1980s came up with the idea of converting some Qur'anic schools into 'mosque primary schools' in the rural areas by adding subjects like mathematics and Urdu that would be taught by part-time teachers in addition to the local imam (mosque leader). The plan faced considerable difficulty as many of the imams themselves had not attended formal schools, and thus were not capable of teaching secular subjects. Some mosque schools did close down, while most are still active and supported by the Awqaf department of the government (that administers religious charitable trusts). At present, there are roughly 25,000 mosque primary schools in Pakistan (Anzar, 2003). However, these mosque schools are not considered madrassahs, though some of them are now transforming themselves into madrassahs for funding purposes.

There are also regional variations in other parts of the Muslim world. It is interesting to note that in many countries, including Egypt and Lebanon, 'madrassah' refers to any educational institute, while in Pakistan and Bangladesh, it commonly refers to an Islamic religious schools (both at the primary and secondary levels) only. For example in Bangladesh, the primary stage of a madrassah is called a maktab or Nurani Madrassah or Furqania Madrassah. There are also the primary education centres giving lessons on reading and reciting the Holy Qur'an are known as Darse Qur'an. Usually the local mosques serve as the centres for primary education for boys and girls of nearby families. The *imams* and *muazzins* of local mosques work as teachers.

The graduating students are called *Huffaz-e-Qur'an* (those who memorize the Arabic text of the Qur'an) or *Qaris* (those who can recite Qur'anic verses with proper Arabic pronunciation); or those with advanced theological training are known as *Ulama* (Religious Scholars) or in South Asian terms often given the title of Maulana.

STUDY AREA SELECTION

Madrassahs are prevalent all across the Muslim world and indeed also in some predominantly non-Muslim countries, especially in Europe and North America. While some social science studies of madrassahs have been carried out in Africa (Brenner 2001), no integrative study of madrassahs and conflict have currently been conducted in South Asia. There is a tremendous need for analysis of madrassahs in Pakistan, due to the proximity to Afghanistan—the focal area of America's 'war on terrorism,' and India's claimed linkage between madrassah graduates and the regional conflict in Kashmir. An understanding of the madrassah phenomenon in Pakistan can thus possibly lead to ways of reducing conflict between two nuclear adversaries or clarifying misconceptions about these social institutions.

While historians differ about the motivation of Pakistan's founder Mohammad Ali Jinnah, regarding the formation of an Islamic state,[6] there is little doubt that contemporary Pakistani identity is anchored in Islam. The conflict in Kashmir is perceived by most Pakistanis to be a continuation of the struggle which led to the creation of Pakistan itself.[7] Indeed, Pakistan was carved out of British India as a homeland for Muslims, and is one of only two countries in the post-colonial world (the other being Israel), to be created solely on the basis of religious identity. The significance of studying madrassahs in Pakistan thus merits specific analysis.

THEOLOGICAL AND HISTORICAL CONTEXT FOR MADRASSAHS

According to early historical accounts, the first formal educational sessions in Islam started at the house of Zaid-bin-Arqam in the valley of the Safa Hills, where the Prophet Muhammad (PBUH) himself worked as a teacher and some of his early followers became his students. After the Prophet's migration to Medina (*hijrah*), a madrassah, namely the madrassah *Ahle-Suffa* was established on a site adjacent to the east of the Prophet's mosque at Medina. Ubada-ibn-Samit was the primary instructor there. Abu Huraira Mu'az-ibn Jabal and Abu Zar Ghifari, two well-known companions (*sahaba*) of the prophet, were among the students. As Islam expanded to other regions of the world (non-Arabic), it became necessary to create uniformity in the teachings of Islam to preserve religious conformity. Henceforth began the tradition of madrassahs worldwide, in order to develop writings and textbooks on *Fiqah* (Islamic jurisprudence), *Sunna* (Prophet's traditions), *Hadith* (Prophet's sayings) and *Tafseer* (the interpretation of the Qur'an).[8]

One of the first known madrassahs is believed to have been established in AD 1005 by the Fatimid caliphs in Egypt, teaching the minority shi'ite version of Islam. It was a fairly well-resourced educational institute complete with a library, teachers for different subjects, including astronomy, architecture and philosophy, and students were provided with free ink, pens and papers. After the Sunni conquest of Egypt, the Shi'ite version of Islam was promptly replaced with the Sunni version. Several Shia manuscripts were destroyed but secular writings on astronomy and other fields of general knowledge were preserved. A number of books were subsequently preserved and taken to Baghdad, where a Seljuk Vizier called Nizam-ul-Mulk bin al-Tusi established the first organized madrassah called the Nizamiyah in AD 1067.

According to Anzar (2003), two types of education were imparted: 'scholastic theology to produce spiritual leaders, and earthly knowledge to produce government servants who would be appointed in various regions of the Islamic empire. Later Nizam established numerous madrassahs all over the empire that provided knowledge in the fields of sciences, philosophy, public administration and governance.' Nizam-ul-Mulk is thus considered to be the progenitor of the Islamic public education system.

Offering food, lodging and a free education, madrassahs spread rapidly throughout the Muslim empire, and although their curricula varied from place to place, it was strongly religious in nature because these schools ultimately intended to prepare future Islamic religious scholars (*Ulama*) for their work.

In spite of the fact that madrassahs during the centuries that followed remained primarily as centres of Islamic education and learning, a large number of them produced distinguished scholars and philosophers who contributed to earthly knowledge as well. *Ijtihad,* or independent thinking, was a notable feature of these madrassahs especially for some in Andalusian Spain which was under Muslim rule for almost 800 years[9]—a much celebrated age for both Islamic and Jewish progress in science, technology and philosophy (Menocal, 2002). Muslim and Jewish scholars jointly pioneered the knowledge of rational thought, mathematics and medicine during this time and this period produced philosophers such as Averroes (Ibn Rushd), the mathematicians

Arzachel (al-Zarqali) and Alpetragius (al-Bitruji), and the physician Avenzoar (Ibn Zuhr). However, while many Muslims nostalgically refer back to these great times, it is important to consider that even then there was considerable dissent between traditionalists and modernists among Muslims as discussed in the previous chapter.

MADRASSAHS IN SOUTH ASIA

At the same time, as Islam spread further east, the Sufi (mystical) order of the Muslim faith were establishing madrassahs in the Indian subcontinent and central Asia, where grammar, poetry, literature, logic, math and other disciplines were being taught with Arabic and Persian being the primary medium of instruction. The first madrassah recorded in South Asian historical accounts was Madrassah Firozi in Multan built by Nasiruddeen Qubacha who was a ruler there (interestingly, this is the largest city near the focal area of the rural case in this book as well). The renowned scholar Qazi Minhaj Siraj (d. AD 1259) took charge of that madrassah in AD 1226. There were two other madrassahs in that period, which are mentioned as Madrassah Ma'zia and Madrassah Nasiriya.[10]

Hakim Sayed Abdul Hayee has divided the changing education system of India into four phases. The below mentioned details are derived from his article '*Hindustan ka Nisab-e-Dars awr us ke Taghaiyurat*' (teaching curricula of India and changes in them) published in monthly *Tarjamn-e-Darul Uloom, Delhi*, (November, December 2000, and January 2001). He had strived hard to find out the syllabi that were taught during different Muslim periods in India. He traced the changes too that took place within due course of time.

First Phase: Stretches from seventh century Hijra to the tenth century. For about two centuries, ten subjects were considered to be high standard education in which seventeen books were taught as a whole. In the beginning, a student was introduced to the Qur'an and Persian. Later he was taught *Sarf* and *Nahwa* (Arabic grammar), Arabic Literature, *Tafseer* of Qur'an (commentary or exegesis), *Fiqh* (jurisprudence or Islamic law), *Usul-e-Fiqh* (principles of Islamic jurisprudence), *Mantiq* (logic), *Kalam* (scholasticism), *Tasawwuf* (mysticism) etc.

Looking at the records of that age it is apparent that *Fiqh* and *Usul-e-Fiqh* were the standard fields of learning. Those who conquered part of Northern India had come from Ghazni and Ghaur—both in

Afghanistan—and the two above-mentioned subjects were on the pinnacle there.

Second Phase: Starts from the beginning of the tenth century *Hijra* when Shaikh Abdullah and Shaikh Azizullah came from Multan to Sultan Sikandar Lodhi. They added some books in Fiqh, Mantiq, Arabic Grammar and *Kalam*, and introduced *Balaghat* (figure of speech) as a new subject in the curriculum of that time. Thus the syllabus altogether comprised nearly thirty books of eleven subjects. In this period Shaikh Abdul Haque Muhaddis of Delhi learnt Hadith in Arabic and tried to introduce Hadith books but he could not gain ground until Shah Waliullah Muhaddis of Delhi (d.AH 1174), came on the horizon.

Third Phase: No sooner did Akbar (AD 1542–1605) sit on the throne that Mir Fathullah Shirazi left Shiraz (Iran) for India. He also made some major additions in the prevailing madrassah curriculum of that time which Ulama accepted wholeheartedly. Shah Waliullah, a student of the third phase, has given details about the books he studied from. According to him, four new subjects Mathematics and Astronomy (fundamentals), Philosophy and *Tib* (medical science) were included in the syllabus besides some books on various subjects mentioned under the first and second phases. The total number of books taught in those times totaled around thirty-eight.

Having studied from the above-mentioned books Shah Waliullah set out for what is now Saudi Arabia, where he completed a specialization course on Hadith study and on his return to India he popularized the study of Hadith in India. From then onward *Sihah-e-Sitta* (six most authentic Hadith books) were added to Indian madrassahs' syllabi. 'Shah Sahib' (as he was commonly known) himself drafted a syllabus but it could not get currency because the centre of Islamic education at that time had been shifted from Delhi to Farangi Mahal of Lucknow.

Fourth Phase: This age is dominated by Mullah Nizamuddin of Lucknow (d.1748). The syllabus that he laid down is named after him as Dars-e-Nizami, a landmark in the history of teaching of Islamic sciences in India. This curriculum laid greater emphasis on the study of logic, philosophy and other sciences and became the most popular curriculum across the Indian subcontinent. While it was revolutionary for its time, the prevalence today of a curriculum that predates the industrial revolution might be deemed anachronistic.

Following the fall of various Muslim empires, some ulama began to disparage earthly knowledge; choosing instead to revive puritanical spiritual knowledge and thus closing doors to independent thinking and reasoning (*ijtihad*). This movement gained momentum in the early eighteenth century under the leadership of the distinguished Delhi scholar Shah Waliullah (1703–62). At the time of the European renaissance, the Muslim education structure was beginning to go into decline and this had an intense effect on the function and philosophy of the madrassahs all over the world. In reaction, many Muslim scholars left the pursuit of rational sciences and followed a survivalist instinct that concentrated completely on preserving the teachings of Islam.

Ironically, madrassahs in South Asia, were at one time considered elite institutions and a certificate of high birth (*sharafatnma*) was often required for enrollment. While the message of Islam was quite egalitarian, there was considerable emphasis in the admission process on family upbringing and training as a prerequisite for being a serious student. The elite status of madrassahs was challenged as the Mughal empire and sultanates began to collapse towards the end of the eighteenth century.

With the advent of European colonialism in South Asia, a 'modern system' of education came to be envisaged as one producing students fit to run the machinery of colonialism, resulting in a strict two category system of education—secular for the rich and elite and religious for the poor. The new western idea of education meant the separation of religion and state which was a direct threat to the Islamic scholars as the new system of governance did not require legitimization through religion.

The colonial authorities at this juncture also tried to co-opt some of the madrassah establishments. Indeed some British leaders were themselves involved in establishing or patronizing certain madrassahs. For example, the Calcutta madrassah was established in 1781 and patronized by the Governor General in Bengal, Warren Hastings.[11] Initial academic accounts of madrassah education by colonial academics were also fairly positive. In particular, a treatise written by the principal of Government College Lahore, G.W. Leitner (a Hungarian orientalist), in 1883 entitled *History of Indigenous Education in the Punjab,* was also quite positive in its description of madrassahs while acknowledging concerns about their career trajectory (Leitner, 1883).

However, overall colonial policy towards madrassahs, especially after 1857[12] was to delink them from mosques—the Anglicists thus were more prevalent than the Orientalists, who wanted some support for indigenous education. Zaman (2002) chronicles some of the colonial accounts in this regard quoting the first Director for Public Instruction of Punjab recording in his memoirs (1858): 'I [have] ordered all village schools to be removed from the precincts of mosques and other buildings of a religious character.... and also directed the disuse of all books of a religious character in these schools.' The ambivalence that characterized this period was also evident in the reform of large madrassahs such as the Madrasa-i-A'zam of Madras (now Chennai) in Southern India.[13]

Apart from some modernist Muslim intellectuals such as Sir Syed Ahmed Khan (1817–98) (founder of Aligarh Muslim University), or Sayyid Amir Ali (d.1928) the theologians of the Indian subcontinent perceived the British system of education as a threat to Islamic identity and, therefore, took upon themselves the task of opposing the British cultural and educational hegemony. There was, however, some disagreement between the scope and breadth of learning and political activism within the madrassah establishment during British rule. Most of the madrassahs followed a curriculum developed by Mullah Nizam Uddin Sihalvi (d.1748) at Farangi Mahal, a famous seminary of a family of Islamic scholars in Lucknow.[14] However, after 1857 there was growing political activism and dissent among religious scholars about the role of madrassahs in Indian society and the struggle for independence.

The Dar-ul-Ulum at Deoband was established in 1867 with two goals in mind: (i) providing a more puritanical interpretation of Islam that would eschew the accretion of other diluting influences such as ritual visits to shrines, (ii) to organize a religious educational movement against British occupation. It is important to keep in mind that the traditionalists, led by the scholars of Deoband, such as, Maulana Husayn Ahmad Madni (d.1957) who had actively campaigned for the departure of the British, nevertheless had many reservations about the proposed state of Pakistan. The primary reason being that they distrusted the leadership of the westernized Muslims such as Jinnah, who, according to the traditionalists often seemed to have a limited understanding of Islam. Another factor was that many, including the founder of the Jamaat-e-Islami, Maulana Maudoodi (1903–79) refused to support the Pakistan Movement, because they believed a nationalist movement defied the universalism of Islam (Abbott, 1968). In this regard, these scholars were not necessarily pan-Islamists, even though some of them may have supported a return of the caliphate via the Khilafat Movement.[15] They recognized that Islamic unity could occur at a scale across nations without necessarily having Islamic states for each national Muslim concentration.

The Jamaat-e-Islami continues to be a revivalist political party in Pakistan and no longer exists as a functional force in India (Nasr, 1995). Maudoodi believed in modernization but only to empower the Islamic community. As such he favoured a more modernist education than the orthodox backers of the traditional madrassahs. He did, however, also lay emphasis on challenging Western culture and intellectual domination.

During the late nineteenth century there was also the emergence of a movement to reform madrassahs within a religio-political context under the banner of the Nadwat-ul-Ulama. This group was led by Maulana Mohammad Ali Mongiri and included the famous Urdu biographer of the Prophet Muhammad (PBUH), and Maulana Shibli Numani (d.1914) who had an opportunity to visit many of the classical madrassahs in Syria, Anatolia and Egypt before embarking on his own reform agenda. Maulana Numani was, however, not impressed by what was being offered in these lands and felt that South Asian madrassahs were quite exemplary in their approach regardless of the need for internal reform (Zaman, 2002). The reforms that were proposed by the Nadwat-ul-Ulama were meant to both make the curriculum more theologically rigorous while also expanding it to more 'worldly pursuits.' While the reforms had measured success, the Dars-e-Nizaami continues to this day to have dominance, though the madrassah established by the Nadwat-ul-Ulama in Lucknow also flourishes and has been a source of moderation in the Indian madrassah establishment producing eminent scholars such as Maulana Abu'l-Hassan Ali Nadwi (d.1999).[16]

There were, however, other ulama from the Deoband school who were in favour of a Muslim state being established to allow for the implementation of Islamic laws. Most notable among these ulama were Maulana Ashraf Ali Thanwi and Maulana Shabbir Ahmed Uthmani. Syed (1982) points out that following independence, the ulama, who had opposed the struggle for Pakistan before 1947, began to demand that the state be made more Islamic. Maulana Maudoodi, founder of the Jamaat-e-Islami party, was the most notable among the ulama for his persistent discussion of the subject. It is interesting to note that when independence came in August, the maulana migrated to Pakistan, notwithstanding his earlier intention of remaining in India to Islamize the entire subcontinent. He began his career in the new state by attempting to pressure its rulers to heed Islam and insisted that the same Muslims, whom he had earlier categorized as nominal Indian Muslims with no awareness of Islam's true goals and mission, struggled for Pakistan in the hope that it would be an Islamic state. He outlined his party's plan to launch an Islamic revolution.

Madrassahs were also a matter of ambivalence for Dr Muhammad Iqbal, the poet philosopher of the Muslims of India, who has also been given the title of *hakim-ul-ummat* (the sage of Islam's community). The eminent littérateur Hakim Ahmed Shuja, has narrated in his memoirs that on one occasion he sought Iqbal's advice on whether or not to reform the Faridiyah religious school in Pakpattan and transform it into a progressive 'Westernized' madrassah. Iqbal responded with the following advice:

> When I was young, I also believed in reform and revolution of Muslims towards Western civilization. However, after spending time in Europe (Iqbal did his doctorate in Germany), my views changed. Let these *maktabs* be as they are. Poor Muslim children should continue to study in these schools— if we did not have *mullahs* and *dervishes*, do you know what would happen? I have seen what would happen. If the Muslims of India are deprived of the influence of these schools, they would fall to the same fate as the Muslims of Spain where the Alhambra and the mosque at Cordoba are devoid of any Muslim presence. In India too we would be left only with Muslim monuments such as the Taj Mahal and the Red Fort but deprived of Islamic vitality.[17]

This quotation shows how madrassahs were perceived by many scholars to be the repositories of culture to be protected by the plebian masses. Iqbal was considered a moderate but devout Muslim by the British who also knighted him—he was generally respected by the Muslims of India though some of his poetry such as Shikva (a complaint to God) drew much ire from many ulama. He also published a rejoinder (Javaab-e-Shikva) that provides a response to the complaint.

It is also important to consider the evangelical aspect of Islamic scholarship—in particular the Tablighi Jamaat. This group of Islamic evangelists was founded in the late nineteenth century by another notable scholar Maulana Muhammad Ilyas Kandhlawi (d.1944), who was trained in a Deobandi madrassah in Saharanpur (Mazahir-ul-Ulum) but wanted to expand the scope of Islamic learning and educational exchange beyond the confines of these institutions. Barbara Metcalfe (2002) describes these tenets as follows: 'The Tablighi Jama'at, nonetheless, took its impetus from a desire to move dissemination of Islamic teachings away from the *madrassah*, the heart of Deobandi activity, to inviting 'lay' Muslims, high and low, learned and illiterate, to share the obligation of enjoining others to faithful practice. It also differed from the original movement because it eschewed debate with other Muslims over jurisprudential niceties and resultant details of practice.'

The Tablighi role in madrassah development is particularly important since their Pakistani headquarters are in Punjab, (near Raiwind) and have come under recent scrutiny by American researchers such as Alexiev (2005), who refers to them as 'jihad's stealthy legions.' However, tablighis have actually not had a strong relationship with any particular madrassah movement and the Jama'at is by its foundation a completely self-funded evangelical movement. While there may be some radical elements within the movement, given its size, the overall texture remains relatively apolitical and often comprises highly trained professionals and academics who could potentially facilitate reform efforts. Thus marginalizing them might not serve the best interests of any effort at educational reform in Pakistan.[18]

MADRASSAH GROWTH AND PROFILE IN PAKISTAN

At the time of independence in 1947, there were only 137 madrassahs in Pakistan. According to a 1956 survey, there were 244 madrassahs in all of Pakistan (excluding East Pakistan, which became Bangladesh in 1971).[19] While there is no comprehensive census of madrassahs across Pakistan at present, a reasonable estimate based on our review of multiple empirical and journalistic sources would suggest that there are between 12,000 and 15,000 madrassahs in Pakistan, with an enrollment of between 1.5 and 2 million.[20] In contrast, there are approximately 150,000 government schools with an enrollment of around 16 million and 35,000 secular private schools with an enrollment of around 6 million in Pakistan, and 25,000 *awqaf* or mosque schools (not madrassahs) with an enrollment of around 1.5 million.[21] However, as noted earlier the absolute number of madrassahs or enrollment across Pakistan is not entirely consequential for understanding any conflict linkages. Instead, we focused on two case studies of particular relevance to conflict dynamics and the demographics within those cases.

More orthodox Muslim sects are believed to have been radicalized by exposure to war, first in Afghanistan and Kashmir, yet the linkage between madrassah education and the perpetuation of these conflicts has not been studied in detail. However, the madrassah problem goes beyond militancy. The curriculum of contemporary madrassahs is also thought to often provide a constrained worldview which bears little resemblance to traditional Islamic education in historical context.[22]

A practical manifestation of how madrassah education in Pakistan is influencing society is the sweeping election victory of radical religious parties in the 2002 general elections. Recent political developments in Pakistan are expected to have immense impact on the democratic polity. The fact that approximately 60 (25 per cent) of newly elected parliamentarians are either madrassah graduates or managers (this ratio in the Senate is 35 per cent) is likely to have a serious impact on policy-making. The Chief Minister and the cabinet in the Northwest Frontier Province belongs to religious parties dominated by madrassah graduates. In Balochistan, the province neighboring Afghanistan nine ministers are madrassah graduates and were actually managing madrassahs before being elected to public office. These developments have important implications for free debate, political dissent, secular thought, civil society and minority and women rights in Pakistan.

Madrassah Categorization

There are five distinct types of Madrassahs in Pakistan, divided among sectarian and political lines.[23] The two main branches of Sunni Islam in South Asia—*Deobandi* and *Bareilvi*—dominate this sector. *Ahle Hadith/Salafi* Muslims have their own schools, as do the Shias—the doctrinal differences of these schools are often irreconcilable in an educational setting. The differences in demographic recruitment and placement between these sects has not been evaluated, and deserves close attention. For example, the largest group of madrassahs is Bareilvi, which are diametrically opposed to the *Wahabbi* doctrine[24] (that has received much media coverage), and yet have been linked to the Kashmiri conflict by the Indian government. Understanding the dynamics of madrassah recruitment, funding sources, and curricular differences between sectarian schools is critically important. Table 2.1 shows the growth of religious institutions in Pakistan by province. These institutions are supposed to include madrassahs as well. However, the data gathering method is relying on those reported to the Institute for Policy Studies (supported by the Jamaat-e-Islami).[25]

Table 2.1: Conservative Estimates of Religious Educational Institutions: 1947-2000

Province/region	1947	1960	1980	1988	2000
Punjab	121	195	1012	1320	3153
NWFP	59	87	426	678	1281
Sindh	21	87	380	291	905
Balochistan	28	70	135	347	692
AJ Kashmir	4	8	29	76	151
Islamabad	-	1	27	47	94
Northern Areas	12	16	47	102	185
FATA	-	-	-	-	300
Total	245	464	2056	2861	6761

Source: Ministry of Religious Affairs 1979 and Ministry of Education, Islamabad 1988-2000, Institute of Policy Studies, 2002.

It is important to note that the government now acknowledges that the number of madrassahs is more than twice what the IPS (Institute for Policy Studies) study estimated in 2002. In his recent autobiography, even former President Musharraf (2006, p. 312) has put the number at approximately 14,000, serving an estimated 1 million students. However, as noted in the first chapter, the actual number of madrassahs is only consequential in terms of record-keeping rather than for ascertaining any conflict linkages.

MADRASSAHS FROM 1947-71

Following independence in 1947, Pakistan, underwent a series of political convulsions as a result of tensions between the military and feudal elite. While most of Pakistan's early leaders followed Jinnah's model of modern education, they did not have widespread support in rural areas. The bureaucracy and the military were modeled after the British system which was resented by the ulama. Though some of these scholars were appointed to government posts their presence was largely symbolic.

The ascendance to power of the military general Ayub Khan in 1958 heralded a defining era in Pakistan's politics. He disqualified 3500 politicians on charges of corruption, thus consolidating his own power. Regarding the role of Islam in Pakistan's political life, Ayub Khan was somewhat ambivalent. He favoured an Islamic identity for Pakistan but with direct control of the government over religious institutions, thus marginalizing the ulama. In global political history this was also the peak of the cold war and since officially secular India had aligned itself with the Soviets, Pakistan was obliged and courted to ally itself with the Americans. Since atheism was a feature of communist rule, a religious identity was also favoured for American allies at this time. It is thus not surprising that the official name of the country was changed from Republic of Pakistan to the Islamic Republic of Pakistan by Ayub Khan in 1962.

As part of its policy of exercising control over religious institutions, the Ayub Khan government established an *awqaf* property (non-transferable religious endowments on which many madrassahs were dependent to meet expenses) department to regulate shrines and madrassahs. To this day there is a high-ranking civil-service position of 'secretary awqaf'—these officers have jurisdiction over *awqaf* properties.[26] In response to some of these moves, the ulama established four *wifaqs*—or federations of madrassahs—along sectarian lines: Wifaq al Madaaris al Arabiya (Sunni–Deobandi); Tanzim al Madaaris-al-Arabiya (Sunni–Bareilvi); Wifaq al Madaaris-al-Salafia (Sunni–Salafi/Ahle-Hadith) and Wifaq al Madaaris-al-Shia (Shia). Interestingly enough the Salafis, who are now most closely associated with the Saudi regime, were the first to take this initiative in 1955 and the other sects followed their example in 1959 (Riaz, 2005). The Jamaat-e-Islaami also initiated a Rabita Madaaris as an additional entity in the 1970s. The government's reform plan included the introduction of secular education in madrassahs similar to what is being attempted at present by President Musharraf. The aim was to enable madrassah students to 'enter public professions' and 'play their full part as citizens.'[27] The reforms proposed the same primary education syllabus and teaching schedule for madrassahs as in the government sector. Religious content would be added but go beyond the Qur'an, *hadith* (sayings of the

Prophet) and other traditional subjects to include issues of national importance, propagation of an Islamic nation or even of an Islamic community *(ummah)*.

As the International Crisis Group contends, 'this meant the transformation of Islam from a theological concept to an ideological one' (ICG, 2002).

The madrassah reform efforts of this period were largely rejected by the ulama except for some initial hints of approval from the Jamaat-e-Islaami. However, there were larger political changes in store for Pakistan in 1970 when a general election left a highly polarized result between East and West Pakistan. The events that followed led to a civil war in 1971 that eventually resulted in the creation of Bangladesh as a separate country in what was East Pakistan and the rise to power of Zulfikar Ali Bhutto in West Pakistan. While Bhutto had won the election in West Pakistan, he had also declared himself chief martial law administrator during the period of civil unrest. He thus followed an autocratic policy on several accounts despite his ostensibly democratic credentials.

MADRASSAH REFORMS AFTER THE CIVIL WAR: 1971–77

After the civil war and the secession of Bangladesh, Bhutto tried to give what was left of Pakistan a new identity for which he needed the support of the Islamic parties. Bhutto attempted to revitalize national identity by conflating theology with socialism. The Islamic parties, which had attained minimal victory in the 1970 elections, were still able to influence the writing of the 1973 constitution, which declared Islam the state religion (Article 2) and mandated the Council of Islamic Ideology to propose measures to Islamize Pakistan.[28] In its preamble, the constitution pledged that the state should 'enable Muslims to order their lives in accordance with the Holy Qur'an and Sunnah.'

The education sector was nationalized; however most of the madrassahs remained independent. According to government data, 1,828 schools, 346 madrassahs, 155 colleges and 5 technical institutions were nationalized (Rahman, 2004, p. 16). Bhutto further tried to build alliances with the ulama by offering to grant madrassahs the equivalence of public sector certificates and diplomas. The highest degree of the Deobandi *wifaq* was to be made equivalent with a Master's degree in Islamic Studies from a government university, given madrassah students cleared a Bachelor's level English course. However, this equivalence was largely implemented and institutionalized during the Zia administration that followed Bhutto. Another important victory for the Islamists during the Bhutto era was the government declaration in 1974 of the Ahmedi sect as non-Muslims—this was a particularly alarming development since the Ahmedis had supported Bhutto in the 1970 elections. However, the *Tehrik-e-Tahuffuz-e-Khatam-e-Nabuwat* (movement to protect the finality of Prophethood), led by numerous ulama in Pakistan prevailed due to their core constituency in many of the areas where Bhutto was most vulnerable.

Reforms for the nationalized education sector included increased religious content. Arabic was made a compulsory subject at middle and secondary school levels, and madrassah graduates were employed as teachers, to widen their horizon of employment. This was also the time when madrassahs began to establish linkages with external sponsors. New madrassahs (mainly in the southern belt of the Punjab) opened to strengthen ties with Arab countries, mainly Saudi Arabia. The clerics, however, were disenchanted by Bhutto's personal habits, particularly his acknowledgement of alcohol consumption as well as his capricious stance on Islamic governance, and decided to join hands with the military, helping to oust him via a military coup in July 1977, after which he was subsequently executed on a murder charge.

THE ZIA YEARS: 1977–88

The new military ruler, general Zia-ul-Haq was known for his strong religious proclivities and he believed fervently in establishing a more ideological state. Zia's Islamization policy was twofold: first, changes were made in the legal system, and therefore, Shariah courts were established, interest free banking was introduced and compulsory deduction of zakat (alms tax) from Muslim account holders were introduced into the system. An elaborate system of provincial, district and village level zakat committees was launched. The second level targeted the print media, television, radio and mosques. Several new ordinances were issued to Islamize public morals, the civil service, armed forces, education system, research organizations and even science and technology.

Zia retained control of some Islamic bodies, such as the Council of Islamic Ideology. The Council suggested at times that parliamentary democracy is non-Islamic and that certain core qualifications were needed for ruling a country—a form of technocracy. *Ulama* of all sects were given representation in 1980 on the *Majlis-e-Shura* (a consensus-building council of technocrats and theologians), who in turn supported the Zia regime. To gain the support of the religious seminaries, the government offered incentives such as the 1979 education policy that promised 5000 mosques schools and a national committee for religious institutes to transform madrassahs into an important part of the educational system. A national survey was conducted by Dr A.W.J Halepota, an educator who had also been associated with Ayub Khan's commission for educational reform in the 1960s, which proposed improving the economic condition of madrassahs and modernizing them with the aim of eventually integrating the religious and the formal education sectors while 'conserving the autonomy of madrassahs' (Malik 1996).

Halepota's suggestions for improving economic conditions of madrassahs included direct government financial assistance, career planning for madrassah graduates and curricular reform. *Zakat* funds were identified as the source of government support. Some modern subjects at the primary, secondary and graduation levels were recommended without altering the theological texture of the curriculum. Following the earlier initiative during the Bhutto years, the government directed the University Grants Commission (UGC), in June 1980, to draw up criteria of equivalence for degrees and certificates from the religious sector. The highest certificates of *wifaq* boards were conditionally recognized as an MA in Arabic or Islamiyat. The primary motivation for this was to fill a shortage of Arabic and Islamiyat teachers in colleges and universities created by making coursework in these subjects compulsory at various levels of schooling. Zia, however, also tried to appease the minority Shia establishment and in 1981 granted them a waiver from the primarily Sunni-mandated *Zakat* contributions collected by the government. Religious parties also flourished during this period. There were only 30 such parties in the country in 1979, and now there are more than 200.

The invasion of Afghanistan by the Soviets in 1979 necessitated a response from the Islamists as well as the Americans. The linkage between madrassahs and the Soviet-Afghan war has been widely contested. While Western writers (Singer, 2002; Stern, 2001) as well as numerous Pakistani intellectuals and nongovernmental organizations (Ahmed, 2003, ICG, 2002) affirm the linkage, the military establishment in Pakistan largely deny any direct connection. When interviewed for this study, General Hamid Gul, who served in the army during the Zia years and was later the head of the Pakistani military's Inter-Services-Intelligence (ISI) towards the end of the Afghan war denied any direct support from the ISI for the madrassahs. However, he acknowledged that the influx of Afghan refugees during this time necessitated the establishment of schools for the education of their children and since the Afghan population had a greater proclivity for religious education, madrassahs started to emerge naturally near refugee settlements and the military provided logistical support to these institutions.[29]

Nevertheless, it is clear that the Pakistani military as well as its allies in the United States at this time encouraged an ideologically-driven war. Islam was certainly used to galvanize action on the part of the Afghans that were fighting the Soviets as well as to garner public support within Pakistan. For instance, special textbooks in Darri (Afghan Persian) and Pashto were written at the University of Nebraska-Omaha with US government support.[30] There are video-taped speeches of the Secretary of State during the Carter administration, Zbigniew Brezinski, hailing the cause of jihad against the 'Godless Soviets.'[31] American arms and money unquestionably flowed to Afghanistan through Pakistan's Inter Services Intelligence as a way of defeating Soviet advances in the region.[32] The US decision to support the mujahideen was, however, guarded because of the Iranian revolution that occurred around the same time. Policy-makers were wary of supporting religious zealots but were comforted by the fact that Iran was primarily Shia and Afghanistan was primarily Sunni.[33] Initially the aid was relatively small, amounting to $30 million in 1979, the year the Soviet invasion took place. However, this was increased considerably both directly to Afghanistan and also to Pakistan as a conduit for arms transfer. At its peak, the aid to Pakistan amounted to $3.1 billion annually and to Afghanistan over $600 million (Tanner, 2002).

However, the fact that the United States helped the jihadists at the time is unfortunately used by some scholars to dignify the radicalism of the jihadists, suggesting that they are giving America a 'taste of their own medicine.' In particular, a recent book by Mamdani (2004) points the finger directly at the US, suggesting that some 'high-level' jihadists were trained in US camps, including High Rock Gun Club in Naugatuck, Connecticut, Fort Bragg, North Carolina and the CIA's own Camp Perry in Williamsburg, Virginia. Citing a Brigadier, Muhammad Yusuf, Chief of the Afghan Cell of the ISI for four years, Mamdani states that in four years some 80,000 mujahideen were trained from 43

Islamic countries. In Pakistan, with active US support, over 2,500 madrassahs were set up with an annual enrollment of 225,000 students. According to Mamdani: 'Fighters in the Peshawar-based Muslim 'international brigade received the relatively high salary of around $1,500 per month.'[34]

Nevertheless, the American government can also claim that their support of the jihadists shows how America has helped Muslims in need. Many American government officials, while reflecting on the terrorist strikes by the Islamists, express a sense of 'betrayal' of the help accorded to Islamists in the Afghan-Russo war, just as much as the Pakistanis and Afghan's feel betrayed by the opportunistic departure of US resources following the collapse of the Soviet Union. Each side claims to have been 'used' by the other for their own ends.

Such rhetoric on both sides, however, detracts from the larger issue of resolving conflicts emanating from any quarter whether from the West or the East. Academics who either castigate or celebrate US involvement are often missing the larger issue of how a balanced foreign policy can now be achieved. While it is important to reflect on past decisions, they should not preclude positive action on current policy imperatives.

MADRASSAHS BEYOND THE COLD WAR

1988 was a defining year in Pakistani history. The Geneva accords to end the Russian occupation of Afghanistan were signed in April. The same month, the largest weapons depot for arms to the mujahideen at Ojhri Camp near Islamabad was destroyed by a mysterious explosion that left errant missiles randomly flying all across the capital, much to the terrified astonishment of the residents. In August of the same year, President Zia of Pakistan, a major supporter of the Afghan mujahideen as well as the madrassahs, was mysteriously killed in a plane crash along with eight army generals, the American ambassador and the US military attaché. The circumstances for the crash are still a mystery but Zia had several enemies both domestically and abroad who could be culpable.[35] These events of 1988 are significant in establishing deeply entrenched conspiracy theories about Western involvement and interference that pervade not only the madrassah establishment but also the general population in Pakistan.[36] The fact that there was no FBI investigation regarding the Zia crash despite the death of two senior US diplomats onboard add to the suspicion of the population.

Following the retreat of Soviet forces in 1989, and the ensuing civil war in Afghanistan, the madrassahs connection to conflict is more clear. For example, the Dur-ul-Uloom Haqqania in Akora Khattak, one of the most well-known madrassahs has direct connections with the Taliban, whose name itself means 'the students'. Mullah Umar, the leader of the Taliban has an honorary degree from this madrassah. The head of Dar-ul-Uloom Haqqania, Maulana Sami-ul-Haq[37] was elected a member of the Pakistani Parliament in the 2002 election, has a student body of 1500 boarding students and 1000 day students, from 6 years old upwards. Each year over 18,000 applicants from poor families compete for around 500 open spaces.[38]

In 1988, civilian rule came back to Pakistan to stay for a decade till 1999 when the military decided to take power back. None of the four elected governments could complete their respective tenures before being ousted by another. In the meantime, the Taliban took over most of Afghanistan in 1994 and the Pakistani government, under Benazir Bhutto,[39] recognized the Taliban government (Rashid, 2000).

In 1996, Bhutto's government was removed from office by a military backed President before it had the chance to impose any of the intended plans it had for the madrassahs, which included the introduction of compulsory audits, new curricula and registration. Her plans were strongly opposed by the religious parties to the extent that the Tehrik Nifaz-e-Shariah Mohammadi (TNSM) in Malakand Division of the NWFP threatened to impose Taliban-style order in the areas it controlled. Nawaz Sharif with his Pakistan Muslim League (PML) and strong support in the Punjab, took some actions against religious extremists in his home province and vowed to remove sectarianism. However, his actions had limited success outside Punjab despite election results in his favour. In 1997, in the general elections, the JUI headed by Fazlur Rehman was the only religious party which won 2 seats in the 217 member national assembly. This ostensibly small victory in the polls by Islamists was used by the government to indicate that popular support was limited for religious groups despite the rise of religious institutions. However, given the limited participation in the polls by various groups, this insight is misleading as we saw a major shift in the dominance of religious parties in the 2002 election.

VARIOUS SECTS AND THEIR MADRASSAHS

As an Abrahamic religion, Islam follows many of the same tenets of monotheism as Judaism and Christianity.[40] There are two primary sects within Islam—Sunni (accounting for 85 per cent of the worldwide population of around 1.4 billion) and Shia (accounting for 14-15 per cent) with 1 per cent or less belonging to marginalized groups such as Ahmedis,[41] Druze[42] or the Nation of Islam.[43] There is also a small sect called Zikris in Balochistan, which are ostracized by most mainstream Muslims.

The Shias believe that the successor of the Prophet Muhammad (PBUH) was his cousin Ali Ibn-e-Abi Talib and not the first three caliphs whom Sunnis take to be his successors. They mourn the battle of Karbala, fought between the Prophet's grandson Hussain and the Umayyad caliph Yazid bin Muawiya in AD 680.[44] The highest density of Shia population in the world is concentrated in Iran (93 per cent of the population) and Iraq (60 per cent of the population). In Pakistan, Shias account for around 20 per cent of the population though in absolute terms, the second-largest population of Shias in the world after Iran is found in Pakistan (around 27 million).[45]

For our purposes, it may be useful to categorize the madrassahs by the sub-sects and then also include Shia madrassahs at par with some of these sub-sects. This is specially relevant since the federation of madrassahs are organized along these lines. The three primary Sunni sub-sects in Pakistan are: Deobandi, Bareilvi, Ahle-Hadith/Salafi. Each sect has its own madrassahs in which their own version of Islam is taught. The two primary wings of Sunni Islam—Deobandi and Bareilvi—dominate the madrassah system in Pakistan.

Madrassahs were created to preserve and propagate what these various sects viewed to be the correct interpretation of Islam—often referred to as *maslak* (creed). Brief descriptions of these sects are as follows:

DEOBANDIS

The most prominent movement towards Islamic revival in India too has its roots in a small city in the United Provinces (now Uttar Pradesh) of India, called Deoband. Founded by Maulana Muhammad Qasim Nanautawi (1833–77) and Maulana Rasheed Ahmed Gangohi (1829–1905), the madrassah at Deoband soon became the most celebrated

Islamist institution in South Asia. According to Rahman (2004), 'while earlier seminaries were loosely organized, Deoband had a rector (*sarparast*), a chancellor (*muhtamim*) and the chief instructor (*sadr mudarris*). Its income was derived from popular contributions and the curriculum was based on the Dars-i-Nizami which emphasized studies based on human reasoning (*maqulat*) but at Deoband the traditional sciences which were transmitted unchanged to the learner (*manqulat*) were emphasized.' Therefore, the Deoband curriculum taught much more hadith than the Dars-i-Nizami had originally prescribed.

The Deobandis were fervently against the notion of intercession by saints in supplication and the commemoration of various saintly death anniversaries (*u'rs*) that were pervasive across the Indian subcontinent. They saw this as an adulteration of Islam's direct doctrine of communication with the Creator and largely dismissed sufi tendencies as a vestige of Hindu and Christian influences. True mystical exaltation to the Deobandis could only be experienced through *taqwa* or piety.

Within a hundred years of its establishment, Deoband had produced 6,986 graduates and established 8,934 maktabs (schools) and madrassahs (seminaries) teaching the Dars-i-Nizami. In 1967, the number of graduates from Pakistan was 3,191 (including those from East Pakistan). Today, the number of students exceeds 102, 865 and the number of those who appeared in the Alimia (MA) examination exceeds 4500 (Rahman, 2004). Some of the more well-known militant madrassahs such as the one in Banuri town,[46] Karachi led by the late Maulana Shamzai as well as the aforementioned Dar-ul-Uloom Haqqaniya are Deobandi.

BAREILVIS

Maulana Ahmed Raza Khan of Bareilly (1856–1921) was the founder of the movement that bears his hometown's name. The Bareilvi vision of Islam is diametrically opposed to the Deobandi's puritanical vision and suggest that saints (*or pirs*) at shrines can intercede on their behalf to God. In India they established several madrassahs, most notably, the Madrassah Islamia Shams ul-'Ulum in Nagpur. They are thus more inclined to some of the Sufi traditions of performances and ceremonies at shrines. The Bareilvis believe in the partial immortality of Prophet Mohammad suggesting that he was made of Divine Radiance (Noor) and had knowledge of the unknown (Ilm-ul-Ghaib). Both these beliefs are vehemently challenged by the Deobandis and the Ahl-i-Hadith ulama since they undermine the unity of God and could lead to personality worship. Often Deobandi ulama disparage Bareilvi veneration of Prophet Muhammad (PUBH) by comparing it to the Christian tradition of apotheosis of saints as well as the Shia veneration of Imam Ali. The Bareilvi madrassahs in Pakistan also teach the Dars-i-Nizami and have great appeal in communities near old saintly shrines. The shrines are an important source of revenue for these communities as well since generous donations by local landlords and pilgrims provide much-needed transfer of wealth. The Jamiaat-e-Ulama-Pakistan (JUP) is the primary political party associated with the Bareilvi movement.

Ahl-e-Hadith/Salafi

Founded by Maulana Sayyed Ahmed (not to be confused with Sir Syed Ahmed Khan, modernist founder of Aligarh Muslim University), the Ahle-Hadith (people of the Prophet's path) are the most puritanical of the South Asian sects. They are often labeled 'Wahabbi' within South Asia because, like Muhammad bin Abdul Wahab (1703–92) of Saudi Arabia, Sayyid Ahmed and his associates also wanted to confine interpretation of Islamic doctrine to the earliest traditions. They shared the Deobandi aversion to shrine worship but unlike the Deobandi, they claimed to follow no particular school of jurisprudence—Hanafi, Shafi, Hambali, Maliki—and were called nonconformists (*ghair muqallid*=one who does not follow a fixed path) by their opponents. The Ahl-e-Hadith resent the epithet of 'Wahabbi' for themselves and appealed to the government of India that the term Wahabbi should not be used for them—hence in 1886 the term Wahabbi was dropped from official correspondence referring to them. However, it remains in currency in Pakistan. The Ahl-i-Hadith madrassahs also teach the Dars-i-Nizami but they emphasize the Qur'an and Hadith and oppose folk Islam and common practices such as the anniversaries of saints, the distribution of food on religious occasions, and popular mysticism.

The Saudi Arabian organization, Harmain Islamic Foundation, is said to have helped the Ahl-i-Hadith and made them powerful. Indeed, the *Lashkar-e-Tayyaba*, an organization which has been active in fighting in Kashmir, belongs to the Ahl-e-Hadith. The *Lashkar-e-Tayyaba* (renamed Jamaat Dawah since being officially banned in 2002) operates a well-known madrassah in Muridke, near Lahore called *Markaz-al-Dawah-al-Irshad*.[47] Interestingly, this madrassah was founded by two highly educated professors from then University of Engineering and Technology in Lahore, Hafiz Saeed and Zafar Khan. The madrassah occupies nearly 200 acres of agricultural land within 50 miles of the border with India. It produces its own agricultural products, fruits and even has an aquaculture business that turns a profit. My field visit to this madrassah showed that there is a clear interest in improving the image of the madrassah abroad and are willing to respond to some government initiatives for transparency. However, the leadership acknowledge that the core purpose of jihad in both intellectual and physical terms against what is termed *batil* (injustice or falsehood in Arabic) must continue.[48]

Many Kashmiri Muslims who deeply revere the Sufi saints suprisingly support attacks against Indian armed personnel by militants associated with the vehemently anti-Sufi Lashkar-i-Tayyeba, associated with the Ahl-i-Hadith school that regards Sufism as 'anti-Islamic'. At the same time they might be vehemently opposed to the harsh 'Islamic' rule that the Lashkar-i-Tayyeba aims at establishing in Kashmir, and only supporting the 'jihad' for operational expediency.

SHIA MADAARIS

In Pakistan, Shias are a minority, accounting for about 20 per cent of the Muslim population. However, they have historically had a strong control on land holdings in central and Southern Punjab as well as Sindh.[49] There is also a clear funding connection between Shia madrassahs and the government of Iran which even had a cultural centre in the central city of Multan where many madrassahs are congregated. This consulate and cultural centre was attacked and looted in 1997 and the cultural attaché was murdered. Several reprisals and counter-reprisals have followed.

While the majority of Shias belong to the Athna-Ashri sub-sect (believing in twelve imams), there is also a sub-sect of Shias who revere only six of these imams and also revere the Aga Khan, whom they believe to be a direct descendent of the Prophet Muhammad (PBUH) (The Ismailis or Sevener sub-sect). Related in beliefs to them are the Daudi Bohras (followers of Burhanuddin) and the Sulamani Bohras (followers of Masood Salebahi). The Bohra community comprises a largely affluent class of business entrepreneurs who migrated from Gujarat in India to the Karachi area. The Aga Khani Shias (also called Ismailis) form an organized group of largely educated entrepreneurs settled in urban areas. They also have a strong presence in parts of the Hunza valley in northern Pakistan, along with twelve Shia sects as well. The Aga Khan Rural Support Programme (AKRSP) has won accolades all over the world and their educational institutions such as the Aga Khan University are widely renowned. Recently, there has been a major controversy regarding the government's acceptance of the Aga Khan Examination Board which madrassah proponents reject (further discussed in Chapter 6).

It is important to consider that the Shias in the Gilgit area (40 miles south of Hunza) started a movement in the 1980s to demand a separate state of 'Karakoram.' During this time, the government began to support Sunni groups in the region. The historical tension between Shias and Sunnis has been accentuated in recent years and is one of the main areas of concern vis-à-vis domestic terrorist incidents in Pakistan. The government has similarly supported other groups in the past as a foil to separatist movements—in particular the support of the Mohajir Qaumi Movement (MQM) in Sindh to counter Sindhi nationalism is widely believed to have sparked sectarian tensions in Karachi since the 1980s (Verkaaik, 2004).

In part this study is an attempt to understand the demographics and possible causes of sectarian politics using madrassahs as a hypothesis. We deliberately selected case studies in areas known for sectarian activity. While all the madrassahs, including the Shia ones, teach the Dars-i-Nizami, they do not use the same texts. They also teach their particular interpretation (*maslak*) which clarifies and rationalizes the beliefs of the sect (Sunni or Shia) and sub-sect (Deobandi, Bareilvi and Ahl-i-Hadith). There has also been a radicalization of mosques adjoining madrassahs. The sectarian differences that manifest themselves in madrassah demographics and change need further study and analysis and that is what the case analyses aim to accomplish in the next chapter.

NOTES

1. The descriptive adjectives 'Islamic,' 'Muslim' and 'Islamist' are often used interchangeably but have different connotations. Initially, the term 'Mohammedan' was used by orientalist scholars but is resented by Muslims as Islam is not just meant to be a religion following the Prophet Muhammad (PBUH) but a complete way of life. A Muslim is an adherent of 'Islam' and this is the basic descriptor—similar to 'Christian.' The adjective 'Islamic' is used often in a more cultural context such as

'Islamic architecture.' The descriptor 'Islamist' specifies political aspirations of Islam and the establishment of a Muslim governance regime.
2. The disagreement between ICG and the World Bank study authors became particularly acrimonious in April 2005 when ICG issued a press release from its Islamabad office that questioned the motivation of the World Bank study since its policy impact had been that the Pakistani government was perceived to become more complacent about the matter. Andrabi et al, asserted that ICG should at least acknowledge the numerical error and strongly resented any aspersions cast by ICG. The US government was also rather defensive about the matter and the 9/11 Commission commented that they had relied on more than just anecdotal accounts in their findings and the head of ICG–Pakistan, Dr Samina Ahmed was asked to testify before the congressional Foreign Relations Committee on 19 April 2005.
3. Tahir Andrabi, public remarks at a conference on 'Pakistan's Educational Reform' held at the School of Advanced International Studies, Johns Hopkins University, 4 April 2005.
4. There are also various transliterations of the word from Arabic to English, such as madrasa, madrassah, maddrassa etc. We prefer using the transliteration 'madrassah' as it is phonetically the closest to the Arabic lettering for the word.
5. The word also has other connotations that mean 'office' or 'forum.' Interestingly enough, Osama Bin Laden and a Palestinian extremist Abdullah Azzam founded an organization in the 1980s, known as *Maktab-al-Khidmat,* to help funnel fighters and funds to the Afghan resistance groups. However, there is no known connection between this group and any particular school (Mir, 2006).
6. See for example Jalal, 1994, Ahmed, 1997.
7. For an excellent analysis of the Kashmir conflict and broader Indo-Pak relations see Bose, 2004.
8. Much of the early history of madrassahs in this section is derived from Anzar, 2003. For a detailed study of madrassah development as a post-Abbasid urban phenomenon see lapidus, 1984.
9. For a detailed review of the history of *Ijtihad* and the controversies surrpounding its legal role in Islam, see Hallaq, 2005.
10. Qasmi, M. Burhanuddin. 'Indian madrassah curriculum and the need for reform.' Paper presented at the workshop on madrassah education at Erfurt university, June 2005.
11. This madrassah has had a fascinating history including several European non-Muslim principals, such as Aloys Sprenger and A.H. Harley, that supervised a largely orthodox Muslim curriculum. Following partition, part of the madrassah was moved to Dhaka (then East Pakistan and now Bangladesh). The madrassah is now known as Kolkatta Madrassah College in India and the Bangladeshi institution is known as the Dhaka Aaliya madrassah. The Bangladeshi institution has been increasingly radicalized and was the site of violent riots in early 2005 leading to temporary closure of the institution by the government.
12. The date marks the official start of colonial rule in India following 'The War for Independence' as it is known in South Asia and the 'Mutiny' as it is known in the United Kingdom.
13. The name of the city of Madras was changed by the Hindu nationalist government of the BJP in 2000 to Chennai—partly because the name 'Madras' is believed to be

derived from 'madrassah,' supposedly named as such by the British because of the prominence of madrassahs in this city.
14. For a detailed account of this madrassah see Robinson (2001).
15. This was a movement following the First World War to preserve the caliphate in Turkey and led by Maulana Muhammad Ali Johar and his brother Maulana Shaukat Ali.
16. The madrassah of the Nadwat-ul-Ulama also has an English web site: http://www.nadwatululama.org. While the credentials of ulama and students at the Nadwa are generally considered impeccable, in 1994, there was a raid at the premises in connection with students' involvement in the kidnapping of foreigners in Kashmir. See Arun Shourie 'Muslims were looking to Pakistan for Help. *The Observer*, 16 December 1994.
17. Narrative of Muhammad Iqbal in Urdu translated by the author. Quoted in Hakim Ahmed Shuja's autobiography in Urdu titled *Khoon Baha*, Lahore: Taj Company 1943.
18. For a detailed history of the *Tablighi Jamaat* see Sikand, 2001.
19. Nadhr Ahmad's 1956 survey quoted by Malik, 1996.
20. According to Dr Mahmood Ahmed Ghazi, the Minister of Religious Affairs, there are about 10,000 registered religious schools, catering for as many as one million to more than 1.7 million children attending classes at least for a short period of time, as most do not complete their education or appear for the final examination. According to ICG, by 1995, 20,000 of them were likely to graduate as maulanas (holders of the highest madrassah certificate) of one sect or the other, in addition to the 40,000 who had graduated since 1947. The majority of madrassah students are in the age range 5–18 years. Only those going for higher religious studies are above that age.' Singer's (2002) estimate of 45,000 madrassahs is unsubstantiated and despite attempts to ask for his sources, no response has been received by the authors.
21. Estimates based on data the Planning Commission of Pakistan. *Education and School Atlas of Pakistan*. (A UNICEF project). 2002.
22. See, for example, the account of traditional Islamic education in Spain: Menocal, 2002.
23. For a detailed contemporary analysis of various Muslim sects and the religious scholars that govern them see Zaman, 2002.
24. For further details on the Wahabbi doctrine refer to the section on Saudi Arabian funding of madrassahs in Chapter 4 of this manuscript.
25. The Institute for Policy Studies (IPS) describes itself as 'an independent think-tank providing a forum for informed discussion and dialogue. The staff are certainly well-qualified but are all affiliated in some form or another with religious institutions. The Academic Council of the Institute includes notable religious scholars such as Justice M. Taqi Usmani, the leader of one of the more progressive madrassahs in Karachi and former judge of the Shariah Appellate Bench of the Supreme Court; Dr Anis Ahmed and Dr Khurshid Ahmed, both senior religious academics who have run Islamic institutions of higher learning. To their credit IPS has been forthcoming in promoting a dialogue between religions and organized an ecumenical meeting in Islamabad including Christian, Jewish and Sikh academics alongside Muslim academics in January 2004. IPS funding comes from individual donors, religious

organizations and some Gulf-based organizations such as the Pak-Kuwait Investment Corporation.
26. The secretaries are assigned through the regular civil service and do not need any approval by the religious establishment.
27. Quoted in ICG, 2002.
28. For a detailed exposition of the Council on Islamic Ideology see Malik 1996.
29. Personal communication, General Hamid Gul, Islamabad, 10 January 2004.
30. As a tribute to the relationship between the University and Afghanistan, President Hamid Karzai was awarded an honorary doctorate from the University of Nebraska in May 2005. Years earlier, the centre also received funding from the American gas company Unocal, to facilitate a business relationship with the Taliban in order to promote a natural gas pipeline project. In 1997, Unocal offered the Centre an up-to-two-year contract worth as much $1.8 million to train Afghan men to build pipelines (Centre for Public Integrity: http://www.publicintegrity.org/wow/bio.aspx?act=pro&ddlC=61). Numerous 'resource war theorists' such as Klare (2002) have linked such transactions to US interest in the region. However, if anything, such interactions, including the Taliban visit to Texas in 1997, may hint how resource cooperation might have lead to cooperative outcomes and persuasive change rather than conflictual change.
31. See the CNN documentary *Cold War*. In this documentary, CIA official Frank Anderson summed up the situation as follows: It is entirely true that this was a war that was fought with our gold but with their blood.' The initial effort was termed 'Operation Cyclone.' See also the film 'Charlie Wilson's War'.
32. Rahman, Tariq. (2004) *The Madrassah and the State of Pakistan. Religion, Poverty and the Potential for Violence in Pakistan.* http://www.himalmag.com/2004/february/essay.htm Pgs. 9-10.
33. Ironically, the US is now having to deal with Sunni extremism in Iraq and the Shias are perceived to be the moderates.
34. Mamdani also suggests with scant evidence that opium trade was allowed to fund these initiatives.
35. For an in-depth review of possible theories explaining the crash see Epstein, 1989.
36. Addressing conspiracy theories is a serious concern across the Muslim world. On the one hand the bizarre denial of facts linking al-Qaeda to the attacks by a large number of Muslims following 9/11 is disturbing because it shows reluctance to reform. However, denial of this kind also suggests a positive sign that the attacks are considered so outrageous by many Muslims that they do not want to believe that one of their own could have carried them out. Either way, the conspiracy theories must be aborted as soon as possible through transparency and candor to avoid further misunderstandings.
37. Maulana Sami-ul-Haq has had a controversial past but had the full support of the Musharraf government when he was stopped by Belgian authorities at Brussels airport on 22 April 2005. The Belgians had Maulana Sami-ul-Haq on a watch list and asked for protracted interrogation that he refused. The Pakistani government promptly lodged a complaint with the Belgian government in this regard and public opinion favoured this position.
38. Field visit to *Dar-ul-Uloom Haqqannia*, Akora Khattak, 12 January 2004.

39. Benazir became highly critical of Talibanization and in an op-ed in the *New York Times*, on 7 November 2007, she stated that the political parties should 'unite in a coalition of moderation to marginalize both the dictators and the extremists, to restore civilian rule to the presidency and to shut down political madrassas, the Islamic schools that stock weapons and preach violence.'
40. For a comprehensive geographic introduction to Islam and the Muslim World, see Al-Faruqi, 1986 or for a popular comparative account of the Abrahamic Faiths see Armstrong, 1998.
41. The Ahmedis have been declared 'non-Muslims' in Pakistan (since the time of President Bhutto). See Kaushik, 1996.
42. Started as reform movement within Shia Islam during the Fatmid caliphate in the eleventh century.
43. This group of largely African-American supremacists is generally regarded a heresy by most mainstream Muslims though at one time the leadership received support from some Muslim governments, particularly Libya.
44. For a detailed account of early Islamic history in this regard refer to Lapidus, 1996.
45. Estimates based on various sources synthesized by adherents.com and Islamicweb.com. Religion demographics are hard to ascertain as many censuses do not measure them accurately and in some cases people erroneously report their sectarian affiliation in a census. In Pakistan this has been the case, specially with Shia demographics where in some cases people may be afraid to associate themselves with a minority sect while in other cases Sunnis may report themselves as Shias to avoid compulsory Zakat (alms due) from the government that is levied on Muslims but given a separate mandate under Shia jurisprudence.
46. One of the accused perpetrators of the Daniel Pearl murder, Amjad Hussain Farooqi alias Mansur Hasnain alias Imtiaz Siddiqui alias Hyder, alias Doctor was affiliated with the Banuri Town madrassah. Farooqi was later also implicated in the assassination attempts on President Musharraf, and killed by authorities in 2004. It is important to note, however, that the alleged mastermind of the ploy, Ahmed Omar Syed Shaikh, was a British-born Pakistani who was educated in a Western-style school in Lahore and then at the London School of Economics.
47. For a history of this organization see. Saeed Shafqat's chapter titled 'From official Islam to Islamism: The rise of Dawat-ul-Irshad and Lashkar-e-Tayyaba.' In Jafferelot ed. (2002).
48. Personal communication with Maulana Zafar Khan, *Markaz Al Dawah Al Irshad*, 4 January 2004
49. Rahman, Tariq. (2004) *The Madrassah and the State of Pakistan. Religion, Poverty and the Potential for Violence in Pakistan.* http://www.himalmag.com/2004/february/essay.htm Pg. 3.

3

EMPIRICAL CASE ANALYSES: AHMEDPUR EAST AND ISLAMABAD CAPITAL TERRITORY

The research presented here on the scope and scale of madrassahs and their potential linkage to conflict is primarily based on a detailed study of two distinct geographical areas, one being a typical rural region that has a substantial madrassah population; the second area selected for research is the federal capital territory of Islamabad, which is highly urbanized, and offers business, employment, education and other economic opportunities. The trends and patterns in madrassahs observed in this research are aimed at providing a framework for the analysis of various reform strategies being considered by the Government of Pakistan, foreign governments as well as international organizations.

The basic methodology for carrying out the research is described in section 1.2 of this manuscript. The data on madrassahs was gathered through primary field visits by individual survey data collectors. Statistics on government and private schools were obtained from secondary sources such as the *Education and School Atlas of Pakistan* (A UNICEF Project in collaboration with the Pakistan Planning Commission). An effort was made to verify these numbers through cross-checking with local officials and civil society groups. A form was devised for the purpose of data collection from each madrassah and contained the following information:

i) Name of police station. (key unit of administration and research analysis)
ii) Name of madrassah.

EMPIRICAL CASE ANALYSES 45

iii) Name of in charge/Manager.
iv) Location (village/street).
v) Year of establishment.
vi) Number of students—residential and non-residential.
vii) Sect to which madrassah belongs.
viii) Whether receiving monetary aid from government (from Zakat fund).[1]

Representative of Special Branch (provincial intelligence agency), local police and administration were also consulted for determining sectarian involvement of madrassahs.

AHMEDPUR EAST

Ahmedpur East Sub-division (APE), in Bahawalpur district of Punjab (Pakistan), has an area of approximately 6000 square kilometers, and a population of 1000,000 (projected), of the total population approximately 800,000 is rural and 200,000 urban.[2] Ahmedpur East comprises of 187 villages, and six police stations. The police station is an administrative unit for law enforcement based on demographic patterns. The sub-division is situated on the left bank of river Sutlej in the southern most part of Punjab (see appendix 4 for a detailed description of administrative delineations in the region).

Bahawalpur has an interesting history as a place of literal and figurative confluence of riparian systems and traditions. As the commentator Ayesha Siddiqa (2007) points out 'much before the age of 'enlightened moderation', Bahawalpur glowed due to its tradition of tolerance and its rich cultural heritage. A certain level of conservatism notwithstanding, the society offered generous space to great men and women of letters.'

During the last decade, however, this region has been the focus of considerable sectarian violence. The region has a history of many fatal and violent incidents involving the *Sipah-e-Sahaba* Pakistan (SSP-*Deobandis*) and Tehrik Jafferia Pakistan (TJP-*Shias*). Ahmedpur East Sub-division is considered to be a stronghold of SSP—the strength of this organization here can be gauged from the fact that during the National Elections of 1993, the candidate of SSP gained approximately 24,000 votes, despite the fact that the candidate was from another province and had no direct connection with the area.[3]

46　ISLAM AND EDUCATION

Figure 3.1 (a) and (b): Map of Ahmedpur sub-district, literacy ratios and madrassah density

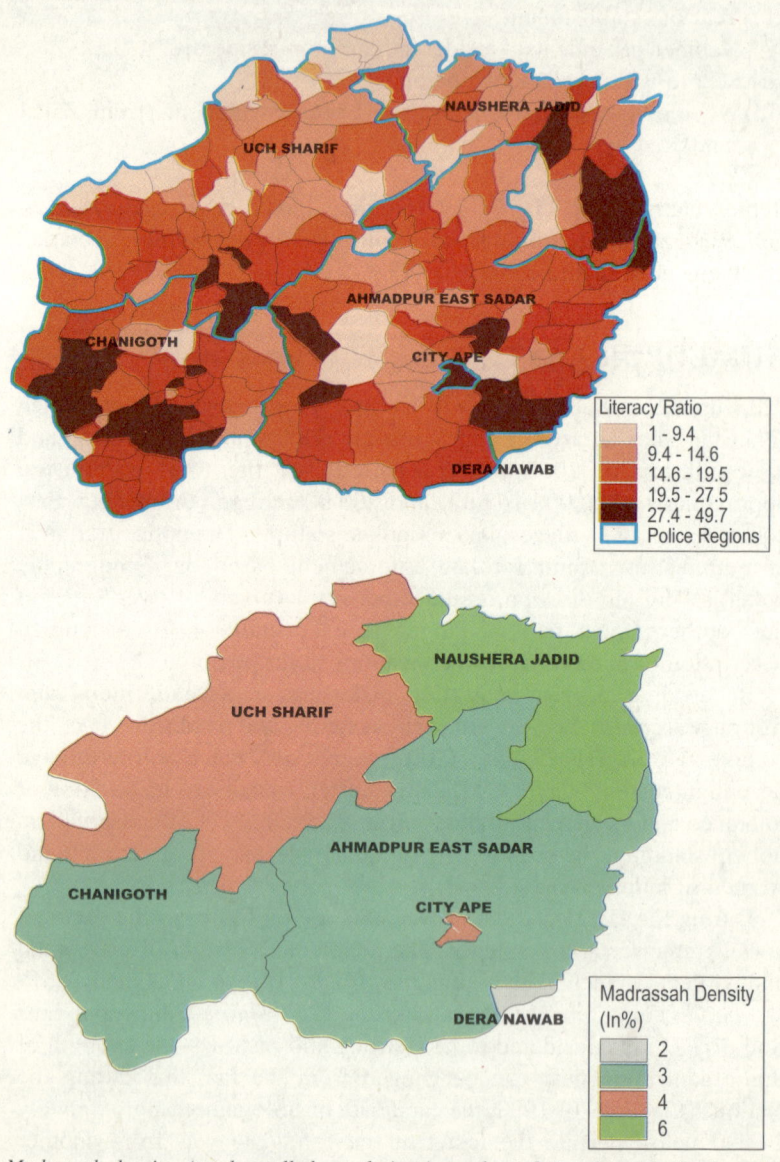

Madrassah density=(total enrolled population in madrassahs/total population in each police station region) X 100

Figure 3.2: Madrassah density with associated sectarian incidents

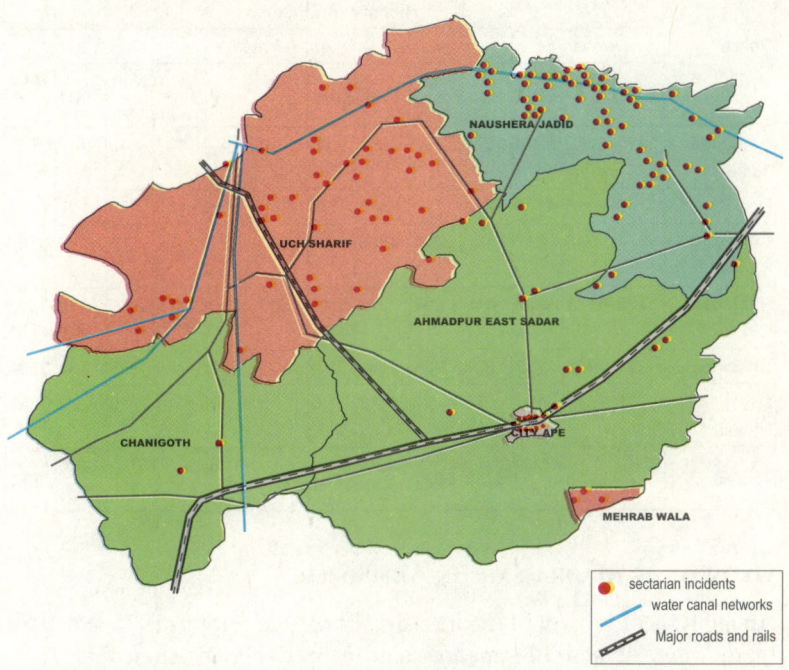

A manifestly militant organization *Harkat-al-Ansar*, which has a Kalashnikov-AK-47 as its logo, started its operations from this area. The organization was banned by the government of Pakistan and declared a terrorist organization by the US in 2001. Another militant organization *Jaish-e-Mohammad* also got many of its founding members from this area. One of the key suspects in the murder of *Wall Street Journal* reporter Daniel Pearl was also from this area.

Table 3.1 shows the aggregate results of the establishment survey documenting the demographics of madrassahs in Ahmedpur-east. The total number of madrassahs in the sub-division is 363, of this 166 belong to the Deobandi sect, 166 to Bareilvi, 21 to Salafi (Ahl-e-Hadith) and 10 to Shia (Ahl-e-Tashee) sects. Percentage-wise distribution between different sects is 45.8 per cent, 45.8 per cent, 5.7 per cent, and 2.75 per cent respectively. It is seen that only 9.3 per cent of Madrassahs (34 out of 363) are receiving monetary aid from the government/zakat fund.

Table 3.1: Number of students by sect in madrassahs, 2004

Police Station	Number of Students											
	Deobandi			Bareilvi			Ahl-e-Hadith			Shia			Total
	Res	Non Res	Total	Res	Non Res	Total	Res	Non Res	Total	Res	Non Res	Total	
Naushera Jadid	3149	2117	5266	1576	490	2066	30	10	40	104	45	149	7521
Uch Sharif	759	3366	4125	667	1796	2463	270	265	535	52	55	107	7230
Ahmedpur Sadar	274	343	617	2185	2111	4296	91	180	271	0	0	0	5184
Ahmedpur City	768	1138	1906	446	524	970	240	280	520	0	0	0	3396
Chanigoth	324	974	1298	207	931	1138	0	0	0	5	175	180	2606
Dera Nawab	100	20	120	72	40	112	0	0	0	0	0	0	232
TOTAL	5374	7958	13332 (51%)	5153	5892	11045 (42%)	631	735	1366 (5.2%)	161	275	436 (1%)	26169

GROWTH OF MADRASSAHS IN AHMEDPUR

An analysis of growth of madrassahs shows that prior to 1975 and 1980 there were 82 and 124 madrassahs respectively in Ahmedpur East. Much of the growth was experienced between 1980–95 and the growth of madrassahs has greatly slowed down after 2001—only 8 new madrassahs were set up between 2001–04. This slowdown in growth can be attributed to a general administrative policy wherein new madrassahs are being registered after an inquiry, and a ban imposed on the registration of new madrassahs was in effect till September 2004, when it was lifted by authorities. However, the madrassahs established earlier on are still largely unregistered and very little effort is being expended in trying to register them.

It is worthwhile to compare this data with the survey done by the field research coordinator of this study in 1994, in the same area—this provides a rare comparison of data pertaining to the same area after ten years. Figure 3.3 provides the ten-year growth comparison for madrassahs in this sub-division.

Figure 3.3

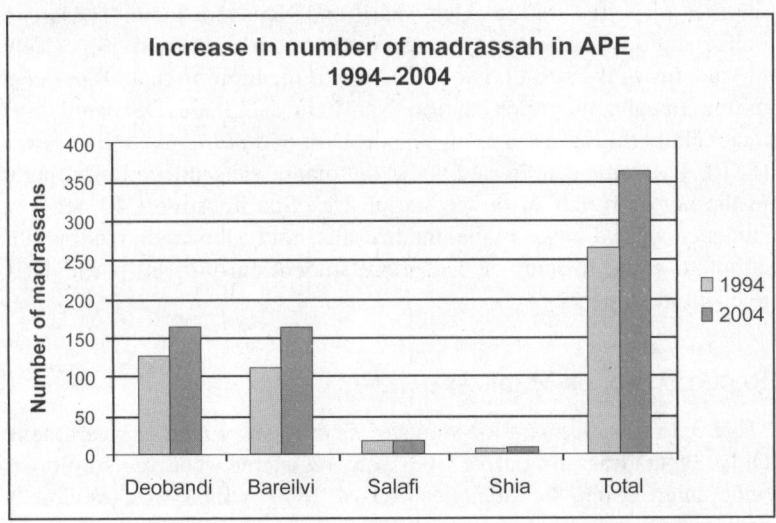

During last ten years the number of madrassahs has increased from 266 to 363 (details for the 1994 data are provided in Appendix 1). There has been a marked increase in number of Deobandi and Bareilvi madrassahs, however, the rate of increase in Bareilvi madrassahs has been more in last ten years. This finding also matches the information gathered during the interviews which suggests that the Bareilvi movement has also gained momentum as a foil to the rise of Deobandi madrassahs. The coverage of zakat to madrassahs during this period remained similar i.e around 9 per cent of madrassahs getting monetary support from the Zakat system.

Table 3.2: Residential demographic of students

Sect	Residential	Non-Residential	Total
Deobandi	5374	7958	13,332
Bareilvi	5153	5892	11,045
Ahl-e-Hadith/ Salafi	631	735	1366
Shia	57	230	287
Total	11,215	14,815	26,030

Our study shows that a major concentration of these madrassahs is in the area of police stations Uch Sharif and Naushera Jadid. These two police stations account for 55 per cent of madrassahs and 58 per cent of students in the sub-division. It is worth mentioning that 68 per cent of madrassahs in police station Naushera Jadid are Deobandi, and incidentally this area is a main support base of *Sipah-e-Sahaba* Pakistan (SSP). The same can be said about the madrassahs situated in villages in the northern half of police station Uch Sharif. Almost 40 per cent students were living in the madrassahs, and Deobandi madrassahs although equal in number, had more student enrollment, particularly residential students.

REGISTRATION OF MADRASSAHS

Table 3.3 shows registration status of madrassahs with the government. Only 39 madrassahs out of 363 were registered. The registration is undertaken under the Societies Act of 1860, which was previously performed by the Registrar Joint Stock Companies on the report and clearance by the district administration. After the administrative reforms called 'The Devolution Plan 2001', the authority to register any organization under the Societies Act 1860 has been delegated to the Executive District Officer (Finance and Planning) in the province of Punjab. In the other provinces this authority still remains with Directorate of Industries at provincial level.

Table 3.3: Registration Status of Madrassahs

Police Station	Number of Madrassahs										
	#	%	Registration by different sectarian affiliation								
			Deobandi		Bareilvi		Ahl-e-Hadith		Shia		
			Total	Reg.	Total	Reg.	Total	Reg.	Total	Reg.	
Naushera Jadid	92	26	62	01	26	00	01	00	03	00	01
Uch Sharif	113	32	58	02	44	04	07	00	04	00	06
Ahmedpur Sadar	77	22	10	01	63	13	04	00	00	00	14
Ahmedpur City	40	09	15	03	16	03	09	00	00	00	06
Chanigoth	36	10	18	04	15	03	00	00	03	01	08
Dera Nawab	05	01	03	02	02	02	00	00	00	00	04
Total	363	100	166	13	166	25	21	00	10	01	39

EMPIRICAL CASE ANALYSES 51

A greater proportion of the Bareilvi and Salafi/Ahle-Hadith madrassahs are registered. As a general trend, larger madrassahs, having an elaborate infrastructure and assets get registered while smaller madrassahs (with fewer than 100 students) are mostly not registered. The role of regulatory agencies and efficacy of departments responsible for registering the madrassahs will be discussed when we look at the Islamabad Capital territory case study.

STATE OF PUBLIC EDUCATION VERSUS MADRASSAHS

Schooling options are an important variable to consider in understanding madrassah prevalence. Table 3.4 shows a comparison of the number of madrassahs and student enrollment in different police station areas. It also shows how many schools are closed. These figures pertain to government schools only and include boys and girls schools of primary, middle and higher standard, whereas madrassahs data shows only male students studying in madrassahs since there were very few girls students in madrassahs of Ahmedpur East.

The data shows that as compared to 363 madrassahs there are 465 schools, of which 69 (almost 13 per cent) are closed due to non-availability of teachers or teacher absenteeism. A total of 55892 boys and girls were studying in public schools as compared to 26169 in madrassahs. It is worth noting that two police station areas having less madrassahs have comparatively more schools and hence more student enrollment. However in Police stations Naushera Jadid and Uch Sharif the number of madrassahs is more than government schools. The student enrolment in Naushera Jadid area is almost comparable in madrassahs and public schools. We observed that student enrollment in madrassahs is almost half of the school system. If one accounts for the girls students, the number of students studying in madrassahs and public schools becomes comparable.

Data on private schools was also obtained from a local association of such schools (the government does not keep any records of private schools). Only aggregate data for the entire subdivision was available and indicated that as of December 2004, there were a total of 17,137 students in 95 private registered schools. Urdu medium students account for 15,842 of this number while there are only 1295 English-medium schools.

Table 3.4: Comparison of government school and madrassah enrollment

Police Station	Madrassah Enrollment	Govt. School Enrollment	Number of Madrassahs	Number of Schools	Closed Schools (per cent)
Naushera Jadid	7521	8166	92	77	20 (20%)
Uch Sharif	7230	15032	113	110	12 (9.85%)
Ahmedpur Sadar	5184	14001	77	162	15 (8.4%)
Ahmedpur City	3396	7554	40	26	0%
Chanigoth	2606	9574	36	87	22 (20%)
Dera Nawab	232	1565	5	3	0%
Total	26169	55892	363	465	69 (13%)

IS THERE MADRASSAH INVOLVEMENT IN SECTARIANISM IN AHMEDPUR?

A major aim of this study is to question the perceived linkage of madrassahs to sectarian violence. This aspect of the research was assessed using proxy indicators—certain features or modes of behaviour were picked to classify a madrassah as being involved in sectarianism. Following are some of the indicators used for the purpose:

1. Any madrassah, which is visited by a leading sectarian leader, whose documented speeches have clearly incited violence towards other sects (records of particular events were gathered to assure quality of the data).
2. If the students/in-charge of a madrassah participate in sectarian processions or gatherings as documented by the police authorities (detailed records are kept by the police authorities regarding apprehensions from each institution).
3. If management of a madrassah lobbies for, or provides leadership to sectarian issues (documented through distribution of material at the madrassah and sermons at adjoining mosques).
4. If managers or students were involved in reported violent sectarian crimes (there will be a more specific analysis of this in Table 3.5).

Madrassahs exhibiting any of the above features, were categorized as positive for sectarian activity. The categorization was done after extensive interviews with local police officials, district administration officers, mosque imams and local community leaders.

Madrassahs situated in police stations Naushera Jadid and Uch Sharif and Ahmedpur City have an involvement rate of 100 per cent, 57 per cent and 45 per cent respectively. Deobandi and Shia sects have very high rates of involvement in violence and sectarianism. Traditionally Deobandi and Shia sects are in most acute conflict; hence we observed that madrassahs from these two sects, are overwhelmingly sectarian. However, Bareilvi madrassahs which were traditionally tolerant and non-confrontational institutions have also started showing violent and sectarian tendencies. In many instances this is a response to violent and aggressive attitudes of some Deobandi institutions and their managers.

Table 3.5: Madrassahs involved in Sectarianism

Sect	Total Madrassahs	Involved in Sectarianism	Not Involved in Sectarianism	Percentage Involvement
Deobandi	166	133	33	80%
Bareilvi	166	42	124	25%
Ahl-e-Hadith	21	03	18	14%
Shia	10	07	03	70%
Total	363	185	178	51%

In addition, our team also analyzed particular incidents of violence or 'hot spots' as they are labeled by local law enforcement authorities. The hot spots are administratively also called trouble spots. The local administration, intelligence agencies in consultation with local police authorities classify the trouble spots or hotspots in A, B and C category. This categorization of trouble spots is an administrative tool used by local police authorities for vigilance, monitoring of sectarian violence and local law and order. It is used for deploying personnel for prevention of serious conflict on different religious occasions. The trouble spots categorization can be general and day or event specific. This helps local police to monitor the situation and make adequate preventative measures.

This categorization or classification is based on the following criteria.

Category A: Any location where a serious sectarian conflict has happened in the past, and resulted in the death of a person (s), such a location is labeled 'A' category. Such locations are specially monitored on national occasions and are closely watched by supervisory officers on religious events. At many A category trouble spots military or paramilitary forces are deployed beforehand.

Category B: These are locations where in the past there has been physical conflict between different religious sects. The reason could be holding of a religious event on a contested venue, or the route taken by the procession. These spots indicate areas of serious conflict but without loss of life.

Category C: These are locations where there is potential for clash or conflict, based on the fact that verbal brawls have occurred in the past, or rival sects have been agitating against each other through demonstrations.

In Ahmedpur East there are 90 trouble spots, of A, B and C category. More that 90 per cent of these are situated in police station areas of Naushera Jadid, Uch Sharif and Ahmedpur city. Geographic Information Systems (GIS) analysis has shown that there are eight 'A' category trouble spots in Ahmedpur sub-division, located in Naushera Jadid, Ahmedpur east city and Uch Sharif police station areas. The trouble spots or hot spots are invariably situated in areas which have more concentration of Deobandi and Shia madrassahs. A closer analysis and study of the background of trouble spots showed that management and students of particular madrassahs were instrumental in the history of conflict pertaining to that trouble spot. Another finding is that the location of category 'A' trouble spots is invariably linked to highly sectarian Deobandi and Shia madrassahs.

The next question that we need to ask is what might be the underlying reasons for the high concentration of madrassahs as well as sectarian activity in Naushera Jadid and Uch Sharif, which are relatively rural areas and not subject to the same urban violence pressures as Ahmedpur.

Table 3.6: Location of 'Trouble Spots'

Police Station	Category 'A'	Category 'B'	Category 'C'
Uch sharif	2	0	23
Naushera Jadid	3	2	26
Ahmedpur East City	2	0	18
Ahmedpur East Sadar	0	0	3
Dera Nawab	0	1	6
Chanigoth	0	0	3
Total	7	3	79

ENVIRONMENTAL AND DEVELOPMENTAL DIFFERENTIATION OF SECTORS

In rural Pakistan and particularly South Punjab, political, economic and social power is closely linked to land ownership. Access to land or land ownership determines the social and political standing of an individual or a group of people in a society. Based on an analysis of landholding patterns from government records we concluded that 96 per cent of the population of Ahmedpur holds less than five acres of land.

Extremist and sectarian groups and religious parties have more following in areas where local feudal land owners have been controlling political and economic (land) power. Districts of Jhang, Khanewal, Multan, Vehari (Mailsi) Bahawalpur are all cases in point. This reaction has been more radical and severe in areas where the local political power was with Shia landed gentry or those more inclined to worship near shrines (often of Bareilvi proclivities).

Madrassahs were frequently the focal point of this movement against the feudal political leadership particularly where it was Shia. For the down-trodden and politically, socially and economically marginalized peasants, the religious political parties were a means of turning the tables on the traditional elite. The state functionaries were particularly receptive and obliging to religious/sectarian leaders, thus adding to their mass appeal. The favourable disposition of administrative machinery towards religious leaders, particularly those belonging to militant radical Deobandi groups, has been a post Afghan-jihad phenomenon. Many of the jihadis returned to their village bases and established madrassahs as a means of livelihood. The government had initially aimed to cultivate local leadership in these individuals and use them as a foil during times of sectarian activity. The administrative functionaries extended patronage to these groups accordingly. This phenomenon brought a fundamental change in the social standing of madrassahs and their graduates since they began to symbolize a revolution against an oppressive feudal system.

In Ahmedpur East land ownership patterns are also extremely asymmetric. Out of a total of 156,977 land owners, only 4 per cent own more than five acres of land, whereas 96 per cent of the land owners have less than five acres of land. In Pakistan, the official economic subsistence holding size is 12.5 acres. This shows that an individual holding less than five acres is living at the margins and needs external assistance or extra employment to meet basic survival needs. In our survey area this phenomenon is seen across the whole sub-division. However, we observed that in Chanigoth and Ahmedpur East Sadar police station areas, although land holding patterns are similar, the phenomenon of sectarian madrassahs is less prevalent. One reason could be the fact that these two areas are near the national highway, thus giving many other economic opportunities and exposure. Further study, perhaps using anthropological methods, may be needed to get a more conclusive explanation of this observation.

Different environmental and developmental indicators were also studied to explore madrassah-conflict linkages due to deprivation. Table 3.7 shows the electrification of the various areas studied.

Table 3.7: Electrification in key study area locations

Percentage of households with electricity	Number of villages falling in each percentile range				
	Uch Sharif	Naushera Jadid	Chanigoth	APE-met	Total in range
1-25 per cent	17	11	5	13	46 (25%)
26-50 per cent	11	11	21	14	57 (30%)
51-75 per cent	4	6	9	12	31 (17%)
76-100 per cent	10	1	10	6	27 (15%)
No electricity	11	2	4	7	24 (13%)
Total # of villages	53	31	49	52	185
APE-met refers to Ahmedpur City and Ahmedpur Sadar combined					

Access to electricity is an important indicator of poverty and standard of living. Almost 13 per cent villages are without electricity, in 25 per cent of the villages less than 25 per cent households have electricity, in another 30 per cent the access to electricity is available to 25-50 per cent households. For Naushera Jadid, which is worst hit by sectarianism and proliferation of Madrassahs, less than 50 per cent of households have electricity in 75 per cent of surveyed villages.

Table 3.8: Infrastructure Facilities

Number of Villages	Uch Sharif	Naushera Jadid	Chanigoth	APE Sadar	Total
	53	31	49	52	185
With water supply	7	0	1	1	9
Without water supply	46	31	48	51	176
No farm to market road	14	2	6	14	36
With Farm to market road	39	29	43	38	149
Extreme Water Shortage	35	31	34	50	150
Mild Shortage	8	0	15	2	25
No Shortage	8	0	0	0	8

The availability of potable water through government provided safe drinking water supply schemes was also studied. Out of a total of the 185 villages in the sub-district only 9 villages have drinking water schemes. Considering that the incidence of water borne diseases is extremely high in the area, the unavailability of safe drinking water is a major development challenge. Here also we observed that not a single water supply scheme is provided in Naushera Jadid and the northern half of Uch Sharif—areas of higher sectarian activity.

The provision of road connectivity has also been documented. In terms of mobility and providing access to market for agricultural produce, farm to market roads are an important provision. Although, generally better than other socio-economic indicators, approximately 20 per cent of villages are still not connected to the farm via market roads. The perennial shortage of irrigation water is one of the key reasons contributing to low productivity and poverty of the area. Scarcity indicators for the villages were developed based on municipal classifications. Given the semi-arid climate in this area, agriculture is highly dependent on the irrigation water. 150 out of 185 villages in the region experience extreme water shortage. Only eight villages have no scarcity of canal water and another 25 villages have mild shortage. In Naushera Jadid the water shortage is most acute—all 31 villages have extreme shortage of canal water.[4]

Table 3.9: Agricultural Productivity

	Uch Sharif	Naushera Jadid	Chanigoth	APE Sadar
Average Yield In *Rabi* (Wheat) maunds per acre	15	16	15	16
Range	30-10	20-10	25-5	30-7
Average Yield In *Kharif* (cotton) maunds per acre	12	12	12.7	12
Range	20-10	16-10	20-5	20-7

In terms of agricultural productivity, although no major variation is seen between different regions of Ahmedpur subdivision (Table 3.9), the average yield of wheat and cotton is almost half of the average yields expected of subsistence farms. The average yield of 15 *maunds* (one *maund* = 40 Kg) of wheat and 12 *maunds* of cotton is half of what some farmers get in the same sub-division. This data shows that agricultural productivity in the region is at sub-optimal or low productivity level.

While resource scarcity alone cannot be an effective explanatory variable, it has many possible manifestations that can compound conflict in certain socio-cultural contexts.[5] One outcome of resource scarcity can also be migration to urban centres. In order to fully understand the dynamics of youth movement and madrassah enrollment, we also studied madrassahs in the urban context of Islamabad.

ISLAMABAD CASE ANALYSIS

The capital of Pakistan was moved from Karachi to the newly planned city of Islamabad in 1960. The city was built near the Margalla Hills to provide greater security and a more pleasant environment and climate for government officials and diplomats. The planning team for the city was led by the distinguished Greek urban planner Constantinos Doxiadis, who had participated in numerous urban revitalization projects and new capital developments across the world.[6] Doxiadis planned the city by residential sectors with a core market area in each sector to avoid traffic congestion. A commercial core area, as well as government and diplomatic enclaves were also planned in close proximity to the residential areas. A key distinguishing feature of the plan was the allocation of several green belt areas which were to be left as environmental conservation zones and no building was to be allowed on these zones.

The name Islamabad was chosen to represent the core focus of Pakistan's creation as a sanctuary for the Muslims of the Indian subcontinent—the name of the city means 'habitation of Islam.' It is thus perhaps not surprising that madrassahs would flourish in the capital. However, the location of these madrassahs emerging on the greenbelt zones was particularly intriguing. Furthermore, Islamabad has always had a reputation of being the most 'westernized' city in Pakistan because of the presence of diplomats and international agencies. It is also a well-fortified city due to government offices and strict law enforcement on most accounts.

The choice of Islamabad as a comparative case study could thus help in understanding how madrassahs can emerge in a more secular ambiance and the impact which they have on communities in the area. The population of Islamabad itself is estimated to be just over a million (in the 1998 census it was 529,180) though the population growth rate from 1981–98 was 5.76 per cent which is almost twice the national average growth rate. Islamabad's neighbouring city Rawalpindi, 15 miles to the south, has a population almost three times that of Islamabad and both cities are now effectively merging into a 'duopolis.'

It is important to note that the empirical analysis for the Islamabad case is less detailed then for the Ahmedpur case because of various developmental variables that are not of relevance in Islamabad as a modern urban centre.

Residential Profile of Madrassahs

A distinguishing feature of madrassahs in Islamabad is that these are almost entirely residential institutions providing complete boarding and lodging to students. This may be due to the fact that a majority of the students come from villages beyond a commutable distance from the city. The size of the madrassahs is also highly varied from 2000 students to 35-40 students. Also, there are separate madrassahs for girls (rarely encountered in rural madrassahs), some as large as 1000 residential students. Tables 3.10 and 3.11 show the demographic patterns of madrassahs in Islamabad based on our survey.

Table 3.10: Number of Madrassahs in Islamabad

Police Station	#	Located on State land	% of total	Sect Wise Detail Number and percentage				No. of Registered Madrassahs
				Deo-bandi	Bareilvi	Ahl-e-Hadith	Shia	
Appara	14	14	12	09	04	0	01	8
Khosar	18	18	15	12	05	0	01	9
Margalla	20	20	17	16	04	0	0	6
Golra	27	26	23	16	10	01	0	6
Tarnol	05	0	04	01	04	0	0	0
Bharkau	09	1	08	06	03	0	0	0
I-9	15	15	13	05	09	01	0	01
Sihala	02	0	02	01	0	0	01	0
Secretarial	07	7	06	04	02	0	01	02
Total	117	101	100	70 (60)	41 (35)	02 (02)	04 (03)	32

Table 3.11: Madrassah Enrollment by Sect in Islamabad

Police Station	Deobandi	Bareilvi	Ahl-e-Hadith	Shia	Total
Appara	3530	290	25	0	3845
Khosar	3257	305	0	95	3657
Margalla	1780	305	0	0	2085
Golra	1245	475	40	0	1760
Tarnol	40	149	0	0	189
Bharkau	687	191	0	0	878
I-9	255	385	250	0	890
Sihala	20	0	0	28	48
Secretariat	391	337	0	144	842
Total	11,205	2437	315	267	14,194

MADRASSAHS VERSUS GOVERNMENT AND PRIVATE SCHOOLS

An urban centre such as Islamabad has an abundance of government and private schools, many of which are far better equipped than their rural counterparts. The enrollment of students in government schools is shown in Table 3.12. The number of private schools in Islamabad is estimated to be 290 with an enrollment of around 43,000 students.[7] Clearly, the madrassahs are a much smaller component of the educational profile here.

Table 3.12: Government School Enrollment in Islamabad 2005

Kind of School	No. of Schools	Girls	Boys	Total
Primary School (Girls and Boys)	209	42,641	42,639	85,280
Middle Schools (Girls and Boys)	54	11,034	11,280	22,314
Secondary Schools (Girls and Boys)	90	11,034	11,280	22,314
Higher Secondary Schools (Girls and Boys)	18	8,803	6,477	15,280
Total	371	73,512	71,676	145,188
These schools are under the Federal Directorate of Education (data source)				

Madrassahs and Greenbelts

However, the relatively small number of madrassahs, here does not detract from their influence and power. The madrassahs are spread out across the city and are situated often in the choicest residential areas. The madrassahs in Islamabad are mostly located at prime commercial and residential locations. A unique and intriguing feature of madrassahs in sectoral Islamabad is that 90 per cent of them are located on state land, in urban areas out of 103 madrassahs, 100 are located on state/public land. The larger ones are situated on green belts, along main avenues, or in reserved or protected areas. This phenomenon is a product of the Russo-Afghan war when many of the madrassahs were given concessions for establishment. Initially, many of these madrassahs were established without a permit but under President Zia, some of these were regularized under planning laws. Since many madrassahs are preceded by the establishment of a mosque, they are protected by cultural reluctance to dislocate a mosque.

We also observed that there were hardly any local students studying in Islamabad madrassahs—most of the students are from the northern districts of the Northwest Frontier Province (NWFP) such as Buner, Swat, Manshera, Kohistan,etc. The students are thus quite disconnected from the communities in which they reside—a phenomenon that has perhaps led the educational linguist Tariq Rehman (2004) to refer to them and their counterparts in government and other private schools as 'Denizens of Alien Worlds'.

During the last couple of years the madrassahs in Islamabad, specially the ones located in major urban sectors, are undergoing extensive expansions and increase in enrollment. The manager of one of the larger madrassahs, whom we interviewed, stated that this increase in enrollment is a post 9/11 phenomenon and a reaction to Western and governmental policies towards Islam and religious education.[8] During our field visit to the madrassahs, we observed that children were having to sleep in corridors because there was not enough space to house the growing demand for enrollment.

Islamabad Madrassahs and Civil Unrest

Unlike the Ahmedpur case, Islamabad law enforcement was reluctant to share the data on 'trouble spots' with us due to security concerns in the capital itself. However, a review of recent acts of sectarian violence does indeed reveal a connection with madrassah proximity and the involvement of several students. Content analysis of newspapers for the past five years revealed that several prominent cases of civil unrest in the city were linked to madrassahs. Here is a sampling of some of the most well-publicized cases:

- The riots involving mostly Deobandi madrassahs on 7 October 2003, when Maulana Tariq Azam was killed, led to serious vandalism and arson of a gas station owned by a US company, a new movie theater and a Bareilvi shrine. According to authorities a majority of those arrested were from local madrassahs.
- In November 2004, the police tried to apprehend the son of the late Maulana Abdullah and brother of the manager of a major Deobandi madrassah on charges of giving refuge to an al-Qaeda operative. In order to resist his arrest hundreds of male and female madrassah students got into violent conflict with police in Islamabad.
- The warrant against Allama Ghazi Abdul Rasheed and Abdul Aziz of the Lal Masjid madrassah in Islamabad in connection with attempted attacks on President Musharraf sparked a series of violent riots in August 2004.[9] The spouses of the accused told reporters that the decree of *irtadad* (apostasy) would be issued against the government (legitimizing killing of government officers) if it did not halt the raids and withdraw the charges against the religious leaders.
- The claim by a federal minister of state of religious affairs and TV-talk show host, Aamer Liaqat Hussain, that there had been 500 claims of sexual abuse in madrassahs also led to riots in several cities, including Islamabad, with sectarian overtones since Mr Hussain is affiliated with the MQM party, and is himself a Bareilvi with controversial credentials.[10]
- The controversy surrounding the allowance of a joint marathon between male and female athletes in May 2005 was also resisted vehemently by religious parties. Of the 40 religious protestors arrested, during these riots, 38 were madrassah students. Additionally, the government also arrested several marathon activists.
- On 27 May 2005, at least 25 people, including a suspected suicide bomber, were killed and approximately 100 others sustained injuries during a powerful explosion at the Bari Imam

shrine of the Shi'ite sect located in the vicinity of the diplomatic enclave in Islamabad (this shrine is also revered by many Bareilvis). The investigation is pending but the perpetrators are being linked to the SSP and local madrassahs by law enforcement agencies.

As a mark of unity, prominent madrassahs organized a joint convocation on 15 May 2005 at the state-owned Convention Centre in Islamabad that is used for high-profile activities like the South Asian Association for Regional Cooperation (SAARC) conventions.[11] This convocation brought together thousands of Deobandi clerics from all over the country including the self-proclaimed 'spiritual leaders' of the Taliban—Maulana Samiul Haq, Maulana Fazlur Rehman, former Inter Services Intelligence Chief (ISI) Hamid Gul, and Qazi Hussain Ahmad. Former Prime Minister Shujaat Hussain, Information Minister Sheikh Rashid Ahmad and Minister for Religious Affairs Ijaz-ul-Haq represented the government. The convocation, ostensibly intended to award outstanding clerics, sent out a strong message, emphasized particularly in speeches by Qazi Hussain Ahmed, Fazl-ur-Rehman and Samiul Haq that politics and religion are intrinsically linked and cannot be analyzed in isolation, and that the mullahs are the greatest custodians of politics.

Maulana Fazl-ur-Rehman stated in unequivocal terms the political intent of the madrassah establishment:

> Politics is the governance of a society the rules of which were set by Qur'an and propounded by the holy Prophet. Therefore, the Prophet was the greatest politician and statesman. Muslims are bound to follow him in all respects of life. Since the mullahs are the true disciples of the Prophet, politics is their religious right. And by doing politics, the mullahs are carrying forward the Prophet's mission. Politics is surely not the business of the Army.

In his highly charged speech, Samiul Haq claimed that the big powers were working on a single-point agenda—the annihilation of the seminaries. 'The international community is against only one thing, the seminaries or madrassahs. Its target is not the Islamic army, the Muslim rulers, generals or the politicians. It is not concerned with our natural resources. Its target is only one—to label our seminaries as hub of terrorism and extremism.'

The convocation passed a 14-point resolution, in which madrassahs figured prominently:

- The five wafaq (coalitions) of religious seminaries should be given the status of a board and their degrees/certificates should be recognized at the national level.
- The Seminaries Reforms Board should be immediately abolished. It is a violation of the agreement that the government had entered into with the five wafaq.
- Seminaries are not involved in any act of terror. Such propaganda is a Jewish conspiracy.
- We condemn the Aga Khan Board (AKB) and demand that it should be immediately banned.
- The proceedings of all the government and private events should start with the recitation of Qur'an and it should be made part of the law.
- The ban on the foreign students who want to come to Pakistan for religious education should be lifted and they should be granted visas.
- The government should stop patronizing Hindu and European culture in the country and ban such NGOs that are involved in this crime.
- The state-media should stop promoting nudity.

The 15 May convocation was extraordinarily well-organized. A media cell, equipped with computers, internet connectivity and photocopiers had been established at Lal Masjid; security was tight, and nobody was allowed entry without invitation. The proceedings of the convocation were transmitted live through the internet at www.defendersofislam.com. Some clerics who could not make it to the Convention Centre participated online. Several observers were inclined to some skepticism regarding the administrative skills of the clerics, and suspicions were voiced that the 'ISI has sponsored this show.'

Arif Jamal—a prolific writer on jihad and rightwing politics—observed:

> The convocation marks a new beginning of relations between the Musharraf Government and the Deobandi ulema. The conflict between the Musharraf Government and the Pakistani Deobandi ulema that started with the fall of the Taliban Government in Afghanistan and reached its climax with the

attempts on the life of General Musharraf appears to be over. The Musharraf Government's reconciliatory efforts towards the ulema in general, and friendly acts towards the Deobandi ulema in particular, have finally convinced them that the government is not hostile towards ulema.

Sectarianism is a serious problem in Pakistan that continues to defy solutions. According to sectarianism researcher Amir Mir, between January 1989 and 31 May 2005, a total of 1,784 Pakistanis were killed, and another 4,279 injured in 1,866 incidents of sectarian violence across the country. This averages out to more than 100 persons per year over the past 17 years. There are some indications that the trends may worsen. Thus, 187 persons were killed and another 619 were injured in 19 incidents of sectarian violence in 2004. Within the first five months of 2005, 120 Pakistanis lost their lives, and 286 were injured in 30 incidents of sectarian violence. No longer can conspiracy theorists cast random blames on 'foreign powers' since in all cases various sectarian leaders have claimed responsibility for these incidents and identities of the perpetrators are public knowledge.[12]

The next chapter attempts to build on the empirical analysis of the Islamabad and Ahmedpur cases to understand how and why violence might be linked to madrassahs more generally.

NOTES

1. Zakat is an Islamic religious tithe collected by the Pakistan government through mandatory deduction from saving accounts in banks and then spent on certain purposes, aid to madrassahs being one of them. Record of the district Zakat office was also consulted for this information.
2. Estimates based on local district records and personal communication with the deputy commissioner of Bahawalpur.
3. Personal communication, Assistant Commissioner, Ahmedpur, January 2005.
4. For a study of feudal control over water and its impact on livelihoods in Pakistan see Mustafa, 2002.
5. There is a wide assemblage of literature on possible linkages between resource scarcity, conflict and security. While much of the linear determinism that characterized the field in the 1980s has been discredited, there are many new nuanced approaches to understanding possible connections between resource scarcity and conflict. For a detailed review of the literature on this topic including bibliographic references on debates refer to the Woodrow Wilson Centre's Environmental Change and Security project.

6. Doxiadis is also known in urban planning as the founder of the field of *ekistics* or the science of human habitation and the author of classics in urban planning such as *Anthropopolis*. For a detailed history of Islamabad's planning see Yakas, 2001.
7. Estimates based on data of the Planning Commission of Pakistan. *Education and School Atlas of Pakistan*. (A UNICEF project). 2002
8. Interview with the *muallim* at the E-7 madrassah in Islamabad, 1 January 2004.
9. This madrassah was slated for demolition by the Pkistani government in January 2007 since it was built on illegally obtained land. A major conflict has ensued between the students (many of whom are women) and the government. The situation has been studied by Farhat Taj, a Norway-based researcher, who visited the madrassah and found the attitudes of the women instructors to be extremely hostile towards any reform efforts.
10. Madrassah leadership are very conscious of these allegations. Some Muslim organizations, particularly in the United Kingdom, are now engaged in training of personnel at Islamic schools and students about sexual abuse. See for example, the guide prepared by the Muslim Parliament of Britain titled: 'Child Protection in Faith-based Environment' London, UK: Muslim Institute Trust, March 2006.
11. The details of this event are derived from a report by Islamabad-based journalist Mohammad Shehzad, email communiqué, 30 May 2005.
12. Data collected from Amir Mir. 'Pakistan's sectarian monster.' *Asia Times*, 8 June 2005.

4

MADRASSAHS AND VIOLENCE: IS THERE A CONNECTION?

Recent scholarship has been largely preoccupied with the absolute number of madrassahs or the size of their enrollment rather than their potential linkage to conflict (Andrabi et al, 2005). Indeed, part of the problem has been that the research is polarized by those who are either viscerally opposed to theocracies and see madrassahs or the role of religion in education more generally as symbolizing such a state of affairs (International Crisis Group, 2004, Nayyar and Salim, 2004) and others who feel obliged to defend the theological roots of Pakistan (Institute of Policy Studies, 2002). In some cases, scholars have attempted to look at linkages to violence but have conflated various variables in their analysis and come up with an interesting but non-definitive analysis (Rahman, 2004). Still others have solely focused on connections to international violence (Bergen and Panday, 2005) and the relatively apolitical tone of traditional madrassah curricula (Ahmad, Mumtaz, 2003), thereby dismissing any cause for concern.

Doctrines of justifiable violence in religious institutions have been debated in many contexts. The Indonesian scholar Muhammad Iqbal Ahnaf (2005) has analyzed various religious traditions and their invocations to violence and nonviolence in greater detail in comparison to Islam. He begins with the primary rationale or moral justification of war and violence that is provided by *the just-war theory*. This theory is based on the writings of western philosophers and theologians like Aristotle, Augustine, Thomas Aquinas, and Reinhold Niebuhr. Just-war theorists have analyzed how and when Christians are to 'break the law for a higher purpose' by undertaking violent actions for a just cause. The first criterion is called *bellum justum*. This requires: (1) that war is conducted to outweigh a higher potential of harm, (2) the probability of success must outweigh the probability of defeat, and (3) all possible alternatives for peace must be exhausted prior to the decision to resort to violence. The second criteria, called *jus ad bellum*, comprises the authority and cause to initiate just-war: (1) war must be initiated by a competent authority (2) just cause must be individual or collective self defense or protection of one's rights. The last criteria, *jus in bello*, deals with the conduct of a just war: (1) It should use proportional utility and (2) it should discriminate in its targets and tactics (noncombatants must be protected). Abdul Ghaffar Khan (a.k.a Bashah Khan), a Muslim tribal leader of the Pathans in Pakistan and Afghanistan, is considered a leading figure in South Asian history who was able to harmonize these Islamic principles of non-violence within political activism and is often referred to as 'The Frontier Gandhi.'

While the positive role of madrassahs as social institutions must be respected, and the role of religious education as part of Pakistan's cultural and political fabric must be recognized, the aim here is to present a dispassionate understanding of various potential linkages to conflict. Rather than casting aspersions on madrassahs themselves, I identify the conflict linkages and then attempt to understand the underlying causes for this conflict.

MADRASSAHS AND JIHAD

The term 'jihad' has been used and manipulated by both proponents and opponents of Islamic doctrine to meet their own ends. For the 'Islamophobes,' jihad is a purely militant concept that focuses on the physical aspect of combating the enemy. For many moderate Muslims, the term jihad has the most benign connotation of 'struggle.' They argue that the most vital and virtuous of struggles is against ones own instinctive impulses to do harm to oneself and fellow human beings. Most ulama, however, consider the pacifist connotation of jihad as only one aspect of *jihad fi-al-nafs* (struggle against negative natural impulses), while the physical nature of jihad of combating injustice through armed struggle to them is just as important. As they rightly point out to dismiss the apologists, Muslims have engaged in numerous battles against oppression and to ensure that their faith is not lost to invading armies. Regrettably, both sides often miss the nuanced nature of Islamic governance, specially during the golden age of the Prophet Muhammad (PBUH) that is supposed to be the hallmark for Muslims to emulate. During this time, the Prophet did indeed fight battles, but all of them were defensive battles and when necessary, he made numerous peace treaties with even his fiercest opponents such as the famous truce of *Hudaibiyah*.[1]

The persistent tenacity of Muslims to jihad has often perplexed western scholars and politicians alike since it shows a remarkable commitment and conviction that some political observers, with a hint of admiration, believe other religions have lost (Buchanan, 2002). Indeed, when we interviewed Muslim religious scholars across the spectrum, they all concurred that jihad against injustice and the preservation of Islam was essential. In the words of Dr Anis Ahmed, one of the most distinguished intellectuals of the *Jamaat-e-Islaami* in Pakistan:[2] 'all this madrassah reform is about trying to stop the spirit of jihad that distinguishes Muslims from other faiths, and that they will not stop.'[3] In his interview, Dr Ahmed also made it clear that jihad is only mandated in the face of oppression and that he fully supports good relations with non-Muslims.

Thus physical jihad is clearly considered a noble concept across the spectrum of ulama. The question to ask then is: under what conditions and permutations is jihad to be allowed and how is this linked to madrassah education? As a fundamental Islamic concept for law enforcement, the tenets of jihad are taught as part of any Islamic curriculum. However, its political applicability in contemporary contexts is usually not taught in the madrassah itself. Usually such commentary is provided in sermons at adjoining mosques where contemporary issues are discussed. However, since madrassah students attend mosques prayers five times a day, they are certainly exposed to this political commentary.

Additionally, it is important to consider whether the jihadist elements are focused on specific causes such as Kashmir or the more expansive globalized campaign of loose confederation of groups such as al Qaeda.

OPINIONS REGARDING JIHAD

Ascertaining the linkage to jihad among madrassah graduates could also be studied with opinion surveys. As part of our study, we chose not to use opinion surveys since the quality of the data would be very doubtful given the high level of suspicion among madrassah students of researchers. Moreover, there is a certain bravado regarding questions of jihad that might affect the responses and lead to inconclusive results.

Nevertheless, it is useful to consider the studies conducted in this regard thus far.

There are only two systematic surveys of opinions of madrassah students and teachers that have been carried out thus far. One was done by the Institute of Policy Studies (2002) and the other by Rahman (2004). However, the results in these studies are somewhat unreliable given the small sample size used, as well as a lack of any statistical testing regarding the output. Nevertheless, some of the findings are striking and at least merit further study and reflection.

According to the Institute of Policy Studies (2002), madrassah students were found to be 'tolerant' of the major Islamic sects and sub-sects (though details are not provided of where these opinions were ascertained despite the acknowledgement that sectarianism can be very regional). However, even in their own analysis, there were some alarming trends which do not bode well for tolerance. Across sects, 43 per cent of respondents favoured a revolution as a process of change in Pakistan, 50 per cent favoured mosque preaching and canvassing and only 6 per cent favoured elections. About 31 per cent of respondents, considered women to be lesser than men, and only 11 per cent considered them equal to men. To the question, 'How can jihad be waged in Pakistan?' only 8 per cent of students agreed with using force. However, 82 per cent of Deobandi students favoured the Taliban as their role model for Islamization in Pakistan, while 95 per cent of Shias favoured Iran as their role model for Islamization (Institute for Policy Studies, 2002).

Rahman (2004) compared opinions on jihad, religious minorities and armed conflict versus diplomacy of madrassahs and government school students and teachers. One of his most revealing findings is shown in Table 4.1. The radicalism among madrassah teachers was found to be greater than among the students. The results for government and private school teachers were substantially lower. However, as mentioned earlier, this study is not definitive by any means and a far more careful analysis, perhaps through anthropological methods might be in order to fully understand opinions and motivations.

It may also be instructive to consider the debate on the use of violence towards non-Muslims in particular. Perhaps the most radical elements among the Islamic clergy derive the sanction to violence against non-Muslims from the writings of Imam Shafai. Modern imams and Muslim leaders generally reject this view and also recontextualize verses in the Qur'an that may be perceived to sanction violence.[4] While there may have been aggressive wars in Muslim history, the reformist scholars are now beginning to suggest that defensive wars are the only justifiable ones under Qur'anic injunctions. However, the question remains how defensive wars are to be defined, since many of the contemporary conflicts in Muslim minds are defined as defensive while they would appear overtly aggressive to Western observers. A perceptual disconnect on these matters can only be resolved through a confluence of historical narratives on the one hand and a willingness to reconcile past injustices through acknowledgement and compensation where possible.

Table 4.1: Results of Survey of Madrassah Teachers, Rahman (2004)

What should be Pakistan's Priorities for Resolving Conflicts? (N=27)		
Open War		
Yes	No	Don't Know
70.4	22	7.4
Funding Jihadi Groups		
Yes	No	Don't Know
59.3	29.6	11.1
Peaceful means		
Yes	No	Don't Know
29.6	66.7	3.7

During the course of our research, we conducted various interviews with madrassah children as well. We were particularly alarmed by the similarity and linearity in the narrative responses of the respondents. An example of a typical conversation with a rural madrassah student is given below. This particular respondent was ten years old at the time of the interview in 2005 and belongs to the largest Sunni sect in Pakistan, the Bareilvis. A comment on each response is provided under the response:

Q: Who are you?
A: *I am a Bareilvi.*
Note: the defining of identity in terms of the sect.

MADRASSAHS AND VIOLENCE: IS THERE A CONNECTION? 73

Q: What is a Bareilvi?
A: *He who believes in the Prophet.*
Note: Linking the sect to a fundamental defining feature of being a Muslim—belief in the Prophet.

Q: And what is a Deobandi?
A: *He who doesn't believe in the Prophet.*
Note: Exclusionary narrative, that makes the other sect inherently alien.

Q: Where is your village?
A: *It is near Ghotaki, about hundred miles from here.*
Note: Willingness of parents to send their son so far from home for madrassah schooling.

Q: Do your other brothers study in madrassahs?
A: *No they go to a government school.*
Note: Often parents might dedicate one child for madrassah education while sending the others to government schools.

Q: Do you have TV in your madrassah?
A: *No TV is not 'Jaize' (Not allowed in religion').*
Note: Non-access to TV excludes a major information resource.

Q: What about computer?
A: *Yes it is allowed, it is a useful thing.*
Note: A clear differentiation between various media of communication.

Q: Have you ever used a computer?
A: *Yes, many times, I know windows, email etc.*
Note: Clear technological proficiency, even in a rural context.

Q: What is the use of knowing computers?
A: *It is a useful thing, it helps in 'rawabit'(networking).*
Note: Clearly well-versed in the importance of maintaining relations with others.

Q: What will you do once you grow up?
A: *I will become a maulvi (religious preacher) and make speeches.*
Note: Clearly defined, albeit limited, career path.

Q: What type of speeches will you make:?
A: *I will invite people towards Bareilvi Islam.*
Note: Clear evangelical intentions.

The psychology of how militancy develops in children following exposure to various ideological and sensory triggers has been widely studied (Bandura, 1973; Anderson et al., 2003). There are, unfortunately, no formal published psychological studies of children in madrassahs of this kind.

However, a graduate student at the University of Punjab did a Masters thesis project in 1995 comparing the level of aggression between eighty government school boy students and eighty madrassah boy students using an adapted Urdu version of an aggression questionnaire developed by psychologists Buss and Perry (1992) divided into four segments: physical aggression; verbal aggression; anger; and hostility. There was a statistically significant difference in the aggression measures between the madrassah students and the government school students in the categories of physical aggression and hostility but no significant difference in the measures of anger and verbal aggression (Saeed, 1995). Some of these findings are attributed by the author to harsh corporal punishment in madrassahs though that seems to be fairly common across all schools in Pakistan.

A recent Indian book in Urdu on madrassahs along the Indo-Nepal border (frequently accused of collaboration with Kashmiri separatists) concluded that the linkage to violence is minimal, though the findings are based solely on an dichotomous (Yes/No) opinion survey. Alam (2004) claims to have administered to some 3500 people at a hundred different madrassahs.

Nevertheless, these findings still need further rigorous analysis and lead us to ask the question of why this aggression might manifest itself in madrassah children. Varying interpretations of jihad might lead us to understand how this radicalization process might be justified in young minds.

Different Forms of Jihad Linkage

If we unpack the notion of jihad further and ask what scale of jihad these individuals may consider engaging in, there can be three possible categories:
i) *Domestic jihad against oppression and the reluctance of the state to allow for implementation of Islamic law*: This aspect of jihad appears to have direct linkages with madrassah establishments since political rallies around madrassahs often become violent (as reflected by our analysis in the Ahmedpur case). The assassination

plots against President Musharraf were also linked to one of the madrassahs in Islamabad where a suspect was given refuge and the imam was later arrested. Such jihadist activity can only be curtailed through greater dialogue between groups on what interpretations of Islamic law can be accepted within a national consensus. Law enforcement to prevent violence is also essential, though this should not be misused as a license to summarily incarcerate Islamists as it will likely only radicalize them further (as happened with the Muslim Brotherhood in Egypt). Internal assessment and contextualized religious reinterpretation within the religious establishment is also in order, and is the ultimate solution as has been the case in other religions as well. In reality, the Afghan jihad was actually motivated by a desire to oust a secular regime and was initially domestic in nature. However, as we saw, with the inclusion of international fighters, it quickly got linked to the second category as follows.

ii) *Pan-Islamist jihad, to help fellow Muslims in need and preserve the vitality of the ummah (Islamic body of adherents).* This form of jihad is perhaps what Western countries are most afraid of since it often implies a willingness to attack foreign targets. In Afghanistan, Arab fighters joined the Afghan cause motivated by a spirit of helping their fellow Muslims rather than any particular domestic interest. Direct madrassah linkage to this form of jihad is relatively remote. However, in some regional cases it became far more direct. For example, in the case of the Kashmir jihad, the linkage of *Markaz al Dawah al Irshad* to the guerilla group *Lashkar-i-Tayyaba* is well established. Similarly, the linkage of some of the Frontier madrassahs to the Afghan jihad is well-known, leading to the Taliban movement. However, contrary to common belief in the West, the aim of the pan-Islamists is not to 'wipe out infidels' but rather to establish Islamic government in historically Islamic lands. Evangelists such as the Tablighi Jama'at who often speak of 'making America' Muslim are not implying to do this through jihad but rather through conventional evangelical means such as those used by Christian missionaries. Of course a double standard does arise in cases where many missionaries of other religions such as the Bahai or Christians are prohibited from evangelizing in Muslim countries. Nevertheless, the two issues of evangelism and jihad should not be conflated.

iii) *Jihad to establish theological purity and prevent adulteration of Islamic doctrine.* This form of jihad is most closely linked to madrassahs in Pakistan because it is the primary motivation for sectarianism. There are two concepts in Islamic tradition that are often misused and manipulated to motivate this form of jihad and often madrassah students are indoctrinated with these. The concept of *murtad*, which is a term used to describe someone who has left the fold of Islam after voluntarily becoming a Muslim. According to most interpretations of Islamic tradition, it is permissible to kill such an individual to prevent doubt from taking hold in the community. This injunction is linked to a strategy used in the early days of Islam by the non-Muslim people of Makkah (Kuffar-e-Makkah). Individuals would pretend to accept Islam at first and then soon reject it leading to doubt among other potential converts. These strategic pretenders are often referred to in Islam as 'munafiqoon' or 'the hypocrites.' In this specific historical context, there was an allowance made to execute such individuals who left Islam and became *'murtad'* according to military doctrine of betrayal (Salman Rushdie was declared a *murtad* by many scholars, and hence jihad against him was permitted). However, this injunction has regrettably been misused by many clerics who declare certain individuals who have converted to another sect as *'murtad,'* and hence jihad is permitted against them. The other concept that is more expansive and can be used in a sectarian concept is the notion of *fitnah* or 'mischief,' that may cause disunity. Often disagreement or dissent is relegated to being *fitnah* and hence jihad is permitted against this. Ironically, the fight against the *fitnah* is usually what leads to most disunity. Usually, the indoctrination is not directly through the curriculum but through peer interaction and mosque sermons. The only way to combat this misuse of *fitnah* and *murtad* injunctions is to directly confront scholars and seek intrafaith peace-building such as what Pope John Paul initiated between various Christian sects. Clearly, there is no hierarchical clergy in Islam, but this can be facilitated by numerous respectable clerics across the Muslim World.

MADRASSAHS AND SECTARIAN VIOLENCE: FEUDAL ROOTS?

Since the most direct connection between madrassahs and violence is in sectarian activity, we need to understand the core causes of such behaviour rather than symptomatically dealing with madrassahs that might only lead to further resentment. As observed in our case analysis, the proliferation of madrassahs in rural areas has been far more pronounced and is highly region-specific. Perhaps the most dominant aspect of life in rural Pakistan is the dominance of the feudal elite. It is interesting to note that Islamic political parties in Pakistan have historically had an ambivalent stance on this issue. While they recognize the importance of social justice, the Jamaat-e-Islaami in Pakistan have come out against socialist policies, branding them as 'kufr' (heresy) because of their perceived linkage to Marxist ideologies (Ahmed, 1994, p. 474).

As noted earlier, madrassahs have been perceived as a counterweight to feudalism in Southern Punjab. Coupled with environmental resource scarcity and underdevelopment, the madrassahs have provided a physical and emotional refuge for many families. Ahmedpur East is an example of this phenomenon. The political leadership here has for decades been with the Nawabs of Bahawalpur (based in Ahmedpur City and Dera Nawab) and the Makhdums of Uch Sharif (Gilani and Bukhari Shias). The religious leadership that rose from madrassahs challenged these ruling families. One of the factors for the growth and influence of madrassahs in Ahmedpur East City, Uch Sharif and Naushera Jadid is the typical social response to feudal social structures narrated above. These are also manifest in some of the environmental and development indicators that we observed for the regions in question.

There have been a series of attempts at land reform in Pakistan. The first was in 1959, when land reforms fixed the ceiling for private ownership of land at 500 acres irrigated and 1,000 acres unirrigated. However, this did little to improve land inequality. A major shortcoming of the proposal was that ceilings were fixed in terms of individuals rather than families. Different family members from the same ruling elite acquired the redistributed property. The reforms also included large productivity exemptions as well as separate provisions for orchards. This often benefited the landlords since they often ended up receiving generous compensation for surrendering uncultivated land.

Hardly 35 per cent of the excess land declared by landowners was actually obtained by the government, with redistribution benefiting only eight per cent of subsistence farmers.[5]

A second attempt at land reforms was made by Zulifikar Ali Bhutto in 1972, following his socialist agenda of *roti, kapra aur makan* (bread, clothes and shelter). This time, the ownership ceiling was reduced to 150 acres of irrigated and 300 acres of unirrigated land. While these reforms were technically promising, the impact was minor when they were actually implemented. Less than 0.9 million acres of land was acquired for redistribution, which was about one-third of the land resumed under the 1959 land reforms. Once again, the ceilings were in terms of individuals rather than families. Thus, large landowners managed to keep their holdings within an extended joint family framework and even now have given up only some marginal, nonproductive, swampy lands. According to the Federal Land Commission, only 1.8 million hectares (or less than 8 per cent of the country's cultivated area) have been resumed so far. Of these, 1.4 million hectares have been distributed to 288,000 beneficiaries.

The strength and tenacity of the Shia landholders in Southern Punjab has clearly fuelled further tensions. In Jhang—the birthplace of the militant Sunni organization called the *Sipah-i-Sahaba*—the proportion of Shias in the affluent urban middle class is higher than in other areas of Pakistan. Moreover, the feudal gentry too have many Shia families, including the Maratab Ali family.[6] The Sipah-i-Sahaba appeals to the interests of the peasantry oppressed by the rich and the influential. Indeed, Maulana Haq Nawaz Jhangvi, the fiery preacher who raised much animosity against the Shias, was himself a man of humble origin and had a reputation for being much concerned with the welfare of the poor and the helpless. He was known to regularly spend time at government courts helping out poor illiterate litigants. Indeed, it was the murder of Maulana Jhangvi on 22 February 1990 which sparked the first large-scale confrontations between Shias and Sunnis. This was preceded by the murder of the head of the Shia Tehrik-e-Jaffria, Allama Arif-ul-Husseini on 5 August 1988.[7]

Another leader of the Sipah-i-Sahaba, Maulana Isar al-Qasimi (1964–91), also preached in Jhang. He too denounced the Shia magnates of the area. In the words of Rahman (2004), 'the peasants, terrorized by the feudal rich, responded as if the maulana were a messiah.' Shopkeepers and professionals alike welcomed the strident Sunni identity he helped create.[8] Rahman goes on to highlight various incidents all over the world where Islamist movements in far afield places as Turkey and Indonesia have claimed the minds of the impoverished. Indeed, poverty and oppression was also a major contributor in the Iranian Revolution against the Shah who were seen as an arrogant aristocrat.

Land reform efforts will require political will to enforce and there will undoubtedly be some friction with the ruling elite to make these reforms workable. However, there is little doubt that equity in land holdings will provide greater opportunities for the rural population and also foster economic growth. As noted in a recent World Bank study 'access to land provides a good social safety net, which induces more farmers to move into non-farm activities, and then produce the boom in small-scale entrepreneurs' (van den Brink, et al, 2006).

Thus the key explanatory variable for the rise of sectarian violence in rural Pakistan, and in some other feudal settings, appears to be class conflict between the feudal elite and peasants. However, there are also several other factors that make the dissemination of the sectarian voice possible.

MINORITIES ON BOTH SIDES OF THE BORDER

In a recent news special, commemorating the sixtieth anniversary of the Partition of the subcontinent, the BBC asked the seminal question: 'Why have Indian Muslims lagged behind?' Indeed, the same question could also be posed to Pakistanis regarding non-Muslim minorities on this side of the border. The reality is that minorities in both countries have under-performed and we need to consider why. In the Indian case, the matter is more consequential since the numbers are far greater and the claims of equality far more strident.

The underperformance of Indian Muslims is not meant to raise hostility or to exonerate Pakistan of its own follies towards minorities but questions must be raised in this regard on both sides of the border. The BBC news article presented some interesting statistics regarding Indian Muslims who comprise 13 per cent of the population but only 5 per cent of employees in India's government. The figure for Indian Railways, the country's biggest employer, is only 4.5 per cent. The article states that the Muslim community continues to have a paltry representation in the bureaucracy and police—3 per cent in the powerful Indian Civil Service, 1.8 per cent in foreign service and only

4 per cent in the Indian Police Service. And Muslims account for only 7.8 per cent of the people working in the judiciary.[9]

For Pakistan, there are no robust statistics available in comparison since minorities are such a small percentage of the total population (less than 5 per cent). However, discrimination against non-Muslims is definitely a major concern in terms of opportunities for these communities to flourish. While there are some notable exceptions of high-profile minorities who have achieved prominence in Pakistan, such as Justice Cornelius, Ambassador Jamshed Marker and Justice Rana Bhagwandas, the overall treatment of minorities leaves much to be desired. Recently, discrimination against the Christian minority forced a notable bishop from Gujranwala, Dr Major (R) Timotheous Nasir, to surrender his Pakistani nationality. In a letter addressed to President Pervez Musharraf, the bishop wrote that he had made this tough decision because he could no longer live with 'the false hope or promise of equal rights for Christians of Pakistan' and ignore 'willful silence of the government'.

On the Indian side, a simplistic response to the statistics about Indian minorities can be that Muslims are not availing of the opportunities provided them. But on closer reflection it is clear that education was a priority for Muslims before Partition (as exemplified by numerous universities and schools established at the time by Muslims) and the quality of access to resources has clearly deteriorated due to governmental policies.

Any talk of minority performance inevitably leads to the larger question of whether Muslims would have performed better in a united India with a larger minority population that could exert greater pressure for acceptance. This hypothesis cannot be addressed empirically, but comparisons with other states with larger minority demographics such as Malaysia (50 per cent Malay, 30 per cent Chinese, 10 per cent Indian and remaining indigenous minorities) suggest that this may well have been the case. On the other hand, if there are inveterate disagreements between communities that have a long-standing historical legacy of conflict, a forced union can also be a recipe for disaster as was the case in the Soviet Union.

In reality, we need to dispense with conjecture about what might have happened in the absence of Partition and instead focus on the social issues at hand on both sides of the border. And the reality is that minorities deserve far better treatment in Pakistan as well as India. No longer can we shield ourselves from criticism by raising isolated success stories of minority supreme-court justices in the case of Pakistan, or ceremonial presidential figures in the case of India. We have a collective responsibility to quell hatred and antagonism between religious groups that exist in equal measure on both sides. While democratic procedures have given India an advantage in due representative processes, it is also important to consider that minorities are often most vulnerable in purely majority-oriented electoral systems. In Pakistan, there have been special seats created for minorities in the electoral process similar to India's reserved seats for *Harijans* (lower castes). However, most of the major Christian organizations in Pakistan have opposed the two electorate system and would rather have a joint electorate. They point examples where the voters of Pakistan have shown the ability to vote for minority candidates in joint elections. For example, in 1970, C. Ayub, a Christian member of the Pakistani Masihi League in Punjab contested an election against Z.A. Bhutto and came in second, securing more votes than other Muslim candidates such as General Sarfraz, Dr Javed Iqbal and Ahmed Saeed Kirmani (Jalalzai, 2005).

Pakistani Muslims' perceptions of minorities vary greatly between social strata and groups, particularly in the realm of education. Elite and upper middle-class Pakistanis often revere Christians for their commitment to knowledge and frequently send their children to Christian schools, particularly to improve their English. On the other hand, the vestige of certain Hindu practices regarding darker-skinned 'castes' have spilled over into religious distinctions and lead to commonplace discrimination. Since many of the converts to Christianity came from the lower 'castes,' they are often victims of discrimination as well and given derogatory epithets such as *choora* (meaning street sweeper). Parsis (Zoroastrians), have always been a highly privileged merchant class and little discrimination is found towards them because of their wealth. The Bhandara family is still licensed to operate the only brewery in Pakistan. Small populations of Sikhs are still found in Punjab near shrines of some of the Sikh saints. A regular pilgrimage programme now exists for Sikhs to visit the shrines and greater tolerance is emerging towards the visitors who provide an important economic benefit to the communities. Award-winning Pakistani director Sabiha Sumar's notable Punjabi film *Khamosh Pani* (Silent waters, 2003), admirably addressed the radicalization of communities in Punjab against Sikhs because of the influence of militant clerics and helped to raise awareness about the treatment of minorities in rural areas where it was specially screened in 41 villages.

Hindu populations in Sindh have come under considerable discrimination but are also being given far greater protection since the Musharraf regime came to power. Nevertheless, the perception of mistreatment of minorities in Pakistan is frequently used by Hindu nationalist groups in India to stir sentiments against their neighboring rival. The narrative can often be highly emotional and laden with vile imagery to maximize its provocative effect. For example, expatriate Hindu Nationalist Vishvas Ghosh, based in Germany, makes the following vitriolic statement about Pakistan:

> ...Pakistan was born—through a blood-thirsty caesarean operation—after a pregnancy of 1100 painful years. It was a strange and defective Siamese twin and had to be separated after 24 years of internal biting and bickering between the two monstrous heads. The habit of blood-thirst has not gone away—neither in the one nor the other, with poor pseudo-secularly governed India inbetween.'[10]

With discrimination and divisive rhetoric ensuing from both sides of the border, it is increasingly important for the issue of minority treatment to be raised within educational institutions and at regional forums. The best way to achieve improved social status for minorities is to work through regional institutions such as the South Asian Association for Regional Cooperation (SAARC) which have until now been toothless tigers. A collective treaty through SAARC on the treatment of minority communities in all member-states is needed with clear monitoring and metrics for improving performance of underprivileged groups. Affirmative action programmes might be needed to prevent discrimination in education and employment at the highest level. In addition, we have to root out prejudice towards minorities, starting from elementary schools where diversity training must be instituted to dispel negative stereotypes about minorities. Islamic and Hindu religious schools need particular scrutiny in this regard to ensure that other Faiths are presented with respect throughout the curriculum. Hate speech towards minority communities must be prosecuted by law as a crime as it is now across Europe (they did so only after learning lessons from the dangers of propaganda during the Second World War). Ultimately, one can only hope that we will learn to embrace religious differences without fear of cultural or moral dilution.

Madrassah Media: Linkages to Violence?

The role of mass-media in instigating violence is widely documented in cases such as the Rwandan genocide (Schabas, 2000). While no such scale of genocide is imminent in Pakistan, the continuing bombings between sects is certainly disconcerting.[11] Understanding how the sectarian message is spread requires an analysis of the media that are employed by sectarian activists. The madrassahs are undoubtedly among the major audiences for many of the publications that are produced on sectarian activities as well as on international jihad. Recently, several investigative journalists have researched the proliferation of various inflammatory publications, internet chat rooms and distribution services that could be fuelling violence. Much of the 'jihadi literature' that is used in militant madrassahs is not publicly available. Indeed, one of the investigative journalists who has done research on this, had to recruit 'student informants' to visit some of the madrassahs who offered themselves to be recruited for jihad over a sustained period of time and gained the trust with the establishment before access was given to some of these materials. However, as noted earlier, the militant madrassahs that are involved in international jihad operations are relatively few, though many sectarian madrassah students might also sympathize with some of these views.

In a publication prepared by a Pakistani NGO called *Ideas on Democracy, Freedom and Peace in Textbooks* (Liberal Forum 2003) in what it calls its 'campaign against hate speech', the organization found that Markaz—Dawah uses textbooks for English in which many responses to questions frequently refer to war, weapons, blood and victory. In their view, these textbooks have been authored to provide a one-dimensional world-view that restricts the independent thought process of the students.[12] In this publication, a Ministry of Education official speculates that 10 to 15 per cent of madrassahs might have links with sectarian militancy or international terrorism. The government admits though that these statistics are unreliable. The lack of credible data makes reform more problematic. It also underscores both the extent of official neglect and, conversely, the special treatment received by a select group of madrassahs.

The rhetoric in many of these publications is indeed revolutionary. It also is often directed specifically at madrassah students and their role in Islam. The director of the Madrassah Education Board set up by the government himself referred to madrassahs as 'the fortress of Islam'

(*Islam ka qilaa*).¹³ In one particular publication of the religious parties of Pakistan, called Al-Muslim, the writer Ali bin Mawiya stated, 'if the 1.8 million students of the religious schools come out on the streets today for the implementation of the rule of Shari'at in the country, no power on earth can stop them, not even the 0.6 million strong army of Pakistan.'¹⁴ The metaphor of fortress is a potent symbol in this regard — as one madrassah leader, Maulana Sharif (who is also the imam at a government mosque), when interviewed by a journalist commented: 'it is we madrassahs who are keeping the Islamic values and traditions intact for hundreds of years. If the religious schools had not been there, Islam and the society of so-called Muslims would have faced irreparable losses at the hands of liberals and Western agents.'¹⁵ The madrassah establishment is thus quite conscious of being an inertial institution and acting as a 'cultural conservatory' as well as their power and influence. A need to instill the dynamism of Islamic institutions and their adaptability through history while retaining core traditions and norms is thus needed, yet few perspectives in this regard ever make it to most madrassahs.

Some of the key publications of the various religious organizations and jihadi groups are listed in Table 4.2 with their sectarian affiliation and readership estimates. Some of these organizations have officially been outlawed by the government but their publications continue to be published and distributed.

Other than the regular madrassahs, religious parties also print militant literature which is distributed among the madrassahs and other institutions.

The role of the internet in allowing for the dissemination of material on various jihadi causes has been widely studied by various organizations recently, in particular the US-based think-tank 'The SITE Institute' (The Search for International Terrorist Entities). All of the organizations mentioned above also have websites that keep shifting domain servers as various counter-hackers try to infiltrate them. The proficiency with which madrassah establishments have used computers is documented in our research as well as in various other accounts as well, particularly with regard to 'cyberactivism' in Asia (Gomez and Gan, 2004).

Table 4.2: Various Islamist Publications found in Circulation at Madrassahs

Organization	Publication	Estimated readership
Lashkar-e-Tayyaba	*Voice of Islam* (monthly, in English), *Al-Ribat* (monthly, Arabic), *Majallah Al-Dawah* (monthly, Urdu), *Tayyibat* (Urdu publication for women, *Zarb-e-Tayyaba* (monthly for students), Web-based radio, Al-jihad (Urdu)	Collectively, Markaz Dawah publishes 400,000 copies
Harkat-ul-Mujahideen	*Sada-e-Mujahid* (monthly, Urdu), *Al-Hilal* (weekly, Urdu),	100,000
Al-Rasheed Trust	*Islam* (Urdu), *Zarb-e-Momin* (Urdu and English)	250,000
Jaishe-Muhammad	*Jaish-e-Muhammad* (Urdu biweekly), *Binaat-e-Ayesha* (Urdu monthly for women)	50,000
Bareilvi organizations	*Zarb-e-Islam* (Urdu monthly), *Dawat-al-Islam* (Urdu monthly)	1,000,0000
Various organizations	*Jihad Times* (Weekly, Urdu)	250,000

Source: Zafarullah Khan. *Genre of Jihadi Journalism in Pakistan*, Freidrich Naumann Stiftung (the Islamabad office of German Research Foundation published this monograph).

The publications of particular madrassahs in the local language are worth considering. Box 4.1 provides a sampling of a review of the newsletter of the madrassah in Binori town in Karachi that shows the tenor of communication among the population. While the Pakistani government has admirably made a major reform of the government school text books to expunge incendiary language in 2006, the informal publications such as newsletters are a major concern for madrassahs. They also reflect the tone of communication within the classroom:

> **Box 4.1:** A sampling of article titles and excerpts from the Binori town madrassah newsletter (Urdu transliteration provided in English alphabet along with a translation by the author):
>
> - *Shiat rafiziat kiya hay?* What is the apostasy of Shias? (author, Ahmed Ali Mardani, September 1999): This article describes why Shias should be considered *mushrikeen* or those who have strayed into polytheism and hence are apostates.
> - *Dunya may munafiqeen ka sab say bara idaara Aqwaam-e-Mutahida:* The world's largest assemblage of hypocrites is the United Nations (March 1998, author Naveed Masood Hashmi). Hypocrisy in the Qur'an is considered a serious sin and this article argues that hence it is worthy of doing jihad against the United Nations which has betrayed the Taliban. There is also a strong anti-Iranian sentiment expressed in the article as a foe of the Afghans.
> - *Aurat or jadeed maghrabi tehzib ka faraib*: 'The fallacy of modernity in the West and Women's emancipation' (May 2002, author Maulana Muhammad Hassan Siddiqui). This article laments how traditional Islamic values about the complementary gender roles are being diluted by the West. To highlight Islam's superiority, the author tries to show that other Faiths have an even worse record on women's rights.
> - *Hindu baniyay ki sifakiat aakhir kab tak?'* How long will the tyranny of the Hindu shopkeepers last?' (Editorial, May 2002). A highly politicized article that focuses on the oppression of Kashmiris in India and urges Muslims to become more pious in order for them to receive Divine strength in countering this oppression.
> - *Duniya par qabza karnay ki Yahudi saazish:* 'The Jewish conspiracy to dominate the world.' This article builds on European anti-Semitic literature that focuses on the dominance of the Rothschild family and also ties this with some of the verses in the Qur'an (arguably taken out of context and similar to verses in the Old testament as well) that refer to indiscretions by the ancient Israelites.

While it is extremely important to preserve the freedom of speech, there are also clear guidelines against publication of erroneous material or inciting violence that is not permitted in any circumstances. Islamic injunctions are also very clear against inciting of violence or indeed even erroneously injuring reputations. One notable hadith (or saying of the Prophet Muhammad [PBUH]) in this regard is: 'It is unworthy of a Mu'min [a person with faith] to injure people's reputations; and it is unworthy to curse anyone; and it is unworthy to abuse anyone; and it is unworthy of a Mu'min to talk arrogantly.[16]

THE EDUCATED TERRORIST

Invocations to exemplify moderate Islam have come under fire by some analysts such as Faisal Devji (2005) who states that: 'However noble in conception, Islamic liberalism is today at its lowest ebb since the 19th century. This is not because Muslims generally are more militant than before, but because the moderation hawked to anxious governments by Muslim notables is itself redundant.' He goes on to then suggest that 'the 'war on terror' should be conducted as a police operation rather than an ideological or even military struggle, as its enemy is not some external power but exists inside liberal as well as illiberal societies.'

There is no doubt that extremism extends beyond the religious schools and highly educated individuals can have terrorist connections. Most of the madrassah revisionists (Bergen and Panday, 2006; Fair and Haqqani, 2006; Dalrymplye, 2005) have focused on the lack of connection between madrassahs and terrorist leadership. While this book does not fully concur with the relatively dismissive approach to madrassahs that the revisionists offer, the larger issue of 'educated terrorism' deserves attention, whether it ensues from traditional madrassahs or secular institutions. For example, Ataur Rehman, leader of the Jandullah splinter of al-Qaeda that tried to kill the Karachi corps commander, was formerly of the student wing of Jamaat-e-Islami (JI) and had broken away from it to form his own extremist group. The two doctor brothers, Akmal and Arshad Waheed, arrested in Karachi for allegedly providing medical assistance to the Jandullah terrorists, were members of the Pakistan Islamic Medical Association (PIMA) and had a history of being active in Afghanistan under the Taliban. The PIMA is said to have the 'sponsorship' of the Jamaat-e-Islami (Shehzad, 2004).

Anti-western sentiment also does not have to emanate from traditionally inclined individuals. South Asia has a peculiar history of highly Westernized anti-Western politicians perhaps symbolized most acutely by Nehru of India. The commentator Khaled Ahmed has characterized this phenomenon as follows:

> The same kind of Westernized anti-Westernism and anti-Americanism haunts the Muslim intellectual who refuses to see that he can be dispatched in short order by the Islamists standing behind him. Nehru's Fabian-socialism was very British and half the time he was defying Britain, it could

be a kind of self-indulgence that one can today associate with the panache that America-educated intellectuals of South Asia display in their unrealistic theories of defiance.'[17]

Let us consider the example of Sri Lanka. What bedevils conflict analysts most about Sri Lanka is that it defies the most common causal factor raised by terrorism experts—a lack of education. Among all South Asian countries, Sri Lanka has the highest literacy rate of an astounding 92 per cent. Yet this is the country where the cult of suicide bombings finds its origin with more than 200 suicide attacks since 1970 that have claimed thousands of lives.[18] The victims include several politicians including the former Indian Prime Minister Rajiv Gandhi, who was killed by a female suicide bomber in 1991. Clearly, the educational development in this country has not had a direct correlation with conflict reduction.

Sri Lanka is not the only example of this phenomenon. Another country that is frequently associated with radicalism, Iran, has one of the highest literacy rates in the Middle East—over 70 per cent.[19] In this case, the gender argument on literacy is not applicable either, since there are now more female college graduates in Iran than men. Yet, this has not translated into a culture of tolerance among the masses, who continue to overwhelmingly support radical ideologies.

The quality or extent of education, rather than literacy itself, may be considered another metric for preventing radicalism, but this too does not hold ground on closer analysis of some of the most charismatic terrorists. America's elusive Unabomber was a Harvard graduate; Abimael Guzman, the leader of Peru's Sendero Luminoso, was a university professor; and the intellectual leader of the Maoist rebels in Nepal, Baburam Bhattarai, has a doctorate in urban planning. Among the al Qaeda hierarchy, Aimen Al-Zawahry is a medical doctor, and Mohamed Atta was an engineering student fluent in three languages.

Such examples clearly show that education is not a sufficient condition for tolerance or conflict reduction, but perhaps it is a sufficient condition for development and can thereby lead to conflict reduction? Here too, the data is not supportive. Analysis by NYU economist Bill Easterly (2001) shows that from 1960 to 1985, sub-Saharan Africa had a remarkably high educational capacity growth of over 4.5 per cent while East Asia's was growing at only 2.5 per cent despite having similar starting points. However, GDP per capita growth in East Asia was over 4 per cent during this period while sub-Saharan Africa languished at 0.5 per cent.

So what are we to make of this dismal linkage? Education is important, and it still may be a necessary (but not sufficient) condition for lasting development since all developed countries do indeed have high literacy rates. Education thus helps to sustain economic development. However, the linkage between education and a reduction in extremism and conflict is much more tenuous. Here, it might not even be a necessary condition for conflict reduction since we have several examples of relatively peaceful indigenous communities where educational indicators are relatively low.

What is clear with conflict linkage is that incendiary information—whether through educational channels at modern schools, madrassahs, or at home—can play a significant role in conflict development. Education in the Internet age is particularly challenging since we are overloaded with specious information that is often absorbed by educational institutions. Indeed, while researching madrassahs in Pakistan, it is remarkable to find how proficient many of the students are in accessing internet chat rooms and radical websites. These sites can of course be accessed by anyone. However, the cultural milieu in certain institutions may lead to an uncritical absorption of this material more so than others. Any conflict reduction strategy must thus try to focus on knowledge-based sources of conflict as well as the institutions—many of which will be educational in nature.

Hence our attempts at reducing radicalization should take place independent of where the targets are. This may lead us to propagandist literature inciting violence, conspiracy theories presented by pretentious intellectuals who distort facts, or a culture of intolerance in some religious and secular institutions. Each avenue should be explored with recognition that human behaviour has complex motivations. We should not let linear solutions beguile us into problem-solving, even when it is that most noble goal of knowledge acquisition.

NOTES

1. See Lapidus, 1998.
2. Dr Anis Ahmed has a doctorate from Temple University in the United States and is frequently part of ecumenical dialogues.
3. Interview with Dr Anis-ud-din Ahmed, Islamabad, 10 January 2005.

4. For an introspective Muslim view on this question see the article by Mohammed Elmasry (2003). 'Does the Qur'an Sanction Violence?' *The Ambition* (Toronto, Canada), January.
5. Data from land reform article on www.yespakistan.com, accessed, April 2005.
6. Notable industrialist and philanthropist Syed Babar Ali, who founded the Lahore University of Management Sciences (LUMS), and was the President of the World Wildlife Fund belongs to this family as does the celebrated politician Syeda Aabida Hussain, who was Pakistan's ambassador to USA in the early 1990s.
7. The state appeal against the acquittal of those charged with the murder of Arif-al-Hussaini still continues to this day. The judge has delayed the appeal on 9 March 2005 on conflict of interest issues with one of the members of the judiciary. The accused are former government officials in the Zia regime, including ADC to the president Majid Raza Gillani, whose apparent motive for such a crime would have been to counter Iranian influence in Pakistani domestic policy. It is also interesting to note that drug trafficking of opium from Afghanistan has also been linked to some of the sectarian activity in this area though without any direct proof (personal communication Zafarullah Khan, 4 January 2004).
8. Rahman, Tariq. (2004) *The Madrassah and the State of Pakistan. Religion, Poverty and the Potential for Violence in Pakistan.* http://www.himalmag.com/2004/february/essay.htm Pg. 9.
9. BBC World Service, 9 August 2007, available online: http://news.bbc.co.uk/2/hi/south_asia/6938090.stm.
10. Vishvas Ghosh, email communication to *Daily Times* and the author, 8 December 2007.
11. Regrettably, conspiracy theorists in Pakistan continue to blame 'foreign hands' (insinuating either Indian or American involvement) for the sectarian violence despite the glaring fact that these are indeed cases of sectarian conflict. The recent spate of suicide bombings in Shia mosques and shrines further shows that these are indigenous fanatics rather than foreign agents (who would be hard to convince to engage in suicide attacks).
12. Future Youth Group. (2002) *Ideas on Democracy, Freedom and Peace in Textbooks.* (Campaign Against Hate Speech) Islamabad, Pakistan: Liberal Forum Pakistan.
13. Interview of Mufti Muhammad Qawi on Voice of America, Urdu radio programme, 9 April 2005.
14. Quoted in Masood Ansari 'The Crackdown Begins,' *Newsline* (Karachi), January 2002. It is interesting to note the number of students which this religious writer quotes—the number is now often underplayed by many madrassah proponents.
15. Quoted in Ahmed, 2003.
16. Hadith from *Sahi al-Bukhari*.
17. Khaled Ahmed's book review of Narendra Singh Sarila, *The Untold Story of India's Partition: The Shadow of the Great Game* (Harper Collins India; Distributed by Vanguard Books Lahore), titled: 'Bilateral Myth-making Over India's Partition' *Friday Times.* 11 November 2005.
18. Sri Lankan demographic and crime statistics from the CIA factbook on Sri Lanka. Accessible online: https://www.cia.gov/cia/publications/factbook/geos/ce.html.
19. For an interesting review of this paradox in the context of Iran see Mehran, 2003.

5
FUNDING OF ISLAMIC EDUCATION

Islamic societies have maintained a strong tradition of capitalist entrepreneurship as well as social redistribution of wealth through government systems as well as philanthropic institutions. Islamic charities, in particular, have come under considerable scrutiny after 9/11 and a large genre of literature has emerged in this regard.[1] Islam also has a strong notion of a 'moral economy' and the role of education within this framework is now beginning to gain greater importance (Tripp, 2006). The use of money for just causes and for ameliorating the condition of other Muslims has a strong tradition within Islam. The Prophet Muhammad's first wife Khadija[2] was a businesswoman who controlled a major trading business and profits from this enterprise were also donated to charity in many cases before the advent of an Islamic state in Medina.

Funding of social projects through private avenues were institutionalized by the concept of *waqf* (plural *awqaf*) which provides for perpetual charitable endowments that are often predicated in land donations. The first religious waqf is believed to be the Quba mosque in Medina which was established as a charitable Trust that would provide returns from any fruits or dates harvested from trees on the adjoining property or other means of return on investment. It should be noted that there is considerable disagreement within Islamic jurisprudence regarding the allowance of interest accrual in terms of modern banking systems. Modern jurists differentiate positive interest from capital usage allowable from usury that was charged on personal loans and considered prohibited (El-Gamal, 2006).

Historically, the *awqaf* in Istanbul, Jerusalem, Cairo and other medieval Muslim cities covered a considerable proportion of total cultivated area. For example, in the years 1812 and 1813 a survey of land in Egypt showed that *waqf* represented 600,000 feddan

(=0.95 Acre) out of a total of 2.5 million feddan; in Algeria the number of deeds of *awqaf* of the Grand Mosque in the capital Algiers was 543 in the year 1841; in Turkey about one-third of land was *awqaf*; and finally in Palestine the number of *waqf* deeds recorded up to middle of the sixteenth century is 233 containing 890 properties in comparison with 92 deeds of private ownership containing 108 properties. Educational institutions were important beneficiaries of these properties. The Ayubites (1171–1249) and the Mamalik (1249–1517) in Palestine and Egypt are good examples in this regard. At the beginning of the twentieth century, Jerusalem had 64 schools and all of them were either *waqf* themselves or supported by *awqaf* properties in Palestine, Turkey and Syria. Of these schools, 40 were made *awqaf* by Ayubites and Mamalik rulers and governors. The fabled University of al Azhar in Cairo, which was founded in 972 was financed by its *waqf* revenues until the government of Muhammad Ali in Egypt took control over the *awqaf* in 1812.[3] The use of such endowments for funding educational institutions is thus well established in Islamic tradition and the usual rationale given us to maintain their independence from the state.

Contemporary Muslims in the West also have their own organizations for this purpose. For example, Islamic Relief, set up in 1984, is the UK's largest Muslim charity, with a worldwide gross income of around £15m–£5m of that raised in the UK.[4] The charity's reputation is exemplified by the fact that it also receives funds from the UK government's Department for International Development. Petrodollars also contribute to many of these charities and to specific projects. However, it's worth noting that many of the larger philanthropic gifts for higher education in Muslim countries have been to establish secular institutions such as the Lahore University of Management Sciences (LUMS) in Pakistan.[5] For the purposes of this chapter, we will focus specifically on funding of madrassahs and educational institutions in Muslim countries rather than examining the full spectrum of educational institutions.

Historically, madrassahs in the subcontinent were supported by land grants and wealthy patrons. The ulama were known for their relatively modest lifestyles. According to Rahman (2004) Maulana Abdul Ali Bahr-al-Ulam of Farangi Mahall, for instance, used in their support all but Rs 40 of the Rs 1000 monthly stipend granted by Nawab Walajah. His 'wife and family suffered and complained, as did those of his grandson, Jamal-al-Din, who suffered in a similar way.' Barbara Metcalf (1982) in her study of Deoband suggests that the average expense of Deoband on each graduate between 1867 and 1967 was Rs 1,314 which is certainly quite modest. Rahman (2004) found that at the Jamia Salafia of Faisalabad, the annual expenditure on the seminary, which has about 700 students, is Rs 4,000,000 (around $75,000). Another madrassah, this time a Bareilvi one, gave roughly the same figure for the same number of students. This comes to Rs 5,714 per year (or Rs 476 per month), which is an incredibly small amount of money for education, books, board and lodging. The expenditure from the government in 2001–02 was Rs 1,654,000 for all the madrassahs in the country and about 32.6 per cent madrassahs do not receive any financial support at all.

The ownership of religious institutions has traditionally been in the form of a trust. In some ways madrassahs are public institutions because of their social service dimension and inextricable linkage between Islam and the state in Pakistan. However, they are beyond government control and hence are private. However, as the funding sources indicate, there is a wide linkage of various interests which thus have figurative ownership of the establishments. Most of the madrassahs are 'owned' by an individual religious leader; they may have a paper management committee or a board of governors, just for fulfillment of regulatory requirements. In fact, even the management committees or boards of governors are close relatives and hand-picked associates of the religious leader. This proprietorship dimension of madrassah management brings in the very important monetary or economic factor. Since it is a private enterprise, which, apart from giving political, religious and even administrative clout to the owner, even fetches huge economic benefits, stakeholder interests get more entrenched. Many madrassahs, since they are built as 'encouragements' on highways and main roads, have commercial properties attached to them. Madrassahs, although religious schools are also political institutions. Many madrassahs are attached or affiliated to a religious political party and may receive support from them as well. For example, the madrassahs organized by the Jamaat-e-Islaami in Mansoora, near Lahore, receive contributions from the party as well. According to estimates provided by the Punjab government, 1256 madrassahs are affiliated with various political parties, with more than two-thirds of these affiliated with the Jamiat-e-Ulama Islam (JUI).[6]

However, the source of the funds in turn to the parties that are earmarked for madrassahs need to be better understood. In addition, the motivation for sending students to madrassahs may also provide some insights into the source of funding, since much of it is intended in the form of scholarships for the needy. Several scholars have studied economic motivation for madrassah enrollment. According to Fayyaz Hussain (1995), a student who completed his ethnographic research on Jamia Ashrafia of Lahore in 1994, nearly half the students joined the madrassah for economic reasons, 41 per cent for social reasons, and only about 6 per cent for religious pursuit. About 3 per cent said they joined the madrassahs in search of education and about 2 per cent described the cause as 'political'. According to a survey conducted by Mumtaz Ahmad in 1976 'more than 80 per cent of the madrassah students in Peshawar, Multan, and Gujranwala were found to be sons of small or landless peasants, rural artisans, or village imams of the mosques. The remaining 20 per cent came from families of small shopkeepers and rural laborers'. According to a survey by the Institute of Policy Studies (2002), 64 per cent madrassah students come from rural areas and belong to poor agrarian families. Rahman (2004) conducted a survey in eight cities of Pakistan in December 2002 and January 2003, madrassah students and teachers were asked about their income. Among those who responded, 76.6 per cent belonged to the poorer sections of society. The teachers of the madrassahs also mostly (61 per cent) belong to the same socio-economic bracket as their students.

Nevertheless, despite their modest needs, the sheer scale of madrassah prevalence still requires a steady stream of funds. Some of the sources of funds that are considered most salient are as follows:

1. Parental Support

Education of children is largely dependent on parental decisions and in the context of madrassah education, the first question to consider is why parents might want to send their children to madrassahs and consequentially support such institutions. This question has been addressed in policy circles by focusing on a poverty-driven hypothesis that assumes that only through desperation or destitution would parents send their children to such schools. Underlying this belief is the assumption that parents want the best quality of education for their children in terms of career opportunities and since madrassahs limit career prospects, few parents would want to send their children there. An exception is made for the ideologically driven parents that are usually relegated to a minority by anecdotal accounts.

Among the few studies of parental choice in school admission processes in Pakistan is a landmark research project conducted by Nelson (2006) in the outskirts of Rawalpindi in which he studied over 100 households in terms of their preferential goals for education of their children. The research sample was chosen in areas where the local madrassah was just one among at least two educational options. In addition the research team chose the study sample according to the demographics of income across the region with a weighting towards lower-middle and middle class households earners. In parallel with these surveys, the study team also interviewed development donors in Islamabad to see what their perceptions would be regarding parental choice of schools. The results are striking at multiple levels. The respondents were asked if they were satisfied with the options for schools (excluding madrassahs) that were being provided by the government and 60 per cent responded in the negative. Furthermore, respondents chose religion as their top priority for the goals of a 'good education', followed by civics, literacy skills, liberal values and vocational training. In contrast, the donor community perceived that vocational skills would be vitally important to the parents and religious schooling would only be important if other options were not available.

In balancing religious versus secular studies, 52 per cent of the respondents felt that they would prefer equal time devoted to religious scholarship and secular subjects while 27 per cent favoured spending less than half of schooling time on religion and 21 per cent favoured spending more than half of schooling time on religious education. In contrast, 67 per cent of the donor community felt that citizens would prefer a curriculum in which less than 50 per cent of the subjects were devoted to religion.

What is clear from this study as well as my own personal experience in Pakistan is that there is indeed a market for madrassahs that is demand driven, not only due to poverty but also incipient ideological leanings of the populace. It may be argued that such leanings are themselves a product of institutional indoctrination over the past few decades but then how are we to confront such matters on purely democratic demand-driven terms?

Is it possible to alter demand through supply-side intervention? Indeed, this avenue must also be explored but in a way that engages with existing innocuous elements of Islamic education. Parental support is certainly not immutable and cultural shift can occur in communities but we need to consider what resources are at play that nurture madrassahs and make them further attractive for parents in some contexts.

2. LOCAL AND GLOBAL PHILANTHROPISTS

Philanthropic donations by local aristocrats, particularly urban based traders and rural land owners, are a major source of funding for most of the madrassahs. Every madrassah has certain identified patrons, particularly in rural areas or small urban towns. These donations are mostly motivated by a feeling of charity called '*Sadaqa* and *Khairat*.' It is also a means of atonement and gratitude to God for the devout. Some individuals also dedicate one of their children to study in a madrassah for a few years as an even greater mark of commitment. A study conducted in 2000 by the Pakistan Centre for Philanthropy claims that approximately Rs 7 billion ($120 million) are given in local philanthropy nationally in Pakistan, out of which a considerable proportion is given to local mosques, madrassahs and religious shrines.[7]

As district administrator and magistrate in Ahmedpur East, the field research coordinator for this study, monitored how local traders and small land owners provide financial patronage to local madrassahs and in the process wield considerable influence over the management of the madrassah, particularly in rural areas and small urban towns.

These local financial patrons have stakes in local politics and play the role of power brokers. By investing in these madrassahs they create immense clout with local police and administration since the level of unrest at religious festivals is often dependent on behaviour of the religious establishment. The land owners and traders on every harvest make donations of wheat and cotton to local madrassahs. The local officers, knowing and appreciating the influence that these local financers wield over a particular madrassah try to maintain a positive relationship with them. They also seek a premium from local administration for these services of conflict control in the form of requests for favours in land cases, municipal licensing issues, police cases, and different issues.

A recent study of charitable giving from the Pakistani Diaspora in the United States, authored by Professor Adil Najam (2006) under the auspices of the Global Equity project at Harvard University, concludes that Pakistani-Americans are a 'generous, giving and active community'. Using a detailed survey of over 400 individuals across America and a series of focus group sessions, the study found that 62 per cent of the respondents reported that religious obligation was of 'high or 'very high' importance in their reason for charity. A slightly higher percentage gave motivational importance to 'helping others in need' (79 per cent) and 'helping family and friends' (69 per cent).

The report also has some sobering news for the Pakistani government. About half of the respondents stated clearly that their contribution would be higher if they had more trust in institutional support across Pakistan that assured them that their contributions were being put to good use. One of the sponsors of this project, The Pakistan Centre for Philanthropy, has undertaken the task of certifying charities through a detailed audit and review process, which can perhaps help in building this trust. This process may have important consequences for addressing concerns about monitoring the financial activity of extremist organizations as well.

Unfortunately, the concentration of wealth among the super-wealthy elite is a phenomenon that pervades the Pakistani Diaspora in the United States just as much as it does the mainstream American population. For example, the upper-middle-class professional organizations such as the Human Development Foundation (which largely comprises doctors of Pakistani origin) raises on the order of two million dollars annually. However, one major gift of two million dollars by a wealthy medical professional to the University of Southern Colorado was enough to establish the Malik and Seeme Hasan School of Business. Tracking the role of individual contributions and channeling them appropriately is critically important.

By far the most significant individual charity in the Muslim world for development is the Aga Khan network of foundations, which have a collective asset base of almost half a billion dollars.[8] Indeed, the Pakistan Centre for Philanthropy itself had its genesis with the Aga Khan Foundation as well. However, this network of charities is run with utmost professionalism and registered in numerous non-Muslim countries as well. While the community derives its funds from giving by a mild Shia denomination within Islam, they also have numerous commercial investments by the Aga Khan's family such as hotels and tourism operations in Asia and Africa whose profits are also funneled into the charitable activities of the network. Much of the educational support from this foundation goes to fund mainstream schools or institutions of higher learning that are considered exemplary in their quality. Aga Khan Education Services (AKES) currently operates more than 300 schools and advanced educational programmes that provide quality pre-school, primary, secondary, and higher secondary education services to students in Pakistan, India, Bangladesh, Kenya, Uganda, Tanzania, and Tajikistan. While the AKDN has not completely escaped sectarian controversy, as noted in the next chapter, their model of charitable giving beyond the Ismaili community itself is worth emulating as a means of bridge-building through charity.

Interviews with madrassah management in Ahmedpur revealed that most of their alumni keep in regular correspondence with the parent institution. Many are working in big cities, particularly Karachi, as mosque clergy and often have side businesses as well. They noted receipt of regular contributions to their alma mater, similar to the way universities in the West gather alumni contributions. Many of the madrassah graduates seek employment in affluent neighborhoods as private tutors of reading and pronouncing Qur'anic Arabic (*Nazarah Qur'an*). It is a tradition in Muslim families (mostly the middle class urban households) that at the age of four or five, children are taught to read the Qur'an—a religious teacher comes to teach recitation of the Qur'an to groups of children in their homes.

Young madrassah graduates provide these services to begin with. As they establish their influence in the new neighborhood, they are on the watch for an opportunity to get a *pesh imam's* (mosque prayer co-leader) position in local mosques or spot a piece of public land (mostly green belts or community purpose plots) to set a mosque-cum-madrassah of their own. Many managers acknowledged that these alumni from the madrassahs are sending a regular subscription to their madrassah. In addition, some madrassah alumni have also got jobs as laborers in the Persian Gulf states. The proximity of these jobs to the holy cities of Makkah and Medina is itself an incentive for many madrassah graduates. These foreign alumni also send regular contributions to their parent institutions.

3. ROLE OF SAUDI ARABIA

The role of Saudi Arabia in funding various Islamic organizations has come under criticism on many accounts. First, there is the role of the state itself in promoting the Wahabbi doctrine of Islam which is perceived to be highly puritanical. The Wahabbi doctrine originated in Saudi Arabia but follows a tradition of puritanical movements in Islam across the ages. The Saudi government and Wahabbi sympathizers have recently attempted to differentiate Wahabbi doctrine from 'Qutbist' doctrine, named after the Egyptian leader Syed Qutb, who traveled extensively in Western countries as well. Interestingly enough, Syed Qutb was greatly influenced by the South Asian scholar Maulana Mauwdudi in much of his work. The government and some of the Wahabbi sympathizers have argued that al-Qaeda leaders follow Qutbist views rather than Wahabbi views. However, this argument is not as compelling if one reads some of the writings of Syed Qutb, who is known for books such as *Islam and Universal Peace* (1977). Much of this book also follows an Islamic supremacist ideology that can be found in Wahabbi tradition as well. In effect, many variations of religious doctrines, including Islam, can be manipulated towards radical ends and hence the focus should be on the manipulation rather than simply on epithets such as 'Wahabbism' or 'Qutbism'.

It is also interesting to note that Indian madrassah educators also had a strong influence on Saudi Islamic education during the nineteenth century. As noted by Zaman (2007), the Sawlatiyya madrassah was established in Makkah in 1875, by a wealthy Indian lady from Calcutta. The first principal, Rahmat Allah Kayranwai was imported from Deoband and is known for his ascerbic anti-missionary writings on the subcontinent. However, despite their initial influence the strong nationalistic fervor of the Saudis, following independence largely eclipsed any such foreign institutions which ended up being absorbed by various government-sponsored programmes.

Saudi laws tend to be more austere than most Islamic countries and there are restrictions on other religious groups that are perceived to be discriminatory. Scrutinizing Saudi Arabia with greater detail following the events of 11 September experts have maintained that Saudi school curricula foster anti-Western and anti-Semitic sentiments. The 9/11 commission report points out that 'awash in sudden oil wealth, Saudi Arabia competed with Shi'a Iran to promote its Sunni fundamentalist version of Islam, Wahabbism.'[9]

The donation towards Islamic education emanates from two primary sources in Saudi Arabia—government institutions and private foundations. The primary government institution that has supported Islamic educational efforts abroad is the *Rabita Aalam-e-Islami* (The Muslim World League) based in Makkah. This organization was established in 1962 to promote unity in the Islamic world. As part of its mandate, the MWL established several schools around the Muslim world as well. Saudi Arabia through the Muslim World League has certainly helped in promoting a jihadist vision, though often with the acquiescence of Western governments. As noted earlier, the Afghan jihad was directly supported by Saudi facilitation of foreign militants. It is widely known and acknowledged by US government sources that in 1980, Osama bin Laden was recruited by Prince Turki-al-Faisal, then head of Saudi intelligence, to help organize the mujahideen supply lines in the Russo-Afghan war.

The second major source of funds for Islamic education comes from a series of private charities. These charities have supported not only direct contributions to madrassahs but also the publication of text books. Following a review of schoolbooks in 2002, the Saudi foreign minister stated that, in light of a Saudi government survey, 5 per cent of the material was considered 'horrible' and 10 per cent questionable, while 85 per cent called for understanding with other religious faiths. Shortly thereafter, the government vowed to remove objectionable parts and to train teachers in promoting tolerance, but skeptics question the extent to which the government is willing or able to instill reforms in its schools. In 2003, the Saudi government announced that it was banning private charities and relief groups from donating money overseas, until new regulations are instituted to ensure that the money is not being channeled to terrorist organizations.[10]

There appears to be a common acceptance in many US policy circles that a majority of funding for Pakistani madrassahs comes from abroad, particularly Saudi Arabia. However, little empirical evidence is provided to support assertions of figures such as those provided by policy research institutions such as the Centre for Security Policy or the Cato Institute that assert that 75 per cent of Pakistani madrassah funding comes from abroad.[11] Our analysis shows that while this may have been true of certain madrassah clusters around the time of the Afghan-Soviet war, it is not a credible assertion based on our contemporary empirical research. The policy implications of simply focusing on Saudi sources of funding can be profound since many of the domestic sources would thus be neglected for regulatory oversight.

4. Zakat

Zakat is a religious tithe that Muslims are obliged to pay and the rate for its payment is 2.5 per cent of savings/assets that a person holds.

Previously it was a private undertaking but in 1979, the government of General Zia-ul-Haq, levied zakat officially and set up an elaborate Federal Zakat Administration, with provincial Zakat Councils and even district Zakat Administrations governed by the Zakat Ordinance.

The purposes for which zakat funds can be spent are clearly mandated by Islamic injunctions. One of the key purposes is welfare of orphans and the destitute. Using this provision as an enabling opportunity, many madrassahs that cater to orphans have been considered legitimate recipients of zakat funds. The Central Zakat Administration which is traditionally dominated by religious leaders devised a policy in the 1980's, through which zakat funds are given to madrassahs specially those that give services to residential students. It is regulated by a policy called 'Revised Zakat Disbursement Procedure for Deeni Madrassahs' as approved by Central Zakat Council on 18 May 2002.

It is generally believed that zakat funding provided the major impetus for growth of madrassahs in 1980s and 1990s. However the research in Ahmedpur East and Islamabad shows that it is no longer a major source of funding for madrassahs. Our survey showed that out of a total of 363 madrassahs in Ahmedpur East, only 34 ever got zakat funding, this figure was 29 out of 266 madrassahs during the survey done in 1994. The official data of Islamabad Zakat Administration shows that 22 madrassahs out of a total of 117 got zakat funding.

Nevertheless, on aggregate, zakat is also a substantial resource flow to madrassahs, approximately 150 million rupees are given by over 100 district zakat committees (DZC) [12] to madrassahs all over Pakistan. In Islamabad, DZC gives approximately 2.0 million rupees to 20 different madrassahs. These funds are meant for food and lodging of students; however, the DZC's give these funds directly to the managers of madrassahs, and these are mostly utilized for infrastructure development and other expenses.

In principle the zakat funding is given directly to the entitled individual beneficiary. However in the case of madrassahs, the quantum of funding is decided on the basis of student enrollment, but funds are not given to individual students, but payments are made directly to the manager of the madrassah. This gives him the authority and freedom to spend the funding. Often, such funding is mostly used for physical improvements and extensions in madrassahs and rarely used for food, lodging and clothing of students, which is its authorized purpose.

OTHER SOURCES OF FUNDS BELOW THE RADAR

Every year after the annual Haj pilgrimage, Muslims all over the world commemorate Abraham's willingness to sacrifice his son by sacrificing a sheep, goat or cow/bull or even a camel. The meat of slaughtered animals is distributed among poor people and close neighbors. Apart from the distribution of the meat of the lambs to the poor and needy, the hides of the animals are also a highly prized and valuable donation. The scale of funds generated through this source is so huge that large political parties, charitable trusts and foundations and many hospitals launch a special campaign for the collection of raw animal hides of scarified animals.

The madrassahs launch very vigorous campaigns for collecting the raw hides of sacrificed animals. These hides fetch a very good price in the market of approximately $20 per hide. It is estimated that approximately 9 million small animals (sheep, goats), and one million large animals (bulls, and camels) are sacrificed every year in Pakistan for this festival.[13] The revenue generated is thus significant and deserves further study to ascertain the exact amount that makes its way to madrassahs.

While the direct contribution of government funds to madrassahs is relatively small, the largest resource transfer to madrassahs is the land grants by the state for construction of madrassahs. As noted in our study, in the federal capital Islamabad, madrassahs have encroached upon prime real estate and green belts. Our survey showed that 90 per cent of madrassahs in Islamabad Capital territory are built on state/public land and invariably in violation of building and land use regulations. Invariably a mosque is attached to a madrassah and this coupling greatly hampers any regulatory initiative by the state. Any pro-active initiative will be taken as (or portrayed as) an interference by the government in the affairs of the mosque and easily dubbed a sacrilegious action. The ban imposed by the federal government on registration of new madrassahs under the Societies Act of 1860, has been recently lifted on the persistent demand of MMA dominated governments of NWFP and Balochistan. This allows for the ostensibly legitimate further expansion of madrassahs though as mentioned earlier, most of the madrassahs are marginally registered and there is limited enforcement of registration of any schools.

The Pakistani government has initiated a reform effort and is also providing funds to madrassahs but not all are accepting this help—it is unclear as to how many madrassahs these funds are being disbursed to. According to Rahman (2004), in 2001-02 a total of Rs 1,654,000 was distributed among the madrassahs which accepted the help. An additional aid of Rs 30.5 million is promised for providing computers and changing the syllabi which will come to approximately Rs 28.6 per student (assuming around 1.05 million recipients). However, as all madrassahs do not accept financial help from the government, the money would not be distributed as evenly as the above calculations might suggest. The next chapter attempts to better understand the dynamics of the government's reform efforts and to provide some insights on whether or not it is likely to succeed.

NOTES

1. See for example the work of Clark (2003) regarding networks of charities in Jordan, Egypt and Yemen or the detailed tracking of militant financing by Ibrahim Warde (2007). Recent scholarship, has challenged the salience of Islamic financial networks and their linkage to terrorists (see for example, Naylor, 2006).
2. Muhamamd (PBUH) was monogamously married to Khadija for 23 years, who was the mother of all his children except one son who was born from a later marriage.
3. These historical statistics are derived from various classical texts cited within the article on *Waqf* on the encyclopedic Islamic web site: http://www.islamic-world.net.
4. Web address for Islamic relief: http://www.islamic-relief.com/
5. LUMS was endowed by the Pakistani Shia industrialist Syed Babar Ali and is considered a leading school of business and engineering in Asia. Interestingly, neighbouring India has received some major donations for the establishment of religio-cultural institutions of learning. The most notable in this regard has been the gift of a staggering $1billion from mining tycoon Anil Agarwal to establish the Vedantic University in Orissa, India, which is scheduled to open in 2012 and will focus on Hindu Vedantic philosophy.
6. Presentation at Civil Services Academy of a report by the Punjab Government, August 2004.
7. Report accessed via the centre's web site: http://www.pcp.org.pk/, January 2005.
8. Aga Khan Development Network web page: http://www.akdn.org/
9. *The 9/11Commission Report*, p. 70.
10. Armanios, Febe. (2003) *Islamic Schools, Madrassahs: Background.CRS Report for Congress*. Congressional Research Service, The Library of Congress. http://www.fas.org/irp/crs/RS21654.pdf Pg. 4.
11. Alex Alexiev is quoted in this regard by Coulson, 2004—who acknowledges in a footnote that there is no citation or empirical basis for these numbers.
12. Central Zakat Council, Annual Report 2002.
13. Estimates from livestock enforcement office, Islamabad, May 2005.

6

MADRASSAHS AND MODERNITY: THE ROLE OF GOVERNMENT AND OTHER STAKEHOLDERS IN CONFLICT PREVENTION

Conventional wisdom suggests that reform in age-old institutions is best accomplished through a combination of external pressure for change and internal initiative and ownership over how such change should proceed. However, in religious institutions, absolutist interpretations usually resist change for its own sake and can make inertia a virtue in and of itself. The metaphor of 'qila' or fortress is frequently used for ulama regarding madrassahs, which can be given a militant connotation but also symbolizes that they are meant to be protective force against the winds of change. In this chapter, the push towards educational reform efforts in Pakistan is compared with some of the more salient regional examples of educational reform. Educational reform efforts are being undertaken by governments and civil society in numerous parts of the Muslim World and all cases could not be exhaustively covered here. However, a sampling of some key efforts of greatest relevance to the Pakistani case is discussed here.[1]

As stated by the Pakistani government, 'the Madrassah Reform Strategy is informed by an overarching objective of eradication of sectarianism and extremism in the country and thus develop friendly atmosphere and national cohesion in the society.... The Madrassah Reform Strategy is based on the belief that madrassah is an indigenous community institution and is performing a commendable service, hence it needs to be fostered and brought into the mainstream educational movement.'[2] The government admits in its policy document that it believes, that some madrassahs may be involved in sectarianism but that it wants a 'hands off' approach while dealing with madrassahs and is committed to maintaining the autonomy and independence of madrassahs. It plans to mainstream them but by teaching formal subjects in madrassahs, and doesn't intend to review the syllabus and internal systems of madrassahs.

The Musharraf government considered this part of the President's policy of 'enlightened moderation' in Islam (Musharraf, 2004). However, the level of cynicism in the population is such that even attempts at moderation and appeasement of various sides are met with hostility. Indeed, in recent columns, Pakistani intellectuals have asked for 'enlightened extremism'.[3]

It is important to note the history of madrassah reform efforts as described in Chapter 2 and to also acknowledge that the initial reform effort that the government initiated was in December 1999, soon after the Musharraf government came to power in the 12 October coup of 1999. The National Security Council of the military government set up a working group to consider madrassah reform. Initially, madrassahs were somewhat responsive and when a form was sent out for soliciting information, more than 2000 madrassahs responded. On the recommendation of the working group, an ordinance on madrassah reform was initiated on 18 August 2001, a month before the tragic events of 11 September of that year. Hence madrassahs were on the government's radar even before the issue was internationalized. Dr Mehmood Ahmed Ghazi, the rector of the Islamic University in Islamabad[4] and the former minister of religious affairs was assigned the task of mainstreaming madrassahs. Earlier efforts by the then Chief Minister of Punjab, Shahbaz Sharif, and also the former Interior Minister, General Moin-uddin Haider had only achieved marginal success.[5] A similar fate was to befall Dr Ghazi's efforts, who is widely respected as a devoutly religious and balanced intellectual. In early August of 2002, Dr Ghazi resigned after failing to bring the religious lobby on board a draft law that would introduce registration of madrassahs. The reform effort, nevertheless, continues though with varying degress of efficacy.

According to the government, the madrassah reforms, in their various permutations, are expected to yield the following results: To strengthen lines of communication between madrassahs and the government; educate about 1.5 million students; provide an opportunity for employment of 32,000 teachers; provide incentives through books, furniture, computers, printers and sports facilities to improve education system of madrassahs.[6] However, we have to unpack several layers of reform efforts that the government intends as part of this ambitious plan.

LEGAL ASPECTS OF REFORM IN PAKISTAN

The madrassahs movement leadership has always contended that they are registered entities under The Societies Act of 1860 and there should be no required registration under a new law. The survey and analysis of madrassahs in APE and Islamabad has shown that out of 363 and 117 madrassahs only 39 and 31 madrassahs respectively are registered under the Societies Act of 1860. This is the same colonial law, which provides the legal framework for registration of NGOs. The efficiency and effectiveness of Societies Registration Act, is extremely doubtful. A study done by the Pakistan Centre for Philanthropy (an NGO) in 2003, revealed that approximately 324 organizations, including NGOs, housing associations, madrassahs were registered with the administration of the Federal Capital.[7] Compliance to regulatory requirements is deemed to be any exchange of correspondence between the registered entity and the government—this could be an annual report, notification of change of address, or any other correspondence. A review of one-fourth of the registered files as part of this research showed that even on such relaxed criteria, the compliance to registration obligations came out to be 4 per cent.

In addition to the Societies Act registration, the government of Pakistan has attempted to pass two laws to control religious extremism in the madrassahs: The first rule called the 'Pakistan Madrassah Education (Establishment and Affiliation of Model Deeni Madrassahs) Board Ordinance 2001' was actually issued on 18 August 2001, a month before the tragic events of 11 September of that year. Hence any causality linking madrassah reform of the present government entirely to 9/11 is unfounded. The plan for a Madrassah Education Board was in some ways modeled after the Bangladeshi madrassah system in which there are two classes of madrassahs: Aaliya madrassahs coordinated by a government board and Quomi madrassahs that are private institutions.[8]

This law aims at introducing secular subjects in the madrassahs in order to bring them at par with government schools. Three model schools were established at Karachi, Sukkur and Islamabad where subjects like English, Mathematics, Computer Science, Economics, Political Science, Law and Pakistan Studies were included in the curriculum. However, the attendance in these model madrassahs is very scant and recent field visits for this research revealed a strong reluctance of parents to send students to these institutions. Part of the challenge with using a 'model' in such a competitive setting is that it deliberately antagonizes other competitors who try to discredit an institution.

The second law has not yet passed the proposal stage, and is known as the Voluntary Registration and Regulation Ordinance 2002 which would require the various madrassahs to register themselves. This is largely an attempt to keep a check on the entry of foreigners into the madrassah system and was motivated by the events of 11 September 2001. However, as mentioned already, there is tremendous resistance on the part of madrassahs to have formal educational registration and this ordinance is largely in abeyance. The Religious Affairs and Awqaf Department of the Punjab provincial government raised strong objections to the ordinance suggesting that 'since the matter is highly sensitive and likely to affect a large number of students and families, it would be appropriate that it be tabled before Parliament in the shape of a bill.'[9]

A very important aspect of the Madrassah Reform Strategy is the institutional mechanism required for successful reform. The Ministry of Interior, Education and Religious Affairs have dealt so far with the reform efforts. All three have different approaches and understanding of the issue. Even on the formulation of the shelved law, the Ministry of Interior and Religious Affairs had diametrically opposing points of view. MOI advocated an effective and foolproof law, where as Ministry religious affairs (MRA) lobbied for an enabling law which should nurture and develop madrassahs. At present there is a lack of concerted effort as far as Madrassah Reform is concerned. The leadership on the issue is being provided by MRA, where as in the provinces and districts where the reform strategy actually has to be implemented, there is no one institution or department responsible for the implementation of the reform strategy. Thus the whole reform strategy is now reduced to the 'Mainstreaming of Deeni Madrassahs,' that is focusing on curricular reform.

ATTEMPTS AT CURRICULAR REFORM

A typical curriculum of what is taught in madrassah schools in South Asian madrassahs is provided in Table 6.1.[10] For a more detailed list

of books used in the *Dars-e-Nizaami* curriculum followed by most madrassahs see Appendix 2.

Table 6.1: Yearly Curriculum of a Madrassah

Year 1	Biography of the Prophet (*Seerat*), Conjugation-Grammar (*Sarf*), Syntax (*Nahv*), Arabic Literature, Chirography, Chant illation (*Tajvid*).
Year 2	Second Year Conjugation-Grammar (*Sarf*), Syntax (*Nahv*), Arabic Literature, Jurisprudence (*Fiqa*), Logic, Chirography (*Khush-navisi*), Chant illation, (*Tajvid*).
Year 3	Qur'anic Exegesis, Jurisprudence: (*Fiqh*), Syntax (*Nahv*), Arabic Literature, Hadith, Logic, Islamic Brotherhood, Chant illation: (*Tajvid*), External study (Tareekh Millat and Khilafat-e-Rashida– these are Indian Islamic movements).
Year 4	Qur'anic Exegesis, Jurisprudence (*Fiqh*), Principles of Jurisprudence, Rhetorics, Hadith, Logic, History, Chant illation, Modern Sciences (sciences of cities of Arabia, Geography of the Arab Peninsula and other Islamic countries).
Year 5	Qur'anic Exegesis, Jurisprudence, Principles of Jurisprudence, Rhetoric, Beliefs (*Aqa'id*), Logic, Arabic Literature, Chant illation, External study (History of Indian Kings).
Year 6	Interpretation of the Qur'an, Jurisprudence, Principles of Interpretation & Jurisprudence, Arabic Literature, Philosophy, Chant illation, Study of Prophet's traditions.
Year 7	Sayings of the Prophet, Jurisprudence, Belief (Aqa'ed), Responsibility (Fra'iz), Chant illation, External Study (Urdu texts).
Year 8	Ten books by various authors focusing on the sayings of the Prophet.'

During the course of our field analysis we verified this structure with the central *wifaq-ul-madaaris* in Multan and they concurred that this characterization of the curriculum was accurate. Pakistani madrassahs stress the teachings of Arabic and Persian. The languages in the Pakistani madrassahs are not taught for their basic value but because they are necessary for the mastery of the religion and because they are obligatory for an *Alim*. Arabic takes centre stage. Persian, which was socially and academically crucial in Muslim India, is still part of the curriculum. Urdu is usually the medium of instruction in Pakistani madrassahs; however, depending on the region this may vary as in the Pashto-speaking parts of the NWFP, Pashto is the medium of instruction while Sindhi is the medium of instruction in many Sindhi-speaking parts of Sindh. Urdu is, nevertheless, the language in which madrassah students become most proficient in most of the madrassahs.

Pakistani madrassahs even today use many of the *Dars-e-Nizami* texts which have their roots in the Farangi Mahal madrassah established in Lucknow by Mullah Nizam-al-din Muhammad. Old Arabic and Persian books written in the AD 1500's or even before are used to teach languages. Anzar (2003, p.16) characterizes the curriculum as follows:

> The student is made to memorize the rhymed couplets from the ancient texts as well as their explanations. As the explanations in a number of texts are in Persian, which is also memorized, the student generally fails to apply his knowledge to the living language. Some ancient texts, such as the *Mizbah-ul-Nah*v, are explained in Urdu. But in this case the Urdu is much Arabicized. The explanation is scholastic and would not be understood by, let alone convince, somebody who is not familiar with the special branch of medieval Islamic philosophy on which it is based. In addition, many of the madrassahs teach *Muallimul Insha* which is written by an Indian *Alim*, which is a response to modernity.... In this book, history begins with the fall of Spain in the hands of Moorish prince Tarik Bin Ziad. It also states that the English were always the enemies of the Muslims and advises that Muslims should adopt certain behaviours to challenge the modern advances that may encroach upon a Muslim's identity.

It is important to note that some of the pedagogic methods used in madrassahs, such as rote memorization, repetition and focus on oral fluency are also followed in many other schools across the region. Linguists such as Tariq Rahman have proposed that the use of such methods is emblematic of a society in transition from an oral learning tradition to a conventional literacy-oriented learning in which reading and writing are emphasized (Rahman, 2004, p. 32). The great Islamic historian Ibn Khaldun noted that the aim of this memorization method was not to 'replace understanding with dogmatism but to plant the seeds that would lead to understanding later' (Boyle, 2004, p. 85).

Madrassahs across the Muslim world have generally resisted calls for reforming the curriculum as it is considered a concession to Western modernism. Even when ulama have gathered to consider reform on their own, the traditionalists have generally won out. For example, in 1994 when the Deoband madrassah in India organized a convention to consider reform efforts, the general consensus emerged that madrassahs were not meant to have modern science subjects but rather focus on religious education. However, the alumni association of the madrassah (based in Delhi) Tanzim Abna-ul-adim subsequently laid out a ten-point plan to consider international affairs and conflict resolution with other religious groups. Nevertheless, how such matters would be included in the curriculum was not considered.

In line with the government of Pakistan's declared objective of reforming the madrassahs, a comprehensive project was initiated by the Ministry of Education at the cost of Rs5759.395 million (US$100 million). The project is planned to be implemented in phases spread over five years (as part of the Public Sector Development Programme). The full details of the reform strategy as articulated by the government are given in Appendix 4. The Major Objectives of the Madrassah Reforms are:

- To introduce/teach formal subjects in 8000 Deeni madrassahs.
- Introduce the subjects of English, Mathematics, Social Studies and General Science in 4000 madrassahs at Primary Level and in 3000 madrassahs at Middle and Secondary Level. English, Economics, Computer Science and Pakistan Studies at the intermediate level in 1000 madrassahs.
- To open lines of communication with Ulama (Religious Scholars). To improve and update knowledge of religious teachers in formal subjects through workshops.
- To improve quality and scope of education by bearing cost of salaries, textbooks, stationary and sports item etc.
- To provide computers and printers at intermediate level in 1000 madrassahs.

The salient features of the project are, to prescribe textbooks in formal subjects in madrassahs. Examinations will be conducted by the relevant Boards of Intermediate and Secondary Education (BISE) at Secondary and Higher Secondary, Levels in the formal subjects. Madrassahs will be selected by the Ministry of Education and Provincial Governments. Funds will be released to provinces, Islamabad Capital territory, Tribal Areas, Northern Areas and Azad Kashmir and other independent areas for distribution amongst the registered madrassahs as follows: Punjab 46.458 per cent; Sindh 19.206 per cent; NWFP 15.696 per cent; Balochistan 8.640 per cent; Islamabad Capital Territory, 10 per cent; and Tribal Areas, Northern Areas and Azad Kashmir.

A total of 8000 madrassahs will be facilitated phase-wise over five years while each institute will be facilitated for three years. Four teachers will be provided to each institution. Appointment of teachers will be made by a committee comprising representatives from the Education Department, Wifaq/Tanzeem/Rabita and a representative of the madrassah concerned.

One-time grants will be released to all madrassahs for purchase of reference books, furniture, and computers and for the improvement of their libraries and buildings etc. Monitoring and evaluation of the madrassahs will be the responsibility of education departments in the provinces. Operational staff will be recruited on full-time basis for five years duration. Monitoring and Evaluation of the project would be carried out by Federal Project Implementation Unit (FPIU), Liaison Officers and Provincial/Area Governments. For this purpose, they may utilize the services of the Executive District Education Officer (EDEO) or assign this task to some other agency/organization considered appropriate. All Project Management Units (PMUs) and Liaison Officers would maintain the record of their provinces/areas and submit quarterly and annual implementation reports to the FPIU regularly.

A National Steering Committee comprising the Education Secretary (Chairman), Joint Educational Advisor (Curriculum Wing), Director of Project, all Education Secretaries to the relevant Education departments including AJK, Northern Areas and Director FATA, Chief Education P&D Division, DFA (Education) will be constituted to look after and check the overall activities of the project and to solve the problems/policy matters faced during the implementation phase. Sub-steering Committees will be set up in each province/area on the pattern of the National Steering Committee. These Steering Committees may be headed by respective Secretaries of Education Departments and include representation from Home and Planning Departments and also include such other departments, persons/organizations, as the provincial/area government concerned may consider necessary. These Steering Committees will seek guidance from the National Steering Committee on policy issues.

The Deeni Madrassah Education Board, set up following the August 2001 ordinance with the sole objective of reforming the curriculum of madrassahs, now has a chairperson, Mufti Muhammad Abdul Qawi from Multan, who is generally well-respected by ulama. The declared policy of government that it will not work on syllabi reform has undermined the rationale for setting up the Deeni Madrassah Board.

Recently, the Religious Affairs Ministry has stated that it will oppose the prime minister secretariat's recent decision to form a Madrassah

Reforms Board under the chairmanship of Federal Education Minister Javed Ashraf Qazi to restructure madrassahs. The ministry is believed to be holding talks with Ithad-e-Tanzimat-Madrassahssa-e-Dinya (ITMD) leaders and the board's formation impeded the process. The ministry took the decision after ITMD leaders rejected the board's formation during the Deeni Madrassah Convention held in Islamabad in March 2005. According to media reports, 'the Religious Affairs Ministry claims that ITMD leaders had agreed to teach conventional education in religious schools, along with the religious education. In return, the government will recognize seminaries' degrees equivalent to Matric, FA and BA, helping their students study conventional education in government colleges, universities and other educational institutions.'[11]

THE AGA KHAN BOARD CONTROVERSY

The Aga Khan Board controversy started when President Musharraf signed an executive order (the Presidential Ordinance of 8 November 2002; CXIV/2002) inducting the Aga Khan University Examination Board (AKUEB) into the national education system. The AKUEB was selected for this assignment due to its excellent record in higher learning and would join the existing 24 examination boards nationwide. As part of the executive order the AKUEB has also been given the task of upgrading and modernizing the declining standards of education and of holding examinations for private educational institutions. The affiliation of these institutions to the Board is voluntary. The Board has not been given any role in government schools, and the system is also intended to help groom teachers in private educational institutions with excellent skills through training. The board would aim to bring modern examinations, both in English and Urdu, at an affordable cost to a much broader section of society, providing parents and schools an option in the style of education they desire from classes IX to XII. National Examination Testing Service has been constituted and the Government Educational Boards have agreed to entertain applications from students who take examinations under the AKUEB.

The government's decision to recognize the Aga Khan Examination Board has drawn much ire from the madrassah establishment. Qazi Hussain Ahmed, the leader of the Jamaat-e-Islaami, in an interview to the English newsmagazine *Newsline* stated that this 'move is part of a well-thought-out plan to globalize education so that any ideological references in text books can be scrapped.'[12] Adding to these conspiracy theories has been the involvement of USAID in funding some of the educational programmes of the Aga Khan Foundation, including a $4.5 million grant for the establishment of the examination board.[13] Sectarian politics was once again sparked by rhetoric from leading madrassah officials such as Hafiz Mohammad Saeed the founder of the Markaz Al Dawah Al Irshad madrassah in Muridke (associated with the now outlawed Lashkar-e-tayyabah). In the internet edition of Weekly Ghazwa (4 November 2004), Saeed said: 'Musharraf is working on making the Northern Areas an Ismaili state. He has been pressured by Christina Rocca (former US assistant secretary of state for South Asia) to hand over Kashmir to Prince Karim Aga Khan so that he could annex it with the Northern Areas and make it his fiefdom.'[14] The rhetoric emanating from madrassah establishments and publications has also been disturbingly similar to the campaign against Ahmadis.

It is also interesting that in addition to conspiracy theories, based on polarized opinion, the jihadists are also providing self-selected nonrandom surveys against Ismailis. Thus the *Daily Jasarat* reported on 19 December 2004: According to a survey by the Islami Jamiat-e-Talba (IJT), 854,000 people have rejected the AKB. There were only 64,000 votes in AKB's support. IJT arranged a special referendum to ascertain the popularity of AKB in Sindh. It set up 140 camps and collected the public opinion. According to their report, around 9,18,855 people took part in the referendum and 93.02 per cent rejected the AKB.

Violence was also threatened as part of this campaign by madrassah leaders and students. The United Students Front (USF)—a union of jihadi students—threatened to attack Parliament if AKF's involvement in education was not ended. The USF's president, Sahibzada Babar Farooq Rahimi said in public interviews that the students will not hesitate to sacrifice their lives if the decision to hand over the education board to AKF was not reversed. Fortunately, these actions have not yet come to pass but as implementation of the board's agenda slowly proceeds across the country, the danger of violence sparked by such vitriolic rhetoric remains high.

Madrassah leadership has also taken up the matter at a political level with the government. In particular the director of the Khair-ul-Madaaris in Multan, Maulana Haneef Jalandari has accused the government of inconsistency—trying to give independence to the Aga Khan Board while restricting madrassah procedures. However, the major difference between the Aga Khan board and the madrassah call for autonomy is that the exam criteria for the Aga Khan programme, and indeed all private schools, are still subject to government approval whereas the madrassah programmes at present have no government oversight.

Clearly there is a communication challenge which the government is facing. Arshad Alam, a researcher based in Germany recently interviewed several madrassah graduates in India from rural Bihar to urban Lucknow (including graduates from the Nadwat-ul-Ulama) and came to the following conclusion that supports our observations of more progressive madrassah graduates as well:

> It seems plausible to argue that contemporary debates about introduction of modern subjects in madrassahs do not appreciate the epistemological dichotomy of *ilm* and *fann* which the madrassahs practice. It was argued that science in madrassahs is primarily a 'skill' to earn one's livelihood. There is a fundamental religious core, the dissemination of which is their primary role. Science and other modern subjects are all welcome to the extent that they do not disturb this fundamental core which is considered to be true for all times to come. Far from being a critical methodology, science here becomes a tool for the further refinement of religion.[15]

HURDLES IN REFORM

The education minister who has led the reform effort thus far is Lt Gen. (retd.) Javed Ashraf Qazi. He has taken an aggressive approach to reform of madrassahs, though his past actions as the former head of Pakistan's Inter Services Intelligence (ISI) between 1993 and 1995 has haunted some of the reform efforts. During his tenure as ISI chief, Qazi admittedly supervised the recruitment of students from Pakistan's madrassahs for the extremist Taliban militia. Commentators have criticized the relatively slow pace for curricular reform even among government schools.

While reform efforts are underway they have been hampered by institutional inertia within the Islamabad-based National Curriculum Wing (NCW). As part of the education ministry, the NCW sets the guidelines for the four provincial textbook boards which publish course material for government schools. The NCW issued a directive in 2002 laying out the following objectives: 'nurture in children a sense of Islamic identity and pride in being a Pakistani and regard Pakistan as an Islamic country and acquire deep love for it.' Such strong Islamic inculcation within the state school curriculum prompted protests from non-Muslims and secular activists. While studying Islamiyat is not compulsory for non-Muslims as it is for Muslim students there is a strong evangelical cadence to the policy. An extra 25 per cent marks are offered to a non-Muslim student who takes Islamic Studies as part of the curriculum. This 2002 directive was issued a month after erstwhile education minister Zubaida Jalal had directed the NCW to revise history books taught in public schools.

There is also a continuing tendency of appeasement of religious parties on the part of the government when it comes to matters of Islamic inclusion in texts. For example, in March 2004, the *Muttahida Majlis-e-Amal* (MMA), the alliance of five religious parties, disrupted the National Assembly proceedings and staged a walkout claiming that a certain reference to jihad as well as other Qur'anic verses had been excluded from the new edition of a state-prescribed biology textbook. The MMA threatened to launch a protest movement if the Qur'anic verses were not reinstated. The education minister at the time Zubaida Jalal immediately clarified that no chapter or verses relating to jihad (holy war) or *shahadat* (martyrdom) had been deleted from textbooks, and that the particular verse referring to jihad had only been shifted from the biology textbook for intermediate students (Classes XI and XII, that is) to the matriculation level course (Class X). It is curious why jihad or *shahadat* might even need to be mentioned in a biology text book to begin with.[16]

Additionally, highly negative material is presented regarding minority religious groups, particularly Hindus and Jews. This is perhaps the area of curricular reform that needs most immediate attention and the government has been quite forthcoming in addressing this issue. However, eliminating hate mongering should not be conflated with an immediate reduction in Islamic curricular content as it is likely to lead to neither policy being implemented. Both hate speech and Islamic content have collectively been the focus of extensive criticism in Pakistan by secular NGOs such as the Sustainable Development Policy Institute (SDPI), whose report titled Subtle Subversion (Nayyar and Salim, 2004) created quite a storm in Pakistan. Initially, the education ministry had supported the study but because of its strong message of secularization, the government, which had initially been supportive of research on curricular reform, had to distance itself from this study because eliminating Islamic content from text books was politically unacceptable to even moderate citizens.

Given the strong identity of Pakistan as a Muslim state, any reform pertaining to Islamic content will have to be approached with trepidation. Imposed secularization of the curriculum is not likely to work. Even many strong proponents of secularization in Pakistan such as Dr Asghar Qadir, former Dean of Sciences at Quaid-e-Azam University in Islamabad, commented that the SDPI study in this context was 'counterproductive'.[17]

Incremental change is most effective in such contexts, and must be pursued as a grassroots effort along side governmental intervention. Examining the lessons of other Muslim countries in working on educational reform initiatives may be instructive in this regard, while considering the peculiarities of Pakistani society.

LEARNING FROM REFORM INITIATIVES IN INDIA

Keeping a balance between theology and pure pedagogy has been a challenge for Muslim communities all over the world. Using the core lessons gleaned from the Pakistani case that has many commonalities across the Muslim world, it is worth comparing some specific connections with other Muslim communities. Let us first consider the case of Pakistan's closest neighbor India.

Madrassah education in India has fortunately been studied in great detail by Yoginder Sikand who is singularly important in providing a rigorous, and cogent analysis of madrassahs history as well as contemporary reform initiatives. I am indebted to his work for this section as my examples are largely derived from Sikand's book *Bastions of the Believers* (2006). There is a strong antipathy which Sikand appears to harbor for the Hindutva movement in India and its abuse of Muslim institutions. However, in order to vilify the extremist Hindus, Sikand has given a rather easy pass to extremists on the Islamic side. Nevertheless, the examples he provides of progressive madrassahs in India are important to consider.

The number of madrassahs in India as with Pakistan is widely contested. Some adhoc surveys have been done by various groups such as the Hamdard Foundation but no definitive number could be reached because of the wide expanse of the country. Former Minister of State for Home in India, Mr Vidyasagar Rao—disclosed in Parliament on 19 March (2002) that there were 31,850 madrassahs in the country and that 11,453 were in the border areas. However, even this number is questionable given the political posturing surrounding this issue.[18] Indian madrassahs have also had the peculiarity of having a sizeable non-Muslim population as well, particularly in West Bengal. According to a report in Kolkata's *Daily Telegraph* there was a 15 per cent rise in the number of non-Muslim students in madrassahs in the state in 2003. Abdus Sattar, president of the West Bengal Board of Madrassah Education attributed this increase to mainly two factors: regular schools running out of seats and the recognition of madrassahs by the West Bengal Council of Higher Secondary education. Additionally, many regular schools seek donations for admission which forces poor students to consider madrassahs. The percentage of enrollment of non-Muslims varies considerably but can be considerable such as the Contai Rehamania High Madrassah where there are 900 students, of whom around 200 are non-Muslims. While most of the curriculum remains the same for non-Muslims, some concessions are also made for example, of the 100-mark paper in Advanced Arabic, non-Muslims can answer questions for 65 marks in Bengali.[19]

Among the madrassah reform programmes, the Markaz-ul-Ma'rif Education and Research Centre, with offices in Delhi and Mumbai is particularly noteworthy. Established in 1982 by a graduate of the Deoband madrassah and member of Deoband Central Advisory Committee, Badruddin Ajmal. Originally from Assam, Badruddin is among a growing progressive cadre of 'ulama who are combining education and development. The Markaz runs a number of institutions in Assam and some other states in northeast India. These include 10 English-medium schools, 550 part-time *maktabs*, three orphanages, a modern hospital and several vocational training centres. The Markaz runs several small social work centres that are engaged in various developmental activities. It also has a publishing wing, which has produced a considerable amount of Islamic literature in various languages, including Assamese, Bengali, Urdu and English.

Similar efforts can also be found in the Dar ul 'Umoor, based at Srirangapatanam, near Mysore. In particular, every Thursday, the students are expected to do some sort of fieldwork, visiting schools, non-governmental agencies, scientific institutions and museums, as well as churches and temples to interact with Christian and Hindu priests.

Establishing appropriate training centres for madrassah teachers, is another area where Indian ulama are showing leadership. The Jami'at ul-Falah, located at Bilariyaganj, near the town of Azamgarh in eastern Uttar Pradesh is exemplary in this regard. Associated with the Jama'ati Islami Hind, it is among the largest and better-organized madrassahs in India, with an estimated 5000 students on its rolls, including some 2700 girls, who study in a separate wing. Falah has acquired a national reputation for providing a broad-based education, that enables them to choose, to go on to regular universities or pursue further theological training. Most consequentially, degrees from the madrassah are now recognized by a growing number of universities in India and in Saudi Arabia and Egypt, thus providing new career opportunities that were not available to traditional madrassah graduates.

In Kerala, which is a state widely acclaimed for its educational achievement, there are estimated to be some 40 high schools associated with the Jama'at, where students train for the 'alim course and simultaneously prepare for a bachelor's degree from a state university.

Surprisingly, despite their austere image in the West, the Deobandis have, in recent years, been among the more active in establishing girls' higher-level madrassahs. One of the largest girls' madrassahs in India, the Jami'at-us-Salihat at the town of Malegaon, in Maharashtra, is linked to the Deoband tradition. It has a large hostel, where girls from various parts of India as well as abroad live together. However, the purpose of this education of girls appears to be geared towards preventing Westernization and inculcating traditional values of subservience. This phenomenon of conservative Islamic feminism is also manifest in the Al-Huda organizations led by Dr Farhat Hashmi, a Pakistani scholar based in Canada, who exemplifies an educated yet extreme version of Islam. Hence, even without a draconian ban on girls going to school (as was the case with the Taliban), one can still have similar outcomes in terms of male dominance and exclusion of women from the productive workforce when women are attending such madrassahs.[20] South Asian reform efforts, particularly, involving women madrassahs must thus be considered with some measure of trepidation.

MODELS OF MODERNITY IN SOUTH-EAST ASIA

The economic rise of southeast Asia, has led many to brand the region as a model of balancing tradition and transformation. Under the leadership of Dr Mahathir Mohammad, Malaysia became simultaneously a modern economy and an Islamized state. Defying the perceived oxymoron of Islamic modernity was considered by many analysts to be Mahatir's ultimate achievement. In contrast, Indonesia tried to crack down on Islamic extremism while following a development path more closely advised by the international financial institutions. The demographic differences between the countries are also important to emphasize. Indonesia has ten times the population of Malaysia while still having an 80 per cent Muslim majority. On the other hand Malaysia has numerous ethnicities and a very financially dominant sizeable majority of Chinese.

A somewhat superficial analysis may reveal that Malaysia was thus able to achieve a balance while Indonesia was not. However, radicalism within Malaysia's Islamic education system has also become increasingly apparent.[21] As noted by both countries, as well as tiny Singapore, nevertheless, have examples of positive transformation of Islamic educational institutions which need to be considered. Malaysian Prime Minister, Abdullah Ahmad Badawi, who is a trained Islamic scholar, has argued that current Islam was almost totally associated with violence and extremism and needed reformulation. Borrowing the concept of 'Islam Hadhari' (progressive Islam), from the fourteenth century Muslim historian Ibn Khaldun, Badawi suggests that the term signifies urban civilization, economic development, civic life and cultural progress. The concept has been explained in a 60-page document published by Badawi that emphasizes the central role of knowledge in Islam; preaches and appeals to Muslims to be 'inclusive', tolerant and outward-looking.

Of particular interest has been the prominence of environmental education in Islamic political discourse in Indonesia. While Islamic theology is not pantheistic, and shares many of the anthropocentric attributes of other Abrahamic faiths, there is a reverence of nature that stems from essential pragmatism within the faith. Due to resource constraints, early Muslims realized that long-term development was only possible within ecological constraints which were shared by all of humanity. Thus, the universality of environmental resources provides a valuable template for peace-building that is realized in Islam.

Nevertheless, there are several systemic challenges to a realization of a sustainable development paradigm within contemporary Islam, largely due to institutional inertia and a reluctance of *ulama* (scholars) to engage contemporary issues. First, the Islamic belief of humans as *Ashraf ul Makhloqaat* (the most superior creation) poses serious challenges to inculcating environmental ethics, particularly with reference to animal rights. However, this can be countered by considering numerous injunctions about the great responsibility which comes with the status of being a 'superior creation'. The concept of *khalifa* (vicegerent) can be considered an antidote to this concept since the role of a vicegerent is to act as a steward for the land and for all creation. Second, the Islamic focus on the after-life rather than the present has also led many Muslims to consider environmental and developmental challenges as trivial compared to the hereafter. This has led to a sense of complacence and fatalism about our developmental predicament, since it is deemed the will of God.

Yet this fatalism is no longer pervasive among the devoutly practicing Muslims of Indonesia. As the host of the United Nations Climate Change Conference 2007, Indonesia's political scene appears to have been resolutely greened and the pesantren can take some credit for this process. Veteran Islamist politician Abdulrrahman Wahid, (popularly known as Gus Dur) has established the Partai Kebangkitan Bangsa or PKB (National Awakening Party) which has a powerful environmental message and is calling itself the country's 'Green Party'. The slogan was officially launched in Bali at a ceremony in which many Islamist activists joined forces with environmental campaigners. Specific nongovernmental organizations that have been most strident on environmental issues such as Greenpeace were invited by the PKB to attend the event. Mr Wahid is backed by the powerful religious seminarian establishment of the Nadwat-ul-Ulama. Beyond the branding and rhetoric, the PKB has a clear strategy to improve Indonesia's environmental performance.

The PKB has proposed to amend the Constitution to make the right to a clean environment a fundamental human right and also strengthen the national laws on environment, forestry and land. Several other Islamic groups in Indonesia are also rallying around the environmental agenda. Another remarkable turn of events has been the *fatwa* (or religious edict) issued by some notable Islamic clerics in Java that nuclear weapons are inherently un-Islamic and that even nuclear energy must be avoided because of its potential for abuse. Several Islamist parties are thus opposing the development of a nuclear power station in Muria of Jepara, Central Java and calling it *haraam* or forbidden. Clearly, there is some disagreement on the matter within theological ranks since previously Muslim leaders had supported nuclear energy as a mark of power and prestige. Ma'ruf Amin, the head of the Islamic Teaching Commission in the ultra-conservative Indonesian Ulemas Council (MU) responded to the *fatwa* by urging caution about hastily declaring external issues as 'forbidden.' However, the PKB is standing firm in its opposition to nuclear energy and its alliance with environmentalists. The pesantren have also played an important part in galvanizing support for this movement. The head of a notable 'green Islamic school' Nasruddin Anshari, frequently uses the refrain 'one earth, for all,' just as much as he does the usual Islamic invocation of 'Allah-o-Akbar' (God is Great). Indonesia's pesantren have come under great scrutiny in recent years due to their perceived connections to terrorist incidents such as the Bali bombings in 2005. Even US presidential candidate Barack Obama felt obliged to distance himself from his childhood days in Indonesia because of a rumour that he too had attended a pesantren, since both his father and step-father were practicing Muslims. Yet the transformation taking place at Pesantren Lingkungan Giri Ilmu would certainly please most constituencies in the West. Children from the village of Bantul are learning about the importance of preserving their ecosystem as a mark of worshipping God. The tenacity of Islamic religious doctrines that often manifests itself in uncompromising stances on political conflicts is being channeled more positively towards environmental ethics.

In contrast to Malaysia's state-spun version of 'enlightened moderation', Indonesia has a more grassroots Islamic reformation. As the world's largest Muslim country and one where some linkages between madrassahs and terrorism have been acknowledged even by revisionist scholars such as Sageman (2005), some comparison is in order. According to Azra (2004) of approximately 44 million children in Indonesian secondary schools, 5.7 million, or 13 per cent, are in madrassahs. The total number of madrassahs is estimated to be around 23,000, of which 4,000 are high schools. Most of these are community-operated, i.e. 'private,' although madrassahs may also be run by the government if they are set up that way or petition the government to take over.

The reformist agenda is being promoted by Muhammadiyah and Nahdlatul Ulama (NU), the two largest and most influential Muslim organizations that boast between 60 and 80 million followers in mosques, schools and universities throughout Indonesia. Lily Zakiyah Munir, a leading Muslim women's rights activist in Indonesia has recently established the Centre for Pesantren and Democracy Studies that works closely with the 'ulama and students of Indonesian Islamic boarding schools or pesantrens. In an interview with Yoginder Sikand[22] she described her organization's role as intending 'to create synergies between the pesantrens and the wider society to produce 'ulama who can harness the humanitarian values of Islam to work along with local communities, Muslim and non-Muslim, for social transformation.'

The notion of Pancasila, the 'five cardinal principles' enshrined in the Indonesian Constitution, are often perceived to be in competition with the five pillars of Islam as providing a more suitable basis for the Indonesian polity. The first sila or 'principle' lays down belief in the one God as binding on all citizens. Hence, Indonesia is neither a theocratic nor a secular state, but somewhat in between the two. Pancasila also mandates the unity of Indonesia, democratic rule and social justice, all of which, according to the late president of Paramadina University, Nurcholish Madjid (2003), are 'in harmony with the principles of the different religions practiced in Indonesia.' Seeking 'Islamic' sanction for Pancasila, is likened to the treaty between the Prophet and the Jews, which guaranteed freedom of religion and allowed for people of different faiths to work together for the defence of Medina. Related to this exhortation for a pluralist Indonesia is Madjid's critique of the post-Qur'anic notion of the world being divided into two competing spheres—dar ul-islam ('the abode of Islam') and dar ul-harb ('the abode of war'). Instead, he invokes the Qur'anic notion of dar al-salaam ('the abode of peace'), which he sees as a society based on peace and social justice for all. Madjid, who was educated at the University of Chicago, and considered a leading Muslim reformist, regarded Pancasila as working in the direction of establishing such a society, and argued in much of his writings that a Pancasila state, rather than an Islamic state, is the best available system for Indonesia.

Malaysia and Indonesia have also been influenced by their small and powerful neighbour, Singapore where the Muslim community has made a conscious effort to unify around some tangible principles of reform in a sort of manifesto. This manifesto was decided by the Majlis-e-ulama-e-Islam Singapura, and announced by Mr Mohammad Alam Musa in January 2003 as follows:

The Singaporean Muslim:

- Holds strongly to Islamic principles while adapting himself to changing contexts.
- Is morally and spiritually strong and is on top of the challenges of modern society.
- Is progressive, practices Islam beyond form/rituals and rides the modernization wave.
- Appreciates Islamic civilization and history and has a good understanding of contemporary issues.
- Appreciates other civilizations and is confident in interacting and learning from other communities.
- Believes that good Muslims are also good citizens.
- Is well-adjusted as a contributing member of a multi-religious society and a secular state.
- Is a blessing to all and promotes universal principles and values.
- Is inclusive and practices pluralism, without contradicting Islam.
- Is a model and inspiration to all.

What is promising according to Sardar (2004), is that 'Malaysia's Islam Hadhari and Indonesia's deformalisation emphasize tolerance and pluralism, civic society and open democracy. Both are likely to spread. Malaysia is trying to export Islam Hadhari to Muslim communities in Thailand and the Philippines. '

FUTURE REFORM EFFORTS IN PAKISTAN

On 6 June 2005, the federal education ministry was allocated Rs4.520 billion under the Public Sector Development Programme (PSDP) 2005–06 with an overall increase of 122 per cent over current year's allocation of Rs2.029 billion. The money will be spent on 59 ongoing and 18 new projects. A large part of this allocation—Rs1 billion—will again go into the ongoing madrassah reforms project, which had been started during the fiscal year 2002–03 with an estimated cost of Rs5.75 billion. The status of this project is unclear.

The project was conceived as a complementary arrangement to the proposed law for madrassah registration. Since there was a need to encourage the madrassahs to register, the project was based on an incentive of one-time grants and teacher salaries. However, although the law is in abeyance, the incentive regimes are being implemented. Some general concerns with the government's efforts are as follows:

- The project states that resources will be given to madrassahs which are registered. It fails to mention under which law? And what obligations does this registration impose on the registered entity, or how efficient and effective is the registering authority?
- The authority to appoint the teachers to teach the formal subjects has been given to a committee dominated by madrassah system nominees, i.e representative of Wifaq and the manager of the madrassah with only one outsider who will be the representative of the district education department.
- The National and Provincial steering committees are very narrowly based, consisting of official nominees with no representation from civil society or any independent expert having knowledge and experience of the madrassah movement.
- The capacity and political will to monitor this project is not clearly articulated. The political will is especially pertinent in NWFP and Balochistan, where madrassah movement leadership are in the government.

Any public policy issue can only be successfully addressed if the 'issue analysis' or problem diagnosis is correct. There is a growing recognition, even in US government circles, that a more nuanced approach is needed in tackling any potential linkage between madrassahs and violence. A recent study by USAID denotes the links between *madrassahs* and extremist Islamic groups as 'rare but worrisome,' but also adds that 'access to quality education alone cannot dissuade all vulnerable youth from joining terrorist groups.' One source reports that even in more moderate ('quietist') schools, students are often instructed to reject the 'immoral' and 'materialistic' Western culture (Aramanios, 2003).

A number of policy options to address the issue are available but will require clear leadership from the government and a willingness to take some political risks. In the case of the Madrassah Reform Strategy the *sine qua non* is to have a formal regulatory mechanism for the guaranteeing efficacy of all educational institutions and ensure quality control whether it is private secular schools or madrassahs. This should cater for registration, create concomitant statutory obligation on the registered entity and its sponsors, by way of governance, financial accountability, and responsibility towards society.

The reform effort should *inter alia* provide for the following elements:

a) Registration of madrassahs as well as private schools for quality control purposes is essential. However, to give more credibility to the effort, this process is best managed at the provincial level with minimal guidelines being set by the federal government.
b) Construction of madrassahs on public lands, must be scrutinized more carefully to ensure the intended purpose of state land use is being met.
c) Inclusion of local council representatives in the management committee or board of directors of madrassah *wifaq* should be suggested in order to ensure the local citizenry are involved in the workings of the madrassah.
d) There is need to set up an interdepartmental committee headed by the Nazim (local-level governor) to steer the reform agenda forward based on local input but with accountability to the federal government.
e) Some measures for ensuring that the local student body representation balances external students enrollment in urban madrassahs should be encouraged so that there is greater connection between the community and the madrassahs.
f) Career placement of madrassah graduates should be encouraged through apprenticeship programmes in which the madrassah graduates can find a way to teach their religious ideals while also contributing as productive members of society. Some madrassahs are initiating such efforts of their own accord. For example, the madrassah of Pir Karam Shah near Sargodha (near the frequent motorway stop of Bhera) is providing facilities to students in order to pursue university degrees after graduation.
g) Exchange of possible practices and ideas between schools and madrassahs within Pakistan and abroad. It is important to promote greater interaction between youth of various schools in Pakistan to reduce class tensions. There are some very promising programmes that a few madrassahs are starting of their own accord in Pakistan and abroad. However, it is important to ensure that the lessons are meant to be mutual and no particular 'role

model' is chosen as that is likely to lead to conspiracies of political patronage.[23]

In August 2006, the government withheld funds for the effort since there was growing reluctance from religious groups to comply and the focus of government efforts shifted to getting a bill passed on women's rights. Although madrassahs are often considered community-owned indigenous institutions, in practice madrassahs, particularly urban madrassahs, are frequently divorced from the community. There is hardly any local student studying in them and there is no representation of local residents in the management of the madrassah. There is often no formal management structure for the smaller madrassahs and the madrassah manager has almost complete control over the operations of the madrassah. Our analysis of the madrassahs in Islamabad revealed that 90 per cent of the students in these madrassahs were from the Frontier province, Northern areas and districts other than Islamabad. Hardly any management committee of registered madrassahs has local residents as members.

The government is beginning to realize the immediacy of issues but the pace is slow. A Centre for Progressive Islam was set up by the government under the leadership of Dr Riffat Hassan, feminist theologian, based at the University of Louisville, Kentucky. However, this centre had limited success in engaging with mainstream ulama and ended up with a 'preaching to the choir' syndrome. The centre's leadership has changed so that it is perceived as an indigenous institution rather than one formed by itinerant expatriates.

The former minister of religious affairs, Mr Muhammad Ijaz-ul-Haq, the son of the late president Zia, carried considerable clout with the ulama because of his lineage. In recent statements, he has acknowledged that there is a problem of indigenous sectarianism. Despite occasional statements underplaying the role of madrassahs, he issued a statement of recommendations in January 2004, following attacks at the Haidry Mosque in Karachi that recommended 'a unanimous code of conduct duly signed by all the religious leaders of all the schools of thought in the country.' In a refreshing turn from the usual conspiratorial rhetoric, he also stated that 'there is no denying the fact that it is the internal elements who are out to create chaos in the country. No foreign elements can go to such an extent.'[24] Nevertheless, far more needs to be achieved to enhance the role of madrassahs in Pakistani society and to quell the tide of sectarianism that they are contributing to.

Enforcement of laws prohibiting arms in schools, violent rhetoric, publication of erroneous facts and libel can all help in addressing this challenge. The radicalization of young Muslims is an insidious phenomenon that goes beyond madrassahs but should certainly be addressed in these vital institutions as well.

The connection between madrassahs and sectarianism is being acknowledged by many madrassah leaders themselves. In an email interview, with Yoginder Sikand, Maulana Zahid-ul-Rashidi a leading Pakistani Deobandi scholar based in Gujranwala stated: 'I think that as far as the question of sectarianism is concerned, the situation with the madrassahs is not at all encouraging. Students are trained to rebut other sects through fierce polemics, but this is really destructive. I feel that instead of this, each madrassah should familiarize its students with the beliefs and proofs of the sect that it is associated with, as well as the basic beliefs of other sects, and train them to dialogue, rather than violently denounce, the other sects. Sectarian differences cannot be eliminated. However, if a culture of tolerance is created, and if dialogue and understanding take the place of polemics, the destructiveness of sectarianism can be considerably reduced.'[25]

The future of madrassah reform in Pakistan remains elusive. In August, 2006, the government withheld funds for the reform effort since there was growing reluctance from religious groups to comply and the focus of government efforts shifted to getting a bill passed on women's rights. The government appears to not have the ability to focus on more than one reform effort at a time and former President Musharraf displayed some ambivalence about how best to reform the madrassahs. In his autobiography (Musharraf, 2006, p. 313) he acknowledges that there is a lack of trust that is hampering madrassah reform but then quickly moves on to conclude the chapter by stating that 'there are many countries around the world that intertwine religious and public schools successfully, and there is no reason why Pakistan cannot do the same.'

There is a need to give these essential Islamic indigenous institutions back to the community, and the suggested changes in domestic government policy may help to bring this about.[26] Nevertheless, we must consider the role of external agents, particularly Western donor countries and also their international relations in the madrassah reform effort as discussed in the next chapter.

NOTES

1. For a coverage of efforts in Northern Africa and Morocco see Eickelman.
2. Descriptive material on madrassah reform strategy provided by the Embassy of Pakistan in Washington DC, January 2005.
3. See article titled 'Enlightened Extremism' by S.M. Rehman on the web site of FRIENDS (Foundation for Research on International Environment National Development and Security, an outfit led by the controversial former chief of the army staff General Mirza Aslam Beg.
4. It should be mentioned that the Islamic University in Islamabad is a highly professional institution offering advanced degrees and a fairly rigorous curriculum including courses and training certificates on the World Trade Organization and Environmental Law. It follows the tradition of strong institutions of higher learning In India as well such as the Jamiya Islamiyah in Delhi that is profiled very positively in Dalrymple, 2005. However, the number of madrassah graduates entering such universities (except for the Islamic studies departments, which Dalrymple focused on) is relatively small.
5. General Moin-uddin-Haider's struggles cost him dearly as his brother was killed in a reprisal attack for his crackdown.
6. Embassy of the Islamic Republic of Pakistan (2004) *Madrassah Reform in Pakistan*. Embassy of the Islamic Republic of Pakistan. http://www.embassyofpakistan.org/pb5php.
7. Report accessed via the centre's web site: http://www.pcp.org.pk/, January 2005.
8. For a good comparison of Pakistani and Bangladeshi madrassahs see Ahmed, Mumtaz, 2004. there has been a common assumption that the Aaliya madrassahs have been quite moderate. However, the recent violent incidents in which the major Aaliya madrassah in Dhaka had to be indefinitely closed questions this assumption. For an excellent visual narrative of Bangladeshi madrassahs, see the feature film nominated by Bangladesh for an Oscar titled 'Matir Moyna (Clay Bird), directed By Tareq Masud.
9. Official response of the Chief Administrator of the Religious Affairs and Awqaf department, Mr Muhammad Javaid Iqbal Awan to the Madaris Registration Ordinance, response dated: 18 October 2003.
10. Darul-Uloom in India, http://www.darululoom-deoband.com/english/ This institution recommends the madrassah curriculum in Pakistan.
11. *The Daily Times* (Lahore), 17 May 2005.
12. Qazi Hussain Ahmed, interview to Sairah Irshad Khan, *Newsline* (Karachi, April 2005).
13. In addition, USAID has also given the foundation a $5 million grant for work in Sindh and Balochistan to experiment with early child education methodologies in 100 schools.
14. Details of this controversy are derived from analysis prepared by Mohammad Shehzad, distributed on the email list Islaminterfaith.org, 15 February 2005.
15. Arshad Alam. *Science in the Madrassas*. http://www.islaminterfaith.org, Accessed, 16 May 2005.
16. This incident is reported by Amir Mir in a web article titled 'Primers of Hate'. http://www.outlookindia.com/full.asp?fodname=20051010&fname=Pakistan+ per cent28F per cent29&sid=1.

17. Personal communication with Dr Asghar Qadir, Islamabad, December 2004.
18. Qasmi, M. Burhanuddin. 'Indian madrassah curriculum and the need for reform.' Paper presented at the workshop on madrassah education at Erfurt University, June 2005.
19. Sanjay Mondal (2004). 'Non-Muslim boom in madrasas—15 per cent growth last year: *The Telegraph, Calcutta,* 26 July 2004.
20. For an investigative article on Farhat Hashmi refer to Kohler, 2006.
21. Noor, Farish. *Malaysia's Home-Grown Taliban: Is this the future of 'Moderate' Islam in Asia?* Email communiqué, 30 January 2005.
22. This interview was posted on the web site: www.islaminterfaith.org in 2004 but which has subsequently closed.
23. There has been a tendency to highlight 'model programmes' that lead to further polarization. For example, the scientifically based curriculum of some Islamic organizations such as the Idaara Minhaj-ul-Qur'an, led by Dr Tahirul Qadiri has been hailed by some as exemplar, without the awareness that Dr Qadiri is a highly polarizing and controversial politician in Punjab. It is thus best to present ideas in a neutral frame of reference rather than providing 'models'.
24. Interview with Mr Ijaz-ul-Haq, 4 January 2004, statement given in writing during this interview.
25. Email interview with Maulana Zahid-ul-Rashidi conducted by Yoginder Sikand and communicated via email on 29 September 2005. He has been a member of the *Jami'at-i-'Ulama-i-Islam Pakistan,* and served for many years as assistant to Maulana Mufti Mahmud, leader of this party, He has set up an educational centre in Gujranwala called the *Al-Sharia Academy,* where he is trying to experiment with combining religious and modern education. He also writes a daily column for the 'Pakistan' (Lahore) and a weekly column for the *'Nawa-i-Haq'* (Islamabad) and is the editor of a web journal: www.alsharia.org.
26. In November 2006, the British Prime Minister agreed to a sizeable donor commitment towards educational reform, particularly with reference to madrassahs.

7

EDUCATION, DEVELOPMENT AND CONFLICT PREVENTION: THE ROLE OF FOREIGN POWERS

The contribution towards educational projects as an overall percentage of government expenditures continues to be very small across the Muslim world. Pakistan spends only 2.7 per cent of its gross national output on public education, one of the lowest rates in the world just behind Congo in UNDP rankings. The government has set a target of spending 4 per cent of GDP and reaching this number in the next ten years.[1] Government-run schools are generally in poor condition. They are often without teachers, books, electricity, running water, and even roofs. Some are even just there on paper and exist only as budget line items as our data has noted with the enumeration of closed premises in Ahmedpur. All this takes its toll on the literacy rate of the country which is at best estimated at being 40 per cent. To overcome this gap in resources and commitment, Pakistan clearly needs some creative incentives as well as strategic pressure to ensure that education remains a priority. Linking education to development, is however, essential. As the lessons of many African countries indicate[2], simply education alone is not enough to ensure stability and vibrancy in an economy. Unfortunately, educational investment from Western donors has had to contend with various political challenges.

According to a senior researcher in the US government's Naval Postgraduate School in Monterey, California, who has studied madrassahs (Looney, 2003), the sources of this extremism and Anti-Western sentiments in Pakistan are complex, but at least four factors have played a significant role:

(1) The extensive Saudi funding for exporting Salafi/Wahhabiism to the subcontinent and for keeping religious reactionaries at bay in seminaries set up in regions at a distance from the Kingdom.
(2) Reliance on religious elements by the military high command and civilian autocrats (like the late Benazir Bhutto and Nawaz Sharif) to promote anti-democratic agendas.
(3) Anti-Americanism generated initially by the perceived pro-Israeli US commitment and fuelled subsequently by the US invasions of Afghanistan and Iraq.
(4) The organizational zeal of the Jamaat-i-Islami which enabled it for the time being to gather disparate religious groups under the umbrella of the Muttahida Majlis-i-Amal (MMA) — the coalition of religious parties that won the provincial elections in the NWFP and Balochistan in October 2002.

While this study does not discount these factors, it proposes some further refinement in the analysis and provides some possible avenues to address the rising tide of anti-Western sentiment, specifically in the context of madrassahs.

CURRENT US PUBLIC DIPLOMACY AND LEGISLATION

In September 2002, USAID committed $100 million over five years for general education reform in Pakistan. The Research Triangle Institute (RTI), a US-based, non-profit corporation, received a USAID contract for $60 million of this aid to implement USAID's Education Sector Reform Assistance (ESRA) project in Pakistan. The United States also has committed additional resources through the Middle East Partnership Initiative (MEPI), which received $29 million in FY2002 and $90 million in FY2003 (through P.L. 108-11). One of MEPI's goals is to encourage improvements in secular education throughout the Arab world, and MEPI's draft strategies have registered concern over the rising enrollment in madrassahs.

A prescient analysis of the US government's public diplomacy efforts has been provided recently by David Kaplan (2005). His review of the 'Muslim World Outreach strategy' shows that the efforts span a range of activities from Intelligence operatives setting up 'fake' jihad websites to dilute militant information to more concerted efforts through USAID. However, unlike the cold war days there is fear of 'blowback.' Some of the key programmes highlighted by Kaplan are as follows:

The CIA's Office of Transnational Issues has created a Global Information and Influence Team, charged with pulling together assessments of key US targets. A public diplomacy conference hosted by the group in February 2005 focused on strategies to influence six nations, according to an agenda for the meeting. On the list are China, Egypt, France, Indonesia, Nigeria, and Venezuela. Regular budget increases since 9/11 have lifted spending on public diplomacy by more than 40 per cent since then to nearly $1.3 billion. The US government's new Arabic broadcasting services—Radio Sawa and Alhurra TV—are showing some success, despite continuing cynicism from critics. According to Kaplan, estimates differ, but an A.C. Nielsen survey last year found that Alhurra, after just six months on the air, was reaching between 20 per cent and 33 per cent of viewers with satellite dishes in a half-dozen key Arab nations.

US funds are supporting the restoration of Muslim holy sites, including historic mosques in Egypt, Pakistan, and Turkmenistan, though many Muslims discount this by saying that even more were destroyed in Iraq and Afghanistan by US bombing. In Kyrgyzstan, US embassy funding helped restore a major Sufi shrine. In Uzbekistan, money has gone to preserve antique Islamic manuscripts, including 20 Qur'ans, some dating to the eleventh century. In Bangladesh, USAID is training mosque leaders on development issues. In Madagascar, the embassy even sponsored an intermosque sports tournament. Islamic media activities of all sorts, from book translations to radio and TV in at least a half-dozen nations are also being funded.

The effort is perhaps most pronounced in Indonesia, the world's largest Muslim nation, with 240 million people.[3] Even the study by Peter Bergen (2005), that largely dismissed linkage of madrassahs to international terrorism found that the Bali bombers had attended madrassahs. According to Kaplan, USAID now helps fund over 30 Muslim organizations in the country. Among the programmes: media production, workshops for Islamic preachers, and curriculum reform for schools from rural academies to Islamic universities. A talk show on Islam and tolerance is relayed to radio stations in 40 cities and sends a weekly column to over a hundred newspapers. Islamic think-tanks with a more 'moderate' interpretation of Islam, showing its compatibility with democracy and human rights, are also being funded here.

Regrettably, the level of US hostility is so great in certain areas that even when the American government should be taking credit for activities, anti-American sentiment can make it tough. During a mission to Cairo by a State Department panel on public diplomacy, visitors were repeatedly told how grateful Egyptians were to the Japanese for building their opera house. Yet they downplayed the fact that Egypt is the second-largest recipient of US aid--nearly $2 billion a year—and that Americans have funded Cairo's systems for clean water, sewage, and electricity. US funds also restored the nation's oldest mosque after water damage, yet Egyptian officials were reluctant to put USAID's signs outside the building.

Regarding madrassah reform, the Pakistani government had declined any direct offers for support (which would in any case be difficult to justify since the US government is not supposed to fund religious institutions).[4] The USAID programme has focused on helping government schools become suitable competitors. However, even in such cases, there can be challenges, as was apparent in January 2005 when the US Embassy ordered an abrupt end to a $1 million contract to supply Internet access to schools due to the arrest of a militant mistakenly thought to be tied to one of the schools.

According to Kaplan's sources, however, in Uganda, which hosts a large Muslim minority and is close to the scene of the al-Qaeda bombings in Kenya and Tanzania, last year, the embassy announced it was funding construction of three Islamic elementary schools as a social service venture. According to Marine Maj. Gen. Samuel Holland, in some cases military officers gather intelligence on where militants plan to start religious schools, they then target those areas by building up new public schools and the local infrastructure (Kaplan, 2005). This is perhaps the most sound strategy, though it must be undertaken with complete local participation regarding development choices.

As part of a State Department programme of grants through the University of Louisville, Kentucky, madrassah teachers from across South Asia as well as other senior scholars have been invited to visit the USA and get training in workshops and participate in ecumenical activities. Indeed, the head of the Wifaq-ul-Madaaris, Maulana Jalandhri, visited the USA for one month as part of this programme in April 2004.

There appears to be some marginal success of these programmes. A poll of Indonesians conducted in March 2005 after the tsunami relief efforts led by the US military found that America's unfavourability rating had plunged from 83 per cent to 54 per cent; support for Osama bin Laden, by contrast fell by more than half (Kaplan, 2005). However, there is still immense trepidation in the Muslim world about trusting the United States. This can only be addressed by focusing ultimately on the core causes of Muslim resentment.

TEMPERING THE TENDENCY TOWARDS FORCED SECULARIZATION

Despite the relatively religious texture of the Bush administration, there has been a strong influence from some analysts to try and use the madrassah issue as a way of imposing secularism in Pakistan. While, Musharraf initially used Turkey as a model of secularism in some of his speeches, he soon realized that secularism is untenable in Pakistan because of popular opinion in favour of some role of religion in public life. In addition, religion is enshrined within the Pakistani constitution and thus poses some interesting legal complexities. The Turkish experience with attempts at secularization of Islamic education deserves greater attention. Following the 1980 military coup and the gradual move back towards democracy, Turkey has followed a gradual move towards reintroduction of Islam in the curricula of schools. The 1982 constitution of Turkey made religious education mandatory in all primary and secondary schools. The military, which has held prominence in Turkey in ways that are perhaps analogous to Pakistan, co-opted Islam to placate the strong resentment towards forced secularization that emerged on the streets. The result has been the emergence of an 'educated counter-elite' (Guven, 2004, p. 199). It remains unclear how workable this strategy will be in Turkey since there is a continuing festering of radicalism. However, what is perhaps most regrettable is that many of these nuanced lessons from specific policy experiments in Muslim countries continues to not be appreciated in the halls of power in Washington and Brussels.

The policy implications of misunderstanding the madrassah phenomenon are evidenced by broader prescriptive monographs such as one published by the highly influential Rand Corporation in 2003 titled *Civil Democratic Islam: Partners, Resources and Strategies.* (Benard, 2003). This report is emblematic of recent prescriptive policy documents from White House advisors that can present a cogent but strategically flawed analysis. The author, Cheryl Benard,[5] somewhat simplistically characterizes Muslims into four categories: fundamentalist, traditionalist, modernist and secularist. Based on accounts of madrassah education and ensuing perceptions, Benard concludes that America should ally itself primarily with the secularists and modernists in the group while distancing itself from even the nonviolent traditionalists. She acknowledges that most Muslims are non-violent traditionalists and yet she does not want the US to embrace this cohort. Rather she suggests that the US can 'at best [...] only make an uneasy peace with them.' This draconian view of traditionalists is partly due to a misunderstanding of madrassahs and other Islamic institutions. As one non-Muslim scholar of South Asian madrassahs has commented on Benard's piece and the broader context of US inclinations to act in this regard:

> No dialogue, other than a dialogue of the deaf, can be expected to follow from the suggestions that this ill-conceived report makes. The report signals a dogged refusal to consider alternative views, a trait that American policy experts like Benard seem to share with their radical Islamist foes. While no one can deny the necessity of progressive and more open understandings of Islam, as indeed of other religions as well, it is unlikely that many Muslims would willingly embrace the brand of 'Islam' that Benard and others see themselves as engaged in fabricating.[6]

In another reaction to this sort of approach to US foreign policy, the Malaysian scholar Farish Noor (2005) responds as follows:

> While there is nothing wrong with being a 'moderate Muslim' per se, one could argue that moderate Islam cannot and will not be born in the laboratories of US think-tanks and policy institutes. Nor should the US or its allies be so cavalier in their issuance of 'fatwas' as to which state or government is 'moderate' and which is not, according to its own jaundiced criteria. Thus far we have seen at least three cases where Muslim states have been bestowed the much-coveted honor of being 'moderate' Islamic states: Pakistan, Malaysia and Indonesia. Yet in all three cases it is clear that the classification of 'moderate Muslim state' has more to do with the needs of US foreign policy than any real commitment to moderate Islam on Islamic terms.

While, one can appreciate the frustration that policy analysts such as Benard feel about contemporary Islamic institutions, considerable more patience, foresight and collaborative effort will be required to prevent the radicalization of nonviolent traditionalists. The complexity of madrassahs needs to be understood and efforts at reform should be encouraged from within the community rather than alienating the masses. The differentiation between domestic sectarian violence and international terrorism also needs to be considered. Both are key issues but have different solutions. Domestic sectarian violence is the result of class conflicts that are rooted in vestiges of the feudal system in rural areas. This radicalization thus has its roots in rural areas and has spread from there to urban centres. It is also the result of a proxy battle of ideas between Iran and Saudi Arabia regarding the supremacy of Sunni versus Shia doctrines. This aspect of violence is analogous to the Catholic-Protestant struggle in Northern Ireland, or indeed the Shia-Sunni conflict in contemporary Iraq and needs to be approached through the facilitation of consensus-building processes between the various sectarian groups. Most of the radicalization of madrassah students in Pakistan is channeled in this context. It is, nevertheless, quite a serious concern for US foreign policy as the sectarian violence in Pakistan, such as the suicide bombing at a Shia shrine in Islamabad on 28 May 2005, or the attack in the Qisa Khani Bazaar in Peshawar in January 2007 can lead to political instability in both rural and urban areas and the potential for further arms proliferation. While some empirical work on suicide bombings by scholars such as Pape (2005), suggests that they are driven by territorial aims rather than religious identity, the situation in Pakistan suggests that a misuse of religion and territoriality both reinforce the pernicious logic of suicidal attacks.

However, US policy responses to this challenge must recognize their limitation in affecting theological change and instead focus on providing alternative livelihoods for madrassah youth. Strong development programmes in areas of sectarian activity that could provide apprenticeships and vocational training for madrassah students to work in agricultural or industrial sectors would likely be more effective than demonizing and disavowing the madrassah system itself. For students who want to continue with a theological career, the establishment of religious hospitals and social service institutions such as those in many other religious missions would also provide students to continue a theological life but one that is also assisting in human development of their region.

The lack of such involvement is accepted by some madrassah graduates themselves. In a highly revealing interview to Yoginder Sikand, a madrassah graduate of the Jami'at-ul-Falah Madrassah in Azamgarh in India, Qari Naseem ur-Rahman, who is now studying for his doctorate at the Jamia Millia Islamiyah, admitted the following:

Many Catholic seminaries insist that their students should do some sort of social work or even work as social activists. This is quite in contrast to the madrassahs, where students are sought to be carefully insulated from the wider society and the problems that afflict it.... Many 'ulama think that training their students in the fine art of fiery debate, particularly against other Muslim sects, is the only form of social work that they should be engaged in....The age of polemics is now long past, and we should be thinking seriously about dialogue instead.... So, I would say, rather than enable or encourage the madrassah students to be socially engaged and to work for the needy, the madrassah system, as it exists today, works to actually further solidify structures of dependence in society.[7]

Within Pakistan, religious fanaticism is further fuelled by a constant questioning of Pakistani identity by scholars, particularly an atavistic reassessment of the partition of Indian subcontinent. More than fifty years hence, there still remains a persistent questioning of Pakistan's value of existence. The 2001 Hindu-Muslim riots in Gujarat, India, partially quelled this revisionist scholarship and many Pakistani nationalists felt vindicated in asserting the value of a separate Muslim state. However, the questioning of Pakistani identity has resurfaced (Cohen, 2004, Jafferelot, 2002).[8] In Pakistan, persistent narrative of partition, reawaken a sense of insecurity. Prior to British rule, India was an agglomeration of over 500 princely states joined together by a series of loose confederate monarchies, yet the myth of pan-subcontinental identity seems to be particularly charming to many commentators. Constant referrals by prominent foreign academics and policy-makers to Pakistan as a 'failed state' or revisiting partition fifty years hence further fuels conspiracy theories. Moreover, the arguments presented in this genre of scholarship are rarely supported by any rigorous study but are rather conjecture, opinion or anecdote, and yet have tremendous policy influence. Furthermore, prohibiting Muslim academics such as Tariq Ramadan from entering the country because of some small errant donation they may have given to a suspicious charity or their family lineage (Ramadan is the grandson of Hassan al Banna, among the founders of the Egyptian Muslim Brotherhood), is also causing further fault lines.[9]

Instead of such knee-jerk actions, there is a need to directly focus on clearly defined analysis predicated on data gathering and engagement with local communities. There must also be a willingness to be introspective on the part of the US regarding grievances from abroad.

THE POWER AND PERIL OF ANALOGY

In his address to the nation on 11 September, President Bush compared himself to Roosevelt and Truman in their face-off with a determined enemy. The agonizing question is often posed to pacifists: how would you contain a menace like Hitler without warfare? The next step in the argument being that Bin Laden and Saddam are comparable to Hitler and hence must be dealt with in a similar fashion. The power of analogy has even fused secular ideologies such as Fascism with contemporary theological movements to give birth to 'Islamo-fascism.' Newt Gingrich recently compared President Bush to Abraham Lincoln and called for congress to 'pass an act that recognizes that we are entering World War III.' This bold assertion also gains legitimacy from historical comparisons for only in the World Wars could we get the unequivocal mandate to 'defeat our enemies—not accommodate, understand or negotiate with them, but defeat them.'[10]

On the other side, al-Qaeda is also drawing strength from acerbic analogies going back in Islamic history. The unintentional slip of language by President Bush in calling the current conflict a 'crusade' was quickly exploited by Islamists to show how the comparison might be taken literally as a clash between Christendom and Islam. Similarly, the antiwar movement is capitalizing on the human proclivity for comparative rhetoric. Iraq is being compared to Vietnam and the war on terror being branded as a vacuous label, similar to the war on drugs. So if all sides are abusing analogical reasoning, might the effect be neutralized on its own?

Unfortunately, the danger of analogical reasoning occurs when we go beyond the explanatory power of this tool and instead start to use it for tactical and strategic purposes. As a conflict resolution professional, one of my goals in any mediation is to ensure that analogies are not misused by any side in their communication strategy. It is far too easy for players on all sides to selectively resurrect destructive memories to fuel fear and rage. However, despite all the clichés, history rarely repeats itself. Our lessons from history should identify patterns and causal mechanisms but not templates for policy intervention.

Analogies are so engrained in the American educational system that there was a major furor when the educational testing service dropped analogical reasoning from its much-feared scholastic aptitude tests (SAT). The purpose of the analogical section had been to help students differentiate between true and false analogies and help in logical argument formation. However, in 2005, it was decided by the College Board that current college curricula are not so 'connected' with this need. As Adam Cohen lamented soon thereafter, 'A nation whose citizens cannot tell a true analogy from a false one is like-fill in your own image for precipitous decline!'[11]

If we were to deconstruct another favoured analogy and perhaps see how it might be framed more constructively, let us consider the comparison of terrorism to cancer. Often we hear of terrorism being referred to as a disease that spreads malignantly like an aggressive tumor. Indeed, several medical journals have published editorials about this remarkably striking analogy. However, as with other ailments there are two paths to treatment: symptomatic and systemic. Both may be important but the latter is probably more effective in the long-term. Targeted chemotherapy against cancerous cells might be comparable to precision bombing against an enemy but to cure cancer clusters in communities the underlying epidemiological causes must be identified. We cannot be complacent about the power of our therapies if the malady is likely to repeat itself. Notice that the analogy here has deliberately avoided historical detail or more specific causal mechanisms. Instead a structural comparison is presented to provide clarity rather than conflating incongruent issues. As we ponder our policy towards current conflicts, we need to consider the limits of analogy more critically and not be too easily compelled to action by comparisons.

The US government should consider some of the more fundamental causes of conflict in this regard. There has to be a clear recognition that territorial disputes between Muslim communities and predominantly non-Muslim states are the root cause of conflict, whether it is Kashmir, Chechniya, Southern Thailand or the Middle East. There is a perception of territorial injustice and of partiality on the part of Western powers that fuels grievance. As noted by Looney (2003), 'clearly the conflict in the Middle-East is a rallying cry for many Muslims–even those who are not very religious.' Unfortunately, this often translates into anti-Jewish sentiments being expressed by Muslim leaders which can only be combated through conflict reduction in the Middle-East on the one hand and positive engagement between Faiths on the other.

The argument propounded that Muslims are 'against the American way of life'[12] does not hold much ground in empirical analysis or opinion surveys of Muslims who are quite discerning in their approval of many Western ideals while being critical of others.[13] The most critical aspect remains the unresolved territorial dispute in the Middle East. Madrassah reform is in and of itself is not likely to change this perception since it is spread out across all strata of society in Muslim countries including Pakistan. As one commentator noted recently in his analysis of the situation for the Asia-Pacific Centre for Security Studies in Hawaii:

> All Muslims, Arab and non-Arab, liberal or conservative, educated and uneducated, share in the agony of humiliation in the form of Israel's occupation of Palestinian territories (following 1967). Public opinion in Pakistan, as elsewhere in Muslim countries, holds the West, particularly the United States, responsible for this grave aggression....Israeli occupation of the West Bank and Gaza has done more damage to Muslim relations with the West than any other issue in the last three and a half decades.'[14]

There is also growing introspection within Islam from various sectors. Younger Muslims are trying to show their multiple allegiances to their adopted homelands such as America,[15] while scholars are trying to rediscover tolerance within an Islamic framework (Eickelman, 1998). Unfortunately, there is a tendency in many orthodox Muslim circles to dismiss such moves as *fitna*—an Arabic word meaning 'mischief', that was used in early Islam to describe people who spread dissent within the community. In addition the term *munafiq* (plural *munafiqoon* or *munafiqeen)* or 'hypocrite' is also used widely by some orthodox Muslims to dismiss such attempts if there is a perceived lack of commitment to Islam on other accounts such as observance of regular prayers and rituals. Some Muslims who are attempting to reform established Islamic organizations in North America are being branded 'neo-con Muslims.'[16] Another concept which is often used to dismiss any attempts at reform is the concept of *bidat* or *bidah* (meaning negative innovation in Arabic). Thus any changes must be presented in a framework that avoids them from being labeled as *bidah*—strong scholarship and linkage to Qur'anic injunctions and Ahadith (sayings of the Prophet) is essential for this purpose. If these tests are met, then the process can be termed *ijtihad* (independent reasoning). Regrettably, the term *ijtihad* is also being easily misunderstood by many progressive Muslims[17] who are interpreting it to mean personal interpretation that is drawing further ire from the clerics.

Instead, it may be advisable to support organizations that are focusing on active ecumenical dialogue efforts such as the Religious

Peace Research Organization (RPRO) or the publication of interfaith journals such as the Insight Forum. However, what is needed, is a more grassroot oriented version of these efforts in local languages and through local leadership at promoting civic discourse between various sects. An effort similar (but more ambitious) to the Karachi Ulama's Convention of 1951 in which various religious scholars from different sects convened to work out a 'peace pact' is actively needed and could be supported through neutral channels.

This is especially important since madrassahs also provide an important 'juristic' service to communities by issuing opinions that may be branded as 'fatwas' (official juristic verdicts) on various social decisions. Large madrassahs in urban centres often receive hundreds of letters per week asking for opinions on common issues such as the use of various kinds of household products as being 'allowable' to behavioural issues and conjugal relations. A dialogue between sects on divergence in opinions on such matters would be an entry point for further discussions as well. The Pakistani television station 'Geo' (in Urdu, this word is also an invocation to 'good living') has initiated a forum for such dialogue between Sunni and Shia scholars through a call-in TV programme. Such efforts are positive developments to promote greater accord between the various sects in a public context, though as noted in the next chapter they can also be ineffective if basic educational changes are not underway.

There is great promise for creative action on the part of Western donors and local action alike, so long as we can be patient and persevere with a sincerity and tenacity of purpose.

DEALING WITH DENIAL AND THE CONSPIRACY FACTOR

Progressive Muslims are often alarmed and amused by how easily populations succumb to fanciful accounts of Western designs against Islam from 9/11 to 7/7 to even the Asian Tsunami! Conspiracy theories appear to be so prevalent among Muslims that Al-Jazeera's website has even set up a separate category to cater to them![18] As noted in Chapter 1, conspiratorial factors within an educational setting can be among the most insidious means of conflict escalation.

Many politicians have once again played the history card in analyzing American relations with Pakistan as well. American and

Soviet follies during the Cold War and the American withdrawal following the decade-long conflict in Afghanistan is repeatedly used to argue why America cannot be trusted. US support for Saddam Hussein prior to the Gulf War is also cited as a mark of American opportunism. Indeed there are worse cases of American indiscretions during the Cold War such as the support of the insufferably corrupt Congolese dictator Mobutu or the nefarious role of the CIA in Latin America. However, harping on these incidents of the past is not constructive. While there is certainly cause for trepidation and caution in blindly trusting any foreign power, we must not let these sentiments translate into hatred and enmity. The US has probably learned from past mistakes and is willing to change.

Of course conspiracy accounts have been a feature of human societies in various contexts. From the lunar landing to the X-Files, human societies like to believe alternative accounts and revel in suspicion. The conspiratorial mind-set is also one of the most insidious legacies of the Cold War—when many conspiracy theorists were actually proven correct. Pervasive secrecy in those dark days incubated these conspiracy theories, but now increased transparency and media scrutiny has made governments more aware of the risk of conspiratorial strategies. In conflict situations, nevertheless, such theories are common—most Serbs, for example, are still in denial about the Srebrenica massacre and the Japanese still obfuscate their atrocities in Korea and China.

However, denial in the Muslim world is far more consequential because it can very easily translate into hatred and violence through misinterpretation of theological tenets. The denial in the Muslim world emanates from three key sources: i) pre-existing distrust of the West, ii) the ease with which misinformation is accepted by public media sources in Muslim countries, iii) a reluctance on the part of Western authorities to confront the conspiracy theories.

All three aspects of this syndrome must be addressed. During our interviews with madrassah students in Pakistan, the single most common cause for distrust of America and anger towards US policy was triggered by the issue of civilian casualties during combat. The reluctance of the US to directly tackle this issue or keep a count of actual civilian casualties in Iraq and Afghanistan has led to the most irate conspiracy accounts. When mistakes are made, the tendency is to dismiss moral equivalence of civilian deaths and casualties of terrorist acts. This leads to further distrust and denial on the part of Muslims.

Furthermore, there is reflexive disdain in US policy circles when any linkage is made between regional conflicts in the Middle East, Kashmir or Chechnya and Muslim anger. Immediately, the prospect is raised that it is all about 'our way of life.' While indeed, some fringe elements might be averse to modern lifestyles, the vast majority of Muslims have no problems with Western ways and have for decades embraced them.

The US government also appears to be in denial about linkages between regional conflicts and Muslim anger—which in turn is fuelling Muslim denial about extremism. Understandably, the US leadership does not want to be perceived as condoning or rationalizing terrorism. However, if we are to have a pragmatic solution-oriented approach, then multiple causality and engagement must be considered. As Yitzhak Rabin is famously remembered to have said—you don't make peace with your friends but you make peace with your enemies.

Nevertheless, denial of extremism among Muslims is also a serious challenge that must be confronted both internally and externally. Muslim organizations must be more scrupulous in publishing unsubstantiated accounts and internet rumours. Deconstructing erroneous conspiracy theories is also essential. The silver lining to this denial syndrome is that it reflects a general repugnance for terrorist acts among the Muslim population—they consider such acts abhorrent and hence wish to believe that someone else must be responsible.

Former secretary of Defense Donald H. Rumsfeld, in a confidential memorandum, posed the central question about the war on terror: 'Are we capturing, killing or deterring and dissuading more terrorists every day than the madrassahs and the radical clerics are recruiting, training and deploying against us?' Starting with Rumsfeld's question, Mark Danner (2005) has commendably approached this issue in detail and his answer is a resolute 'no.' Danner quotes counterinsurgency specialist John Arqullia who compares the US reaction as highly *mercurial*: 'We have taken a ball of quicksilver, and hit it with a hammer.'

Exaggerated accounts and manipulation of statistics to spin conspiracy theories are of course not just confined to Muslims. Every community seems to have its share of such spin masters and conspiracy cultivators. For example, in India, Hindutva activists have on numerous occasions used census data to give the impression that Muslim population increase is a targeted effort to outnumber Hindus and cause a diminution of India's Hindu identity. The controversy became specially acute since when the results of the Indian census were released in 2001. Of the total Indian population of 1.028 billion at the time of the census, the Hindus totaled 827 million and 80.5 of the population. The Muslims numbered 138 million, comprising 13.4 per cent of the population. The next in size were the Christians (24 million or 2.3 per cent). Census data since 1951, the year of the first Indian head-count, suggest that the Muslim population increases by about 1 per cent every decade. Activists used this data to suggest that it will take three centuries for India to become a Muslim-majority country! The figures, turned out to be inaccurate because the census of 2001 included India's only Muslim-majority State of Jammu and Kashmir which had been excluded in the 1991 exercise, and the Northeastern State of Assam, excluded in 1981. After two days of mounting tensions, the commission came out with 'adjusted' figures, which told a different story altogether.

They showed that that the growth rate of the Hindu population had declined from 22.77 per cent over 1981–91 to 20.02 per cent over 1991–2001, and that of the Muslim population from 32.86 to 29.33 per cent. In other words, the decline in the population growth rate has been greater for Indian Muslims. J. Sri Raman (2004) has described this propaganda campaign by Hindutva activists in detail along with an exposition of how Hindutva activists continue to mislead with erroneous analysis of statistics. This is of course a continuing embarrassment for the Indian government since it prides itself on being the world's largest secular democracy. It is interesting to note that, in the tradition of Gandhi, many left-leaning non-Muslims in India are leading the struggle to protect Muslim rights in this regard.[19]

Such episodes as well as the support of some authoritarian regimes by Western powers have led to an unusual alliance between secular leftists and Islamists. The Kefaya ('Enough') Movement in Egypt exemplifies the willingness of Islamists to form coalitions albeit reluctantly with other secular movements for reform. This diverse coalition of oppositional movements-new Islamists, liberals, Nasserists, and Arabists has demanded change from below and an end to the rule of President Hosni Mubarak as well as American influence in the region (Lynch, 2005). Unequivocal support of authoritarian regimes at the behest of security is thus problematic. At the same time, tolerating the intolerant among the Islamists is also a recipe for disaster. Perhaps the best way out for Western powers is to intervene on humanitarian grounds where needed, and build a reputation for non-opportunistic action. There may be initial setbacks as was the case with the well-intentioned US intervention in Somalia but slowly, there may be a mark to be made. The Western intervention in Bosnia and Kosovo are cases where Muslims were advantaged by US and European intervention. Such efforts should be given more coverage in historical accounts of east-west relations in text books and media outlets in the Muslim world.

Specific skill-based programmes within Islamic schools such as USAID's culturally tailored programme on AIDS education in the madrassahs of Tanzania may also be considered as workable models of intervention. In late 2006, USAID launched an environmental education programme in Tanzania in partnership with NGOs such as the Baraza Kuu la Waislamu Tanzania (BAKWATA) and the Jane Goodall Institute. The 'Roots & Shoots' programme will target 12,650 primary school students and 12,650 madrassah school students. As part of this effort, two hundred and twenty primary school teachers and 220 madrassah teachers will be trained on coastal and marine ecosystem issues, techniques for sharing this information with other teachers and students, and how to create and support environmental initiatives in their schools and 'Roots & Shoots' clubs.[20]

A more ambitious programme started by USAID in the Philippines and Nigeria is known as the 'Livelihood Enhancement and Peace' (LEAP) project. The project in partnership with the Philippine Government is designed to assist former combatants of the Moro National Liberation Front (MNLF) make the transition from combatants to commercial-level farmers and fishermen. It is important to note that this programme started in July 1997 (before 9/11) and has provided over 24,000 former MNLF combatants with technical assistance and training, agricultural and aquaculture production inputs.[21]

The LEAP programme in Nigeria was launched in November 2001 and is working with 327 primary schools (including 78 Islamic schools) from the three target states of Kano, Nasarawa and Lagos. Over 90,000 primary students attend these schools. In addition, 194 Parent-Teacher Associations (PTAs) affiliated with the participating schools have been engaged in this effort that includes a series of workshops aimed at improving teaching and learning skills (Boyle, 2004).

Such cases, at broader levels of recognition may slowly help in transcending conspiracy theories. Most social psychologists who study conspiracy theorists believe that they are rooted in a lack of information and candor within societies.

CONTEMPORARY CONFLICTS AND CALLS FOR INTERNAL REFORM AND MODERATION

Foreign powers can play an important role in highlighting some particular internal conflicts within Muslim countries and use these as a means for leveraging reform. Sudan is an interesting case in point in this regard.[22] The once obstinate religious leader of the Sudanese Muslim Brotherhood, Hassan-al-Turabi is showing astonishing signs of moderation. In a recent interview to the London-based newspaper Al-Sharq al-Awsat, Dr Turabi spoke of allowing women to become Imams, promoting greater allowances for inter-marriage between Muslims, Jews and Christians and even venturing to call for radical Muslims to seek penance for their indiscretions. The Sorbonne-educated Turabi has been an enigmatic and somewhat chameleonic figure in Sudanese politics for the past thirty years. The 9/11 Commission Report referred to him as 'Sudan's longtime hard-line ideological leader' who gave sanctuary to Osama bin Laden. He was a spiritual leader of the current Sudanese government until 2004 when he was imprisoned for fomenting a coup plot. However, he was released in the summer of 2005 and continues to command considerable respect in many parts of the Muslim world.

Turabi's newly found moderation has left many Islamic scholars aghast and several Sudanese clerics have branded him an apostate. However, the mere fact that such clear calls for moderation and reinterpretation of Islamic texts is coming from such an old ideologue such as Turabi is very promising indeed. Even if we discount these proclamations as opportunistic attempts to seek help from the West, the call for reform emanating from one of al-Qaeda's oldest friends is a dramatic change to consider. It is equally significant that this call is coming from Sudan, which has been at the crossroads of conflict at multiple levels.

The fault lines in the civil war in southern Sudan had been about religion and race–Christian Africans versus mostly Muslim Arabs. The conflict was used in the West to highlight the most macabre face of Islamic and indigenous cultural extremism, from slave trades to forced conversions. Accuracy of these accounts were disputed and conspiracy theories about oil greed and imperialism raged on for years. Thankfully, most of these came to rest following the peace agreement between the government and the Sudanese Peoples Liberation Movement (SPLM) in January 2005. More than a year has passed and this agreement has withstood continuing turmoil in Darfour as well as the death of the SPLM leader John Garang in August 2005. Hence, extremists who had repeatedly concluded the incompatibility of Muslims and Christians to live together in Sudan have been proved wrong.

However, the Darfour crisis has been far more vexing for Muslim clerics such as Turabi to understand. All sides in the conflict are Muslims of the same sect. Hence sectarian strife such as the case in Iraq or Pakistan cannot be implicated either. There is not even a clear racial distinction to be drawn in the crisis since there have been Arab-African alliances during some phases of the conflict as well. The perpetuation of the Darfour crisis has thus led to some soul-searching on the part of ideologues such as Turabi who now conclude that a culture of violence is to blame for such conflicts. Inequality of resource distribution and competing land use policies, sparked by a cultural acceptance of weapons to resolve disputes are the key ingredients of Sudan's predicament. If there is any silver lining to this tragic tale, it would be that extreme elements such as Turabi have been forced out of their martyring determinism. Whether the peace agreement in Darfour holds or not, the West should pay close attention to the way this conflict is transforming the vanguards of Islam in Sudan.

Malaysian scholar Chandra Muzaffar is widely respected for articulating the needed reforms in Islam as moving from a ritualistic approach to a value-based approach that marries development paradigms with theology. In one of his essays, he describes the most fruitful approach may be one that links policies and programmes to values not only to ensure that the moral dimension of the goal at hand is sustained but also to emphasize that the task itself is an act of virtue.[23] As noted by fellow-Malaysian Farish Noor (2006), 'due to the apparent ossification of debate and self-critique within the Muslim world, the respect for alterity and difference among Muslims has waned to an all-time low. The oppositional dialectics between the West and Islam have further entrenched the cultural, religious and ideological divide between the two sides, making dialogue itself a hazardous venture that few would attempt.'

First, let us consider the larger issue of moderation as it is a tempting invocation for most human endeavors. Even in our own cultural and religious traditions *miyana ravi,* (following the middle path) has been a frequent refrain. However, moderation is applicable to human phenomena when two preconditions are met: i) the behaviour itself is not predisposed to addictive excess, ii) the impact of that behaviour does not lead to involuntary risks on others.

Let us now consider the most common exhortation for moderation these days—religious doctrines versus scientific inquiry. Can we apply moderation to religious doctrines? Again if we apply my two tests for moderation applicability to religion we find that for many exclusionary doctrines, reform is a losing battle because of systemic issues in the theology. Hence the only avenue for moderation in religious doctrines exists where there can be accommodation for equal respect and coexistence of other Faiths, an acknowledgement of scientific inference and differentiating societal law from personal belief. Contrary to many secularist ideologues, I believe these criteria can indeed be met for religious doctrines as well. However, in the case of Islam this would require a departure from some mainstream belief structures that are rooted more in culture than theology. Some theological tenets may also need to be contextualized, particularly with regard to women's rights (Hassan, 2006). No matter how difficult this transition might be, it must take place and indeed many Muslim organizations worldwide are struggling with these challenges. These struggles for reform must be supported without disparaging the Believers. It would be strategically fatal for both scientific humanists and theologians to think that either science or religion are obsolescent and will simply fade into oblivion. Sensationalistic and linear monographs such as *The End of History* or *The End of Science*, and most recently *The End of Faith* are generating more heat than light on these issues and must be read with some measure of skepticism.

I had an opportunity several years ago to interview the late Stephen Jay Gould, an eminent evolutionary biologist, about the confluence of science and religion and finding some moderating channel between the two. He referred to both as 'non-overlapping magesteria.'[24]–each having its own locus of operation which should not compete with one another. Gould admitted that scientists and theologians alike can be a trifle arrogant in their approach to these matters. Religion, after all, could itself be an important evolutionary strategy that has sustained human societies through many adversities and brought much-needed meaning to human societies. While many individuals can transcend this need for meaning, no one should show condescension towards those who need spiritual sustenance, which happens to be a majority of the world's population. As a politician in Carl Sagan's novel *Contact* asks the central character, an atheistic scientist, 'do you really think that 90 per cent of the country's population is delusional simply because of their beliefs?' It should be mentioned that Sagan was himself an agnostic but one who appreciated uncertainty and the value of respecting religion so long as it did not infringe upon science.

Similarly, theologians must not disavow science for lack of understanding and should always remain steadfast to the search for facts and consequential truth.[25]

Finally, we must not confuse three related but different issues: moderation, tolerance and neutrality. Tolerance must be reciprocal and hence tolerating the intolerant is a recipe for disaster. Similarly neutrality is only appropriate when subjective opinion that does not impose risks on others in society is at play. When asked to mediate a conflict, foreign powers must make it clear to all parties that they will be neutral only when the debate is operating within mutually agreed rules and never neutral on matters of process. Thus if the voice of one side is not being heard, one would have to show a measure of advocacy to ensure that voice is heard in order to be fair. Erstwhile colonial powers will have to recognize that, whether they like it or not, they will be expected to play the role of mediators by many in the Muslim world. In this context they must recognize that assumed role to ensure that existing power structures do not subvert neutrality. As the famed holocaust survivor and Nobel peace prize recipient Elie Wiesel once said: 'neutrality often favours the oppressors.' The many travails of ostensibly neutral Swiss foreign policy in recent years exemplifies how hollow neutrality can be in the face of oppression. The final chapter that follows attempts to bring some closure to our quest for balance, moderation, tolerance and neutrality when necessary within Islamic education.

NOTES

1. Presentation by Javed Ashraf, Minister of Education in Pakistan at the School of Advanced International Studies, Washington DC, 12 March 2005.
2. Many African countries have had very high literacy rates but poor development. Part of the challenge has been the tendency of development donors to focus on 'panaceas' and linear solutions rather than integrative solutions that incorporate and link multiple factors. For a critique of development errors, by the World Bank in particular, see Easterly, 2000.
3. Indonesia is believed to have 23,000 madrassahs. Azra, Azyumardi (2004). *Mainstreaming Islamic Education in Indonesia*. Address to the United States Indonesia Society, Washington DC, 31 March.

4. In 1991, the American Civil Liberties Union won a case against USAID to stop it from funding 20 Catholic and Jewish schools overseas. However, given the current security climate, such a lawsuit would unlikely carry favour.
5. Director of Research at the Boltzmann Institute in Austria. Considering the influence of this report, it should be mentioned that Ms Benard is the wife of Zalmay Khalilzad, US ambassador to Afghanistan, and a key adviser to President Bush.
6. Yoginder Sikand's review of Benard's report on http://www.islaminterfairth.org Accessed 27 May 2005.
7. Transcribed and translated interview of Qari Naseem-ur-Rahman to Yoginder Sikand, 19 July 2004.
8. Cohen's book *The Idea of Pakistan* presents an interesting commentary on the country that should be taken as such—a commentary—rather than as an academic piece or a policy prescriptive document. It has received favourable reviews by Indian officials but is resented by many in Pakistan. His section on madrassahs is regrettably not well-researched and even misplaces the Haqqania madrassah in Balochistan when it is widely known to be in the NWFP. The former Indian defence minister Jaswant Singh's review is titled 'Pakistan, a definition' and appeared in the *New York Times Magazine* section on 21 February 2005.
9. Ramadan was offered an endowed professorship at the University of Notre Dame and then denied a US visa twice in 2005 and 2006 because of ostensible violations of the Patriot Act because he had given donations to a European charity that was later linked to Hamas. While he may have some controversial views on the Arab-Israeli conflict, his writings are far more moderate on the matter than US academics such as Chomsky. Much of his academic work is in fact totally apolitical such as his most recent book on the life of Muhammad (Ramadan, 2007).
10. Newt Gingrich 'Bush and Lincoln: Echoes of the past in today's strategic mistakes.' *Wall Street Journal*, online exclusive, 7 September 2006: http://www.opinionjournal.com/editorial/feature.html?id=110008905.
11. Adam Cohen. 'An SAT without Analogies.' *The New York Times*, 13 March 2005.
12. This idea has been used often by commentators such as Ann Coulter. While such anti-modernity views do exist in some fringe circles, the opinion polls suggest that overwhelming Muslims do not have anything against Western values. Even in countries like Iran, the sentiments are overwhelmingly friendly towards Western culture: Scotten (2007).
13. See the recent opinion survey conducted by Zogby International *Impressions of America* (2004).
14. Mohammed Waseem (2004). 'Origins and Growth patterns of Islamic Organizations in Pakistan' in Limaye et al eds. 2004.
15. See for example the web site of the organization Muslims Against Terrorism that rejects violence while holding firm to a stance against perceived oppression or The International Centre for Islam and Pluralism in Indonesia: http://www.icipglobal.org/ or the organization called Future Islam the web site http://www.futureislam.org
16. Kaleem Khawaja email communiqué on Islaminternfaith.org, *Neo-con Muslim: Nuisance or Threat,* 18 April 2005.
17. See for example recent books by ultra-progressive Muslims such as Manji, 2004, Wadud, 2003, Nomani, 2004. Calls for an Islamic reformation from agnostic writers such as Salman Rushdie (2005) are unlikely to gain any acceptance in Muslim

countries. Other efforts at moderation of Islamic doctrine include the Centre for Islamic Pluralism, established by Stephen Schwartz, a convert to Islam who has found particular proclivity for Bosnian interpretations of Islamic doctrine, which have not gained traction with the mainstream Muslims.

18. The web site referenced here is www.aljazeera.com—a popular magazine, based in Dubai, UAE. The TV station of the same name, based in Doha, Qatar has a different web site: www.aljazeera.net
19. Gandhi was assassinated by a Hindu fanatic because he was perceived to be too friendly to Muslims. This is of course reminiscent of Yitzhak Rabin's assassination by a Jewish fanatic or Anwar Sadaat's assassination by a Muslim fanatic. In all cases the conflict within the community to resist change was the most potent.
20. http://www.usaid.gov/stories/tanzania/ss_tz_lessons.html
21. USAID LEAP programme description at: http://philippines.usaid.gov/mindanao_leap.php
22. I am indebted to Sudanese scholar Mahmoud El-zain of the University for Peace bringing this matter to my attention. We coauthored an op-ed on this topic in *The Daily Times* on 20 May 2006 titled 'Salvaging Islam in Sudan' from which this segment is largely derived.
23. Paper presented at the Asian Muslim Action Network (AMAN) conference in Dhaka, Bangladesh in November 2000 and published in Chandra Muzaffar's compilation of essays, *Muslims, Dialogue, Terror*. (Selangor: International Movement for a Just World, 2003).
24. Gould also expounded on these matters in his monthly essays for *Natural History* magazine.
25. The perennial debate on religion and Science has once again reached a feverish pitch since the publication in late 2006 of Richard Dawkin's book *The God Delusion* and Daniel Dennet's book *Breaking the Spell: Religion as a Natural Phenomenon*. My approach to the matter is one of policy pragmatism–whereby religion as a social phenomenon cannot be ignored or wished away. Indeed, it can be a means of providing some very useful civic outcomes. However, the importance of science and critical reasoning must be an essential ingredient of religious manifestations in our educational system.

8
WAYS TO RECONCILE TRADITIONAL EDUCATION WITH MODERNITY

Islam like many other religious traditions has an inherent struggle with modernity since its anchorage lies in historical traditions at various levels. The infallibility of the Qur'an and the Sunnah of the prophet for Muslims leads to a tendency for temporal nostalgia. The time of the Prophet is considered sacred and emulation of even the most basic daily acts of the Prophet such as the use of an acacia twig for brushing one's teeth is considered an act of worship. In this context educational reform faces tremendous challenges that are not new to Islamic scholarship as the struggle between those who have advocated *taqlid* (following tradition and precedent), and those who have advocated *ijtihad* (individual reasoning).

Contrary to popular opinion, modest reformations have occurred throughout Islamic history and have usually come from within rather than being prompted from the outside. In the Medieval period there were reform efforts within various caliphates by scholars such as Ibn-Rushd/Averroes (d.1198). These reform efforts have been more pronounced within the last two centuries by notable activist scholars such as Jamal-uddin-Afghani (d.1897) or Sir Syed Ahmed Khan (d.1898) in South Asia or Rifa'a-al-Tahtawi (d.1873) and Muhammad Abduh (d.1905) in Egypt or Ali Shariati in Iran (d.1977). In the case of Shariati, despite his modernist views, he came at a time of intense secularization under the Shah and was thus perceived as an Islamist despite his relatively moderate vision of Islam. His assassination, allegedly by the Shah's security police, provided impetus towards the radicalization of Iran.

Within the Indian subcontinent, Islamic educational reform in Kerala was led by Moulavi Chalilakath Muhammad Haji who was appointed as the headmaster of the Tanmiyath-ul-'Ulum Madrassah at Vazhakkad in Malabar in north Kerala. In his attempt at reform, he renamed the madrassah as 'Arabic College' to emulate a modernist approach to education. In this case it may be argued that the reform effort was prompted by the British since Malabar was under British control at the time. Around the same time Vakkam Muhammad 'Abdul Qadir Moulavi (1873–1932) established several modern madrassahs in the state of Travancore and also arranged for government schools to teach Arabic to Muslim students. Similarly, in Cochin, Sanaullah Makti Thangal and Shaikh Muhammad Mahin Thangal opened schools where modern disciplines were taught alongside Islamic subjects. The work of these reformers was carried on further with the establishment of organizations set up with the purpose of reforming the traditional Muslim educational system, including the Malabar Muslim Educational Association (1911), the Lajnat-ul-Muhammadiya Sangham (1915), the Muslim Mahajana Sabha (1920), the Kerala Aikya Sangham (1922), the Kerala Jami'at-ul-'Ulama (1924) and the Hidayat-ul-Muslimin Sangham (Sikand, 2005).

However, what is remarkable is that all of these efforts have met with such intense resistance that their impact on mainstream Islamic theology has been limited. Conservative ulema are quick to credit the resilience of Islamic tradition in this regard while many contemporary commentators are now beginning to consider if this inertia is symptomatic of structural issues within Muslim societies that must first be addressed.

Educational institutions may lie at the core of this structural impediment to temporal adaptation. Gesink (2006, p. 334) describes how the Egyptian Islamic modernist Muhammad Abduh considered the role of madrassahs as an impediment to reform in the nineteenth century: 'Abduh accused the madrassah scholars of deliberate obstructionism, preferring mediaeval texts to subjects that would save the community...and warning them that they must pursue new fields of knowledge or perish.'

Madrassahs are clearly an important social institution across the Muslim world and are often described by proponents as the Muslim world's largest network of NGOs (nongovernmental organizations). However, the noble purpose of education and enlightenment for which madrassahs were originally intended, has been challenged by various sectarian elements within Pakistan. This study finds evidence of linkage between a large number of madrassahs and sectarian violence, particularly in rural Punjab. We also found that the number of madrassahs has increased over a ten year period and that in some areas they are competing with government and secular private schools for enrollment. Many madrassahs are residential and cater to relatively poor students in these areas. However, in urban madrassahs, this pattern is not always followed as affluent families may also send their children to madrassahs for disciplinary and theological reasons.

The empirical analysis of Pakistani madrassahs presented in Chapter 3 of this book clearly showed that sectarian activity in areas of greater madrassah density per population size was found to be higher, including incidents of violent unrest. Unfortunately, most urban observers in Pakistan tend to cast aspersions on 'foreign elements' for any sectarian activity, without conducting in-depth analysis of causality. While Iran has funded Shia madrassahs and Saudi Arabia has funded Salafi and Deobandi madrassahs, there is no other external linkage to be found with regard to the violence observed on religious festivals and other occasions. Sectarianism is a serious and palpable internal challenge for Pakistan and madrassahs in this case study were found to be contributing to this challenge. At one level this is more of an internal challenge for Muslim countries like Pakistan or Iraq rather than a direct contributor to international terrorism. Nevertheless, we are living in a world of increasing linkage between domestic politics and international networks that are fuelled by discontent at multiple levels. Averting a cognitive clash between sects as well as between civilizations thus requires a recognition of the linkages between these political spheres.

RECOGNIZING THE INHERENT POLITICS OF EDUCATION AND RELIGION

Political Islamic movements have capitalized on educational institutions in the same way as their secular corollaries and their influence needs to be recognized more acutely. The role of the Islami-Jamiat-Tulaba (IJT), the student wing of the Jamaat-e-Islaami in Pakistan and Bangladesh is perhaps the most striking example of the power of student activism in politics. As Mumtaz Ahmed observed in his contributive essay to the University of Chicago's monumental project on global fundamentalism: 'much of the political strength of the Jamaat, especially its ability to mobilize the masses to confront the government, depends on the IJT.'[1]

The Students Islamic Movement of India (SIMI), is another example of a group emanating from an educational setting that has been radicalized and is advocating a need for Indian Muslims to respond to the threats that they are faced with by resorting to armed jihad. Established in 1977, the SIMI was banned by the Government of India in 2001 on account of its militant tendencies, even though there have been no convictions related to their work. The movement has a revivalist cadence that goes back to the calls for a new caliphate during India's struggle for independence led by scholars such as Maulana Muhammad Ali Johar. In the absence of a caliphate, the SIMI believes that Muslims cannot lead their lives fully in accordance with Islam.[2]

While the politicization of higher educational institutions is widely recognized in many cultures, what is most striking about Islamic education has been its ability to politicize even elementary education—hence the madrassah phenomenon. As noted in Chapter 6 numerous Ulema have themselves declared that madrassahs are considered the most foundational fortification to preserve tradition (calling them *Islam ka qila* in Urdu). Therefore, if a departure from tradition is on the political agenda of any government, the madrassahs will inexorably be used as a means of political resistance.

The politicization of elementary education has become significant in the West in a few cases such as the teaching of evolution and sexual norms. These issues are just as salient for Muslim educators as well and provide an interesting entry point for considering the merits and limits of systemic reform efforts. As noted in Chapter 4 of this book, informal education through the popular media must not be discounted in terms of its influence on impressionable minds.

Higher educational institutions can be used for lasting politicization of social movements through activist scholars such as Hafiz Saeed, founder of the Salafi madrassah that has been linked to the militant Lashkar-i-Tayyaba. They can also be a place for more theoretical reflection that might galvanize social movements but can, nevertheless, convey a strong political message. Secular scholars such as Pervez Hoodhbhoy, who was awarded UNESCO's Kalinga Prize in 2000, may also be active in such a locus.[3] In more tempered ways, Islamic scholars are also asserting their views through reflective publications and reaching out to the west as has been the case with Iranian scholar, Abdol Karim Soroush, whose work has been called 'The Islamists' Theory of Relativity.[4]

There is also a common theme of perpetuating narratives of historical persecution in most contemporary conflicts. Osama Bin Laden's vitriolic speeches have urged Muslims to reflect on 80 years of subjugation since the demise of the Ottoman caliphate. Christian fundamentalists are urging their adherents to consider the genocide of Armenians by the Turks. Serbian nationalists refer back to the invasion of the Balkan lands by the Caliphate in the seventeenth century. Jewish extremists are promoting the idea of a primordial Holy Land that was originally inhabited by the Children of Israel, driven out by Gentiles. African-American activists constantly remind us of the injustices of slavery in the US. Hindu militants have lamented the onslaught of Muslim dynasties that overcame their age-old control on the subcontinent's indigenous population.

Even venerable writers such as the recent recipient of the Nobel Prize for literature, VS Naipaul have succumbed to an atavistic remembrance of pre-Muslim India and Malaya in his controversial book entitled *Beyond Belief*. The phenomenon is clearly widespread and is reinforced by exhortations to learn from history, no matter how anachronistic the lessons may be.

However, there is a difference between learning from history and being governed by the past. Contemporary political discourse in many parts of the world, particularly in the pan-Muslim world, is unfortunately sliding into the latter category. There is reluctance to exorcise memories of past injustices that are irrelevant to contemporary times. Regrettably, some Muslims often remember only the first clauses of Qur'anic verses which urge caution in friendship with non-Muslims and forget the subsequent Qur'anic injunctions to forgive past iniquities and move forward without prejudice.

The life of the Prophet Muhammad (PBUH) which exemplifies a forward-looking approach to public policy in his benevolent dealings with the Makkan tribes rarely make their way into the curriculum of madrassahs. Indeed, the first hijrah (or migration) of the Muslims was from Arabia to Abyssinia (present-day Ethiopia), whose Christian ruler Najashi gave sanctuary to Muslims, including the Prophet's daughter, and was repeatedly called a great friend of Muslims by the Prophet. The current exhortations by many to divorce Muslim and non-Muslim territorial presence are thus even more disturbing.

Let us consider the example of the Arab-Israeli conflict. Based on interviews for this study, in the minds of many Pakistani Muslims, the Palestinian conflict is still anchored in the Balfour declaration which created the state of Israel. In reality most Palestinians are now willing to live alongside Israel so long as their right to a state is protected—yet this narrative usually does not effectively reach much of the Muslim world. Thousands of Palestinians have worked in Israel until the second Intifada and the economies of both Palestine and Israel are inextricably linked. The legitimacy of Israel might also be linked to Pakistan's own creation, which has similar ideological roots of statehood based on religion. Yet such comparisons are taboo for many in the region because the analysis is not presented with care and a goal of conflict resolution.

Unlike Judaism, both Christianity and Islam have attempted to go beyond tribal identity as a binding force. All ethnic groups are welcome to join without any requirement of matrilineal association or ethnic descent as was traditionally the case with Judaism. However, the darker side of this universalism in the later two Abrahamic faiths has been their propensity to proselytize and claim exclusivity over salvation. This makes the confluence of religion and politics inevitable, specially in a democracy since both the evangelists and the politicians are vying for demographic control and voting power.

By claiming that only their adherents can reach heaven, many Muslims and Christians have themselves formed tribal identities that are connected by scripture rather than ethnicity or genetics. The international community is confronted with the dilemma of whether or not religious identity should be subsumed within the broader categorization of 'culture,' when it serves to negate other cultural attributes such as music and art. Furthermore, the exclusivity of salvation also leads to a default tribalism which can certainly lead to cooperation and organizational action within the community but can lead to external conflict.[5] If we are to mitigate such threats to national unity and conflict escalation, the only way forward is to develop a truly global identity which trumps the divisive aspects of tribalism at multiple levels.

Once we are able to recognize our mutual interdependence on global resources, the positive aspects of tribalism, as exemplified by indigenous languages, art and learning can shine through. Religious devotion and patriotism to national identities could also coexist in such a world but with due deference to the larger goal of a truly 'civil' society.

DEPRIVATION, DEMOCRATIZATION AND EXTREMISM

This book also considered possible environmental and developmental factors that may be contributing to economic deprivation and consequential radicalization of the population. The continuing prevalence of feudal elite and economic inequality have given madrassahs a greater sense of legitimacy as a social movement in this region. Areas of higher madrassah prevalence had lower development indicators, such as electricity or roads and access to natural resources such as water for irrigation.

Development of these areas may thus also reduce radicalization and open other career opportunities for madrassah graduates. Vocational training programmes for madrassah graduates following their seminary education and clear ways for them to be channeled into such programmes should be funded independently of the madrassahs themselves. In addition, the economic disparities that are perpetuated by the feudal elite need to be addressed through establishment of trust funds for each village serviced from property tax revenues that the landlords must be obliged to pay in order to retain title to their land. While major land redistribution is unlikely to occur in Punjab, there can be better management of existing land-use patterns to ensure more equitable distribution of resources and local involvement in economic decision-making.

It is also important to appreciate that much of the al-Qaeda Movement is not concerned with development per se. This makes the movement somewhat unique in comparison to other extremist movements, such as the Maoists of Nepal or the *Sendero Luminoso* of Peru, that have emerged from deprivation. In his introduction the first English translation of Bin Laden's speeches Bruce Lawrence (2005) has highlighted this 'The absence of any social programme separates al Qaeda not just from the Red Army Faction or the Red Brigades, with which it has sometimes mistakenly been compared, but—more significantly—from the earlier wave of radical Islamism in the mid-twentieth century. Both Sayyid Qutb in Egypt and Abu'l Ala Mawdudi in Pakistan tried to transform their societies into a just Islamic order (*nizam-i mustafa,* the model order of the Prophet, in Mawdudi's elegant phrase). In place of social objectives, Bin Laden accentuates the need for personal sacrifice. He is far more concerned with the glories of martyrdom than with the spoils of victory. Rewards belong essentially to the hereafter' (Lawrence, 2005).

According to Fukuyama (2005), 'radical Islamism is as much a product of modernization and globalization as it is a religious phenomenon; it would not be nearly as intense if Muslims could not travel, surf the Web, or become otherwise disconnected from their culture. This means that 'fixing' the Middle East by bringing modernization and democracy to countries like Egypt and Saudi Arabia will not solve the terrorism problem, but may in the short run make the problem worse.'

The question of whether democracy will be a cause or a consequence for reform is very salient to consider in Islamic educational reform. There has been a complacence among leadership in some Muslim countries that Islamists would not have the clout or the resources to win elections. This has been proven false in Algeria, Palestine and to some degree in Turkey and in the Frontier province of Pakistan. The reaction to this reality has often been the unquestioning support of authoritarian leaders by western powers. Secular and religious authoritarianism must both be given the same treatment across the world. Preventing democratically elected Islamists from subverting basic human rights is essential but the way to do so is not to exclude them from the process but rather to ensure that structural changes in governance institutions such as constitutions, regional trade organizations and civil society oversight prevent such domination. Once such efforts have been exhausted and as many of the militants are brought from the periphery to within the mainstream, the residual hardliners might ultimately need to be fought. However, if a due process is followed, such a fight will be deemed more legitimate by the public and also operationally easier.

As democratic institutions and channels for political conflict resolution start to gain acceptance, grassroots change is possible even among the most radical elements. An interesting example of this has been the recent rise of dissent within militant organizations in Indonesia. Al-Jama'a Al-Islamiya, the largest jihadist group in Southeast Asia has been engaged in considerable introspection. Since 2002, imprisoned leaders of the organization have published eight books with titles such as *The Correction of Concepts*. In his detailed ethnographic study of such manuscripts, Gerges (2006, p. 200), notes that the organizations are now advancing 'a new paradigm based on peaceful engagement with state and society. The ideological revision represents a revolutionary rupture with and departure from doctrinaire jihadist theory and practice.'

REWARDING INTROSPECTION AND SELF-CRITICISM

Efforts at reform are always likely to be far more successful when there is buy-in from the constituents in question. The government's efforts at 'mainstreaming' madrassahs, as exemplified through programmes such as the 'model madrassahs,' is not likely to succeed because it is perceived as an external imposition. While the allocation of resources for madrassahs, such as the Rs 1 billion allocated for madrassah reform announced on 7 June 2005 (20 per cent of the entire budget for the education ministry's public sector development programme) is laudatory, these resources might be channeled more appropriately. Instead of trying to convert madrassahs into conventional schools, there should be an attempt made to expose madrassah leaders to alternative voices of Islamic learning and facilitating dialogue between various sects. Curricular reform would naturally follow from such interactions and could complement the vocational training programmes for madrassah graduates mentioned above. As noted by Rahman and Bukhari (2006, p. 337), the government's imposed reform and its perceived linkage to Western powers has 'perversely hindered the reform movement that was launched by the madaris' own initiative. This is because maintaining the status quo in a defensive mode itself becomes a need in a hostile environment.'

Just as there have been attempts at ecumenical dialogue between faiths, a concerted and deliberate national dialogue between Shias and Sunnis (and within Sunni sub-sects) is essential. Apart from their educational activity, some of the larger madrassahs also serve the purpose of providing theological opinions on various community concerns. Deliberative dialogue on some of the issues that are raised by community members in these solicitations could be a formal means of initiating dialogue between sects as well.

At the same time, violence and incitement to violence must be treated as any other law enforcement action. There should not be any exception made for particular establishments where communal violence is concerned as this sends a mixed message to agitators. While censorship of madrassah literature or any publications and sermons is to be avoided to preserve freedom of expression, the publication of erroneous data, inflammatory rhetoric that can be suggestive of violence is not protected under any freedom of expression legislation. Indeed, the role of mass-media in instigating violence is widely documented in cases such as the Rwandan genocide. Hence promoting a culture of responsible dissemination of information is essential in this context as well. Indeed, even in Islamic tradition, there are very strict injunctions and responsibility for giving inaccurate sermons and admonition for inciting violence. Such injunctions should be invoked in this regard. There should be closer scrutiny of any misinformation or incitement to violence in publications, particularly in areas of high sectarian activity. Combating a culture of victimhood is a responsibility for Muslim communities themselves.

Let us consider the example of the Nobel Prize as an illustrative parable of how Muslims consider their place in the world of knowledge and ideas. While many Islamic countries continue to claim victimization in the ' war on terror', it is interesting to note that since 11 September 2001, three of the six individual Nobel peace laureates have been Muslims. Their area of recognition has spanned the spectrum from human rights activism (Shirin Ebadi, 2003) to nuclear vigilance (Muhammad Elbaredei, 2005) to micro-credit entrepreneurship (Muhammad Yunus, 2006). What is perhaps even more astonishing is that in the 106-year history of the Nobel peace prize there are only two other Muslims who have been so honored. Anwar Saadat (1978) and Yassir Arafat (1994) shared the prize with Israeli leaders for highly variable and controversial contributions to peace-building in the Middle East.

Out of more than five hundred Nobel laureates in the sciences—only two have been of Muslim lineage. Pakistan can claim one of them: Abdus Salam, who shared the prize in physics in 1979, and memorably wore a *shervani* and turban to the award ceremony in Sweden. However, as a member of the Ahmadiya community, he was regrettably spurned at home as a non-Muslim. The other Muslim science laureate is Ahmed Zewail, an Egyptian-American chemist based at the California Institute of Technology who received the prize for chemistry in 1999. The reason for the paucity of Muslim laureates in the sciences is perhaps the relative intellectual inertia in educational institutions in many Muslim countries. There is a tendency to atavistically celebrate the accomplishments of tenth century Muslim mathematicians, while investing little in developing contemporary educational capacity. Far too often we hear from imams about the etymology of algebra coming from Arabic and the pharmaceutical accomplishments of Avicenna but do we ask why more of such great scholars have not been seen for a thousand years in Islamic countries?

Those Muslims who are educated and proceed to develop successful professional careers find contentment with a comfortable job but would rather not invest in cutting-edge creativity. An interesting example is the medical profession in which many Muslims, specially Pakistani Muslims have excelled considerably and formed organization such as the Association of Physicians of Pakistani Descent in North America (APPNA).[6] However, most of these brilliant doctors are focused on making money in clinical practice rather than in creative research which would lead to laurels such as the Nobel Prize. There is cultural complacence that leads to a mindset where success is marked by simply making a good living for the family, contributing some earnings to charity and then living a lavish life. As for the recent Muslim peace laureates what is even more striking is that many Muslims have rejected their efforts and refused to accept them as role models, and instead label them as stooges of the West.

As with Shirin Ebadi and Muhammad Elbaredei, frequent charges were also leveled by many Muslims that Dr Yunus was also a 'stooge of the West.' The same criticism was also leveled against Orhan Pamuk of Turkey who won the Nobel Prize for literature in 2006. The late Egyptian writer Naguib Mahfouz is the only other Muslim writer to have won this prize. Both of these writers have been known to marginalize their Islamic identity at various times, and perhaps the literature prize mirrors the peace prize in its political message.

Just as Gandhi was denied the peace prize despite being an inspiration to so many later laureates, some Muslim writers may claim a measure of discrimination here, contending that only a certain liberal elite are even considered seriously. Perhaps many Urdu poets such as Iqbal who were widely known in the West were deprived of the prize for being too 'Islamic?' In the case of Mr Pamuk, one Turkish writer commented in the *Wall Street Journal* that he 'has not taught anyone anything they didn't already know but has made precisely the right noises that the progressive arbiters of taste in Europe like to hear.'[7]

As the Nobel Prize parable suggests, the tone of arguments in many Muslim countries is highly polarizing between the secular elite and the masses who continue to populate mosques. On the one hand, the intelligentsia feel so liberated by the West that they disparage or caricature their own cultural roots, while on the other end of the spectrum the fanatics become even more entrenched in their dogmas. Indeed, both sides reinforce each other's worst stereotypes and feed off the distortions which they label against their perceived opponents. Healthy self-criticism is often supplanted with self-hatred or self-glorification.

Religious clerics continue to spill vitriol and conspiracy theories about the West while the secular elite spare no opportunity to resurrect orientalist visions of mediaeval morality that has become a self-fulfilling myth. The situation is perhaps more acute in Pakistan than in India because moderate opinions are far more easily labeled as being the proverbial 'CIA plot' by the mullahs or 'fundo-talk' by the secularists. In many of the debates between religious clerics and secularist academics on channels such as Al-Jazeera or Pakistan's Geo-TV, both sides continue to talk past each other. The civil tone that is maintained remains momentary and in some cases the occasional insult that may ensue from such encounters ends up ruining any vestige of positive relations that might have existed prior to the conversation.

Mediators are often asked the seminal question: how can one 'respect' opponents when there is a fervent belief that they are delusional. My response is to state that most conflicts arise primarily because we assume too much about an opponent and rarely question our own assumptions. For example, some of my other research on land-use conflicts between Native Americans and miners shows that community interactions become extremely spiteful when some tribal group might suggest that a particular mountain is 'sacred' and hence cannot be mined (Ali, 2004). Mining companies may consider such a claim to be delusional but there are laws which protect such sites simply because beliefs, no matter how far-fetched, cannot be trampled without care. The term 'sacred' in many cases reveals complex environmental interactions which that community might have with the landscape rather than just a *prima facie* theological belief. On the other hand, cultural practices that violate basic tenets of human rights that are now part of globally accepted norms should be confronted head-on. There can be no compromise on such matters and good leadership can emerge from both secular and sacred sources in these arenas.

Finally, the most significant feature of fruitful public arguments is to pursue them with a goal of collective learning rather than convincing the other side. Unlike a court of law where there is often a polar verdict, public discourse can lead to many complex solutions that can often please many constituents. In this regard, secular commentators are correct that many religious systems have denied the public from even engaging in such collective learning experiences. However, this can often change and evolve with different religious traditions. The Bahai community has been particularly astute in developing a workable confluence of such processes across their Faith. Larger religious groups are struggling with such norms but there are voices of dissent which are now being heard with greater clarity. In Islam, such a transition may take longer than in other faiths due to potent radicalization of Muslim communities due to territorial conflicts. However, notable Muslim initiatives such as the Zaytuna Academy in California that was recently profiled by the *New York Times* are hopeful signs that the inertia of Islamic imams is being overcome through introspection.[8] Similarly, Egyptian preacher Amr Khaled has struck a chord with young Arab Muslims with his blend of contemporary culture and conservative tradition. As noted by Shapiro (2006), Khaled is willing to say that Islam is also about having fun. Such an upbeat tone of blending popular culture and religion is gaining traction in North American Muslims with TV shows such as Canada's *Little Mosque on the Prairie*.[9]

The Islamic Cultural, Educational and Scientific Organization (ISESCO) based in Morocco is a nascent pan Muslim-organization with similar objectives and deserves greater support at an international level. Among Arab countries, in particular, the curricular reform efforts are proceeding at a more glacial pace.[10] The case in places such as Lebanon or the United Arab Emirates is not one of ostensible cultural modernity which is quite visible but rather of peace-building at a broader level across communities. This is where the matter cannot be confined merely to madrassahs but must permeate educational institutions at all levels.

ISLAMIC EDUCATION AS A MEANS OF CONFLICT PREVENTION

The most systemic strategy for preventing conflict linkages with madrassahs is to invigorate peace education within the curricula of madrassahs and other schools across Muslim countries and among the Muslim Diaspora in the West. While occasional references to Islam as being etymologically linked to 'peace' is often made by Muslims, a comprehensive peace education curriculum is generally absent. Most notable among recent scholarship on nonviolence and peace-building within Islamic learning is a book by Mohammed Abu-Nimer (2003) in which he uses theories from linguistics to argue that there is enough of a repertoire of peace-building narratives within Islamic tradition to be utilized for conflict mitigation even within a theological context.

The Council on Islamic Education, based in California is also trying to professionalize the curriculum in Islamic schools and promote greater tolerance and context to Islamic texts by differentiating between *jihad* (a just struggle for rights) and *hirabah* (unjust war) through a detailed training programme. According to the training manual: 'The jurists prohibited *hirabah* because Islam places an absolute value on public safety and protection as God-given human rights. These rights belong to 'the sphere of God.' A right of God in Islamic law is one based on universal rights, whose penalty is not subject to the discretion of the judges; neither can acts of *hirabah* be ignored. *Hirabah* is punishable by the most severe penalty mentioned in the Qur'an, where it is called *fasad* in Chapter 5, verse 33, meaning in this case mayhem and destruction.'[11]

The work of the International Centre for Religion and Diplomacy (ICRD) and their growing partnerships with madrassahs in Pakistan, to promote peace education within Islamic tradition is quite promising. What is remarkable about the work of ICRD is that their leadership have strong historical ties to the US government but through careful planning of their workshops and partnering with receptive local organizations they have generally avoided being stigmatized by extremists. They have also gone beyond preaching to the choir and visited some of the more radicalized madrassahs such as the Binori Town madrassah and the Markaz-al-Dawah-al-Irshad in Muridke. There appears to be palpable impact of the ICRD's programmes in Pakistan as exemplified by the following quote from one of the madrassah administrators: 'I felt all the anger and rage I have carried for so many years about the Americans washed away from my being...the ten days spent on learning and in reflections helped me put the pieces together to reach out in peace instead of constantly burning with anger.'[12]

The United Nations mandated University for Peace, based in Costa Rica has also held a series of peace-education efforts in the madrassahs of Bangladesh and Tajikistan. They are now expanding their efforts to include programmes at Islamic schools within diaspora communities in Canada with support from the Canadian government.[13] The role of madrassahs in Central Asia is particularly interesting to consider since many of the leadership studied in Pakistan. As observed by Rashid (2002), at one time hundreds of Tajiks and Uzbeks could be found in Pakistani madrassahs. However, most of these leadership lost traction back home after the political conflict subsided and the reform was spurred partly by market forces of diminishing demand.

It is also important to consider that some local imams in many parts of the Muslim world have also tried to find paths of moderation but they are often unrecognized or can be lumped together conveniently with extremists for political purposes. Of particular note is the unfortunate incident of Mukhtaran Mai that gained considerable press coverage in the west. Her tragic tale of gang-rape on orders of a village council or *panchayat* has alarmed human rights activists, journalists and greatly embarrassed the government of Pakistan.

Much as Mukhtaran Mai deserves to be congratulated for her courage, there is another unsung hero in this saga. In a patriarchal and highly restricted society such as what is found in rural Pakistan, one may wonder how Mukhtaran Mai was able to get her voice heard and approach the police about this awful crime. Initially Mukhtaran Mai felt so desperate and humiliated that she swallowed a bottle of pesticide, hoping for a merciful death but she was saved in time. Her cries for help and call for justice were initially, not picked up by any urban women's rights group but rather by the local mosque *imam* (religious cleric). Maulvi Abdul Razzaq defied the stereotype of a misogynistic Muslim male and stood by Mukhtaran Mai's story. He gave a detailed sermon at the Friday prayer that a great sin had been committed by the village council and the criminals responsible for Mukhtaran Mai's rape must be brought to justice. He then went beyond his pulpit and brought a local journalist, Mureed Abbas, to meet Mukhtaran Mai's father, and persuaded the family to file charges against the rapists. The family was convinced to do so primarily because of the Imam's stature in the community.[14]

It was at this point that Pakistan's excellent assemblage of women's rights activists embraced Mukhtaran Mai and helped her through the convoluted judicial process. As the trial unfolded, the sordid behaviour of the Mastoi clan became apparent. The unfortunate series of events began with the forced sodomy of Mukhtaran Mai's 14-year old brother, Shakoor, and a cover-up that would involve falsely accusing him of adultery against a Mastoi woman. As reprisal, the village council subsequently followed the appalling custom of ordering forced fornication against Shakoor's sister, Mukhtaran Mai. As the judicial process unfolded, those responsible for this crime were charged, but in March 2005, a civil high court in Punjab overturned the conviction for lack of 'convincing evidence.' At this point there was yet another positive intervention by the religious establishment. The Islamic Shariah Court intervened and ordered that the criminals be apprehended again. This was particularly remarkable since the Islamic courts have generally favoured men in cases of rape and adultery. Indeed, there are many cases of women who were accused of adultery when they had actually been raped and are serving sentences for the former due to Shariah laws. However, in this case, the Islamic courts as well as the clergy played a very positive role for which they should be commended. Eventually, the Supreme Court of Pakistan intervened and took jurisdiction over the case and the role of the Islamic establishment received little press coverage.

As former President Musharraf tried to paint the image of Pakistan as a progressive Muslim state, the positive role played by the clergy in this high-profile case was a missed opportunity. Instead, the president embattled himself with defensive rhetoric and rows with the *Washington Post* over an interview in which he claimed that rape victims were getting easy visa passage abroad, suggesting ulterior motives in such criminal claims. The 'rape to riches' theory became the focus of this sad story when the positive role of the *imam* who championed Mukhtaran Mai's cause or the Islamic court that supported her was lost. To his credit, the President gave Ms Mukhtaran Rs 500,000 ($8,000) to start a school in her village as compensation but the larger message was one of denial.

Unfortunately, even the women's rights activists and human rights groups were also not keen to give credit where it is due. Instead of championing a progressive *imam* such as Maulvi Abdul Razzaq, the secular elite of Pakistan remained quiet. Instead of being applauded, the *imam* was even accused of being a terrorist during the trial by the village police to discredit his support for Mukhtaran Mai.

When such positive actions go unappreciated cynicism sets in among reformers. Acknowledging the efforts of this cleric is exceedingly important. It is also high time secular and religious forces try to find common ground on such pivotal human rights issues as a means of furthering the education process.

A SYNTHESIS OF SCALE

The relationship between education and conflict must be considered as a multiple scaled phenomenon in which religious schools interact with secular institutions and networks of radicalism can transcend the confines of each category. This book has attempted to provide both a general analysis of potential for linkages between Islamic education and conflict and also a detailed empirical case of the Pakistani experience with madrassahs in this context. What has emerged is a complex causal linkage between Islam, education and conflict escalation in which culpability is shared with religious institutions and the state. I have resisted the contrarian approach that might then lead people to exonerate madrassahs from this linkage as argued by recent popular scholarship on this topic that focuses only on the upper echelon of terrorist networks. Scholars such as Sageman (2004), or Bergen and Pandey (2006), Fair and Haqqani (2006) have used empirical evidence from major terrorist incidents such as the 9/11 attacks, the Bali bombings and the 7/7 attacks in London to show that many of the perpetrators of these attacks came from western educated schools and not madrassahs. However, what such analysis often misses is that the groundswell of support for these technically savvy executers may often come from a wide array of institutions, including madrassahs. The organizational structure of the Jamaat-e-Islaami in Pakistan provides some insights in this regard. Upper echelons of the organization comprise well-educated and trained individuals who are given full membership (*rukn*). The second tier of associate members (*karkun*) are the workers and fund-raisers who volunteer their time for specific projects of the organization and are usually college graduates. However, the largest base of support for the organization are the street supporters (*muttafiq*) many of whom come from madrassahs. These are the people the organization can rely on for mobilization at political events and give the organization democratic legitimacy.

Furthermore, the lack of critical thinking skills in contemporary madrassahs can often make their support for extreme causes more unequivocal and dependable than the average university or high school. Apart from this tacit support of fanaticism, there is a larger concern with regard to career placement that must also be considered for madrassah graduates as population rises in Muslim countries and employment opportunities become limited. So far madrassah graduates have been able to find jobs as teachers and evangelists with charitable support. However, such professional development can only lead to a proliferation of even more madrassahs, since the graduates act as religious entrepreneurs to spread their message far and wide. While there is nothing wrong *per se* with such entrepreneurship, there can be a serious concern about educational quality across the Islamic world if we do not adequately address curricular reform. Some donor agencies have now started to consider how madrassahs could be used as a means of social capital for educational development (UNESCO, 2005). Madrassahs indeed have a noble history of use in furthering the cause of science and learning in medieval Islam but that tradition has been largely forgotten. The rigidity of most mainstream interpretations of Islam make this matter even more troubling. Until we are able to have a reformation within Islamic theology that adequately appreciates pluralism and context, the use of madrassahs as a conduit for general education seems highly unlikely. Philosophy scholar Ghazala Irfan (2006) sums up this challenge by tracing back a fundamental epistemological challenge with madrassah learning claims that 'tradition is the only competent authority or criterion of truth.'

Given this rigid and confined concept of learning that most madrassahs espouse, infusing a peace education curriculum within the current Islamic theological domain may be the only significant contribution that can be made with minimal resistance among the ulema. There is a credible and substantial amount of material on peacebuilding, ecumenical dialogue, political compromise and tolerance within Islamic tradition to counterweight the more austere traditions of jihad. However, such an effort must also be undertaken with two synchronous policy efforts to achieve success in decoupling violence justification and Islamic education.

First, public school curricula in Muslim countries must be improved and the accessibility and quality control of these institutions in rural areas augmented. Islamic education must remain a part of the curriculum in government schools but provided in the context of global religious studies. This will provide greater incentives for parents to consider mainstream schooling while not feeling that religious awareness is being compromised. Towards this end, Muslim governments may indeed have to take an uncompromising stance towards the most radical theologians who would oppose any conciliatory or ecumenical approaches. However, such radical elements must still be given due process in their curtailment rather than giving them further fodder for claiming victimization.

Second, misinformation campaigns at all levels of society must be curtailed through transparency on the part of Western governments and donors. The power of conspiracy theories in the context of education and specious arguments and pseudo-science must not be underestimated. To facilitate this effort Western governments will need to pay more attention to regional political conflicts in the Muslim world. In particular, conflicts that have a clear historical connection with colonialism must be addressed in ways similar to Portugal's' approach in resolving the East Timor territorial conflict. Providing alternative historical narratives through a revitalization of foreign policy efforts to resolve disputes in Kashmir, Chechniya, the Middle East and Africa will limit the recruiting power of radical elements.

Apart from these possible actions, we should also have a more humane vision of madrassah children and address their needs as those of any other child. In the words of retired General Talat Masood, a distinguished observer of Pakistan's foreign policy and a renowned peace activist. 'the people in madrassahs are neither demons nor heroes... they have insecurities, pain, hopes and frustrations... they are human beings just like us.'[15]

The challenge of preventing cooptation of Islamic institutions by external interests for political conflict, while preserving their independence and social service is reaching a critical juncture in Pakistan and across the Muslim world. A multifaceted strategy is essential to tackle this challenge—one which accepts the empirical insights that are provided by research and avoids sensationalistic or sanguine accounts of the problem.

NOTES

1. Mumtaz Ahmad's essay on the Jamaat-e-Islami and the Tablighi Jamaat (p. 492) in Marty and Appleby, 1994.
2. Sikand, Yoginder, email communiqué titled: Islamist Assertion in Contemporary India: The Students Islamic Movement of India, 1 November 2004. Two doctoral dissertations on Indian *madaaris* and social movements are of particular relevance here: Irfan Ahmed, *From Islamism to Post-Islamism* (University of Amsterdam, 2006) and Marieke Winkelman. *The Construction of Islamic Knoiwledge in Girld's Madrasas in India* (Leiden University, Netherlands, 2002).
3. Hoodbhoy has written extensively on educational issues in Pakistan and has generally been a critic of Islamization. However, like other secularists of his genre, he finds particular sympathy in the Palestinian cause and like his friends Noam Chomsky, Edward Said and Eqbal Ahmed, takes exception to a demonization of

Muslims (and perhaps more significantly Arabs) in this regard. For example, see the correspondence between Hoodhbhoy and Paul Kurtz (founder of the Council for Secular Humanism) in response to an article by self-proclaimed apostate Ibn Warraq (a pseudonym for protection) who authored the book 'Why I am not a Muslim.' Details at: <http://www.chowk.com/show_article.cgi?aid=00002692&channel=civi c per cent20centre>

4. Soroush has been a visiting scholar at various Western universities while maintaining a presence in Iran. Wright (1995).
5. This behaviour has been studied in detail by conflict theorists in the natural and social sciences. For an excellent review of the 'dark side' of tribal cooperative behaviour patterns see Ridley 1998.
6. APPNA has been involved in development work in Pakistan through the Human Development Foundation. However, their overall contribution to building cutting-edge educational capacity or increasing the research and creativity potential of their own members remains highly limited.
7. Melik Kaylan, 'Pamuk's Reality.' *The Wall Street Journal*, 16 October 2006.
8. The founder of the academy Shaikh Hamza Yousef, an American Muslim-covert, who received theological training in the United Arab Emirates, Saudi Arabia and in West Africa has not escaped criticism either. His *fatwah* denouncing the burning of the American flag raised ire with some Muslims though he continues to be profiled with suspicion by 'jihad-watchers' like Robert Spencer and Daniel Pipes (see sites: www.jihadwatch.org and www.danielpipes.org).
9. Artists and comedians are also gaining some prominence in Muslim Diaspora communities across Europe, north America and Australia. For an upbeat account of such activities see Abdo, 2006.
10. ISESCO's web site is http://www.isesco.org.ma/: Recently the organization has been involved in bridging the sectarian divide prompted by the Shia-Sunni violence in Iraq.
11. Council on Islamic Education web site: http://www.cie.org
12. The ICRD is led by Douglas Johnston, who is an evangelical Christian but also has a strong academic background and was a planning officer in the President's Office of Emergency Preparedness, Director of Policy Planning and Management in the Office of the Secretary of Defense, and Deputy Assistant Secretary of the Navy (Manpower). Some of his approaches on peace-building can be found in Johnston (1994).
13. The University for Peace programme is led by Amr Abdalla, an Egyptian-American and his wife Sharmin Ahmad, a Bangladeshi-American. Details at http://www.upeace.org
14. Several interviews with Mukhtaran Mai have confirmed the role of Maulvi Razzaq in this case, including the BBC and a detailed follow-up visit by investigative journalist Jack Morris. Details at http://www.thepalmerpress.com/Mai.html. commenting on this aspect of the case Morris wrote back to me in an email, dated 4 May 2006, 'I share your support for this fine man and what he has contributed to on behalf of Islam, Mukhtaran Mai, and women the world over. I asked to meet Imam Razzaq while I was with Mukhtaran and Shakoor, and I was told in swift reply by the police commander that it was not to be. He gave me no recourse but to turn away and continue my visitation.'
15. Quoted in Ahmed, 2003.

EPILOGUE: BEYOND THE RED MOSQUE

The summer of 2007 will no doubt be remembered by historians of Pakistan as a pivotal period in the country's history. The subtitle of Hussain Haqqani's notable book on Pakistan *Between Mosque and Military* was most literally captured by the events that unfolded at the Red Mosque in Islamabad. The city's population had been polarized for several years between the radical traditionalists that immigrated from the Frontier on the one hand, and the extreme modernists who were gaining momentum from economic growth on the other. A clash was perhaps inevitable since the government was allowing both extremes to grow unabated. Calls for 'enlightened moderation' by former President Musharraf became more of a polemical exercise than a policy intervention and by the time the government finally decided to act, the militant elements within the traditional Islamists had already armed themselves to the teeth. The warning signs were clear for the past several months when weapons had been seized in Maulana Abdul Aziz's car heading towards the Red Mosque. Yet, in an effort to placate the religious parties, the Minister of Religious Affairs, Ijaz-ul-Haq had managed to get such indiscretions pardoned. As noted in this volume, his sympathies with the religious establishment harkened back to his father General Zia-ul-Haq's days in power during the 1980s when many of the mosques in Islamabad and their accompanying madrassahs had been built.

Even so, the religious establishment were not pleased with Ijaz-ul-Haq either and as the siege began, he was singled out by most of the religious clerics as a primary cause of the failure to amicably resolve the matter—such are the perils of alliances with absolutist forces: If matters do not go exactly as they please, friends are quite quickly branded as foes. When I interviewed Maulana Abdul Aziz Ghazi in the winter of 2004, he came across as someone who regarded most foreign researchers with suspicion and felt that Islamabad was being indoctrinated by foreign elements. There was little doubt that this was a madrassah with a mission of sanctimonious 'reform' of the urban corridors of power.

The Ghazi brothers began their professional careers at very different starting points, even though they had a devoutly religious upbringing by their father Maulana Muhammad Abdullah, who established the Red Mosque in 1965. The older brother, Maulana Abdul Aziz was inclined to assume leadership of the mosque and initially came across as more conservative than his younger brother, Maulana Abdul Rashid who attended a modern university in Islamabad and worked as a government officer for many years. However, after the assassination of their father in 1998, the younger brother became far more radical in his views but used his articulate demeanour to debate the public vociferously on moral reform in the capital. This was particularly striking, since the father had always considered Abdul Rashid to be a rebellious son and had even struck him from the will for not being Islamic enough in his lifestyle.

The madrassah establishment, under the leadership of the radicalized Ghazi brothers, were quite adamant that the most fundamental purpose of educating Muslims was to claim political ascendancy in the world. The confusion over what this 'ascendancy' really means continues to bedevil policy-makers in the West. Interestingly enough, a year later when I went for Hajj, one of several muftis from Lal Masjid (Red Mosque) who usually respond to scores of query letters from villages about *deeni masail* (religious issues) was in our pilgrimage group. His rhetoric only reinforced my view that the situation of this particular madrassah would reach a critical pitch. As I personally watched the events in Islamabad unfold, the issue became much clearer and far more acute than the revisionists had assumed. The governing board of madrassahs was well aware of this radicalization but kept a low profile on the matter until early 2007 when they finally expelled the Red Mosque family of madrassahs from their board.

The madrassah leadership had taken it upon themselves to purge the city of vice and enforce laws against pornography and brothels in the city. President Mushharaf's personal habits and the notoriety of many military elite in terms of alcohol abuse were already part of parlour conversations around town. The liberal elite in Islamabad had clearly had some easy years under the Musharraf regime and the much larger conservative population of the city was seething with resentment. Pakistan remains a very conservative society and any call to purge a city of such 'dins of sin' usually garners support without much forethought from the populace. While most residents of the city would not subscribe to the absolutism of the Lal Masjid, the clarion call of the mullahs against the more cardinal sins of alcohol and sex gained easy traction with even the enlightened 'moderates.' What they soon realized, however, was that the mullahs were also against some of the more benign forms of entertainment such as a Bollywood movie or a billboard showing a woman sipping Lipton tea. Several years earlier, students from the same madrassah had taken out their wrath concerning the assassination of a notable religious cleric on the city's entertainment industry as well by burning down the Melody cinema (the capital's only venue of its kind).

Initially, the regime tolerated the vigilante acts of the madrassah in terms of closing down video shops and apprehending an alleged brothel owner. The mosque students even took some law enforcement officials hostage without much response from the government. However, when the madrassah establishment attacked a Chinese massage parlour and held its owners hostage, the matter was too serious to ignore. As Pakistan's strategic ally and a major economic investor, the Musharraf regime could not afford to alienate China. The mosque establishment were beginning to feel that they could carry out their 'missions' with impunity, and after timidly surrounding the compound for six months, the government finally decided to act.

On 3 July 2007, an exchange of gunfire between militants at the madrassah and government rangers outside the building quickly escalated and within hours, the environmental ministry building was randomly attacked and set alight. Scores of people on both sides had been killed. Yet the perpetrators of the arson as well as numerous other acts of vandalism across the city were not just from the madrassah itself but from an entire network of seminaries spread out across the city. In a country where one-third of the population has cellular phones, it is quite easy to mobilize action when a network of militancy exists as it does with the madrassahs.

An interesting factor of this madrassah network was that it ostensibly was intended to stand up for women's rights and had a separate seminary for young women known as Jamia Hafsa that was led by the wives of the Ghazi brothers. In several interviews before the Western media, including one for the BBC, Abdul Rashid Ghazi rejected any comparison between his group and the Taliban by saying that unlike the militant Afghan groups, he was in favour of educating women as leaders for social change. Indeed, we saw the activism of the women students throughout the virtue campaign initiated by the madrassah, where images of staff-wielding burka-clad women were seen across the media. It is interesting to note that Maulana Abdul Aziz was less resilient than his younger brother during the siege, despite being far more strident in his rhetoric. In fact, he tried to escape during the siege wearing a *burka* (fully covered dress for women) and was paraded by state-owned television in a rather humiliating interview that actually created more sympathy among the public for the clerics. The siege also highlighted the role of the nascent independent media in Pakistan which covered the entire episode with live reporting and even tried to play a mediating role by directly calling the cell phones of the clerics inside and forging negotiations with the clerics that greatly complicated the situation.

One week after the siege of the mosque, as I went for Friday prayers at a mosque in the relatively elite Lahore suburb of Gulberg, a rather distraught young man handed me a flyer in Urdu lamenting the role of the government in the Red Mosque siege and calling for a national uprising against the government. The flyer also branded conspiracy theories of how the government had tried to use the chaos generated in this episode to divide Muslims and obfuscate their own 'ill intentions'. At the end of the diatribe was a clear statement of this group's intentions—the establishment of a caliphate. It addressed the readership in Urdu as 'Ahl-e-Quwat', meaning 'People of Power' and exhorted them to join together to establish the authority of Islam in the government and indicated that no other form of governance was acceptable to them. The note was signed 'Hizb-al-Tahrir'—a well known militant organization that has its roots in the United Kingdom. This was clearly a sign that the Red Mosque episode was now going to be used as a recruitment tool by international militant organizations. Indeed, a spate of suicide bombings ensued soon after the mosque episode and continue to haunt many parts of the country.

The siege of the Lal Masjid in Pakistan has ended but there are lingering questions about the causes and ultimate consequences of this unfortunate incident which might possibly have been prevented by earlier action. The vestiges of extremism continue and Lal Masjid loyalists have now set up a new website for the mosque with the slogan of '*shariat ya shahdat*' (Islamic Law or else fight till martyrdom) and a subtitle which reads 'you can kill the body but not the passion.' How is one to negotiate when there is such absolute conviction about only one worldview?

Several Pakistani governments countenanced the extremism of this group for years and tried to placate their behaviour in the interest of winning favours with the Islamist parties. Occasional arrests were made but then perpetrators were released on mild assurances. Arms and ammunition accumulated in the compound and then the government claimed it was too dangerous to engage the group. The authorities could have exerted nonviolent pressure on the institution far earlier on by cutting off communication, power and water but they decided to be reactive rather than proactive. In many ways, this siege was reminiscent of a fanatical hold-up by the Branch Davidians in Waco, Texas more than a decade ago which ultimately led to the death of dozens of women and children. The Waco siege showed us that prevention must occur at a much earlier stage when weapons are being accumulated by such groups. Once the matter reaches a siege stage, there are no winnable options since suicidal fanatics are in question. While the Waco raid was also assailed by the news media and was the motivation for Timothy McVeigh's Oklahoma bombing, in retrospect there were few options that the Clinton administration could have pursued at that point.

The Waco comparison shows that non-Islamic fanatics are also capable of many horrors. Yet the reality is that mainstream churches in America condemned the extremist's behaviour and largely distanced themselves from the group. In contrast, Pakistan's Islamist politicians and clerics offered very mild condemnation of the mosque's fanaticism and only a few months before the siege did the Wifaq-ul-Madaaris (federation of madrassahs) suspend the membership of the Lal Masjid seminaries. The media-savvy Maulana Abdul-Rashid Ghazi continued to give interviews to Western news outlets with aplomb. As noted earlier, Maulana Ghazi, dismissed comparisons with the Taliban by stating that unlike the Afghan strains of Islamists, they were in favour of educating women. Yet what this education entailed, few cared to ask or question and by each passing minute the group was further emboldened.

It is high time that we become more aware of the perils of extremist educational institutions which have a far broader base in Pakistan than we care to admit. The only way to address the problem is for Muslim countries to encourage skill-based madrassas while independently monitoring and controlling vigilantes and ensuring curricular development in partnership with the reformist ulama. Ensuring that 'peace education' is part of the entire curriculum (both in madrassahs

EPILOGUE: BEYOND THE RED MOSQUE

and regular government schools) is also essential. In one such effort sponsored by the United Nations mandated University for Peace and in which I have recently been involved, lesson plans on peace education are being developed for madrassahs in Tajikistan, Indonesia and Bangladesh in partnership with religious scholars. Such proactive approaches are important to ensure that incidents such as the one at Lal Masjid are not repeated.

Muslim governments must make it clear to all clerics that the most important verse in the Quran regarding such matters is in Surah 2 Verse 252 which states quite clearly that 'there is no compulsion in religion.' At the same time, the proponents of modernization should consider that there are certain baselines within Muslim countries that are far more elemental and must be considered: prohibitions against alcohol and pornography are part of the law in most Muslim countries and their enforcement and continued prohibition will ensure that vigilantes do not gain traction with the public.

Some level of constructive conflict between various perspectives on interpretation is positive but conforming to basic tenets of human rights as articulated in various international charters and indeed within Islamic jurisprudence is essential.

Yet the absolutist ideologies that are sweeping the Northern areas of Pakistan are particularly disturbing. Violent means of achieving political ends have sadly seduced far too many of the Pathan tribes, who were once known for non-violent revolutionary leaders such as Badshah Khan. There was a time when even a seditious call for secession was preached through peaceful means by such leaders, bringing them wide acclaim, despite their controversial message. Yet now, the only attribute of Pathans that commentators can remember is that they are 'fierce warriors' who challenged even the most resolute colonials. It is high time that the valiant Pathans reclaim their identity from the frightful dogma of cultural superiority and fanaticism to which they seem to have fallen prey.

Peshawar University at one time was among the most prestigious in South Asia and produced some of the leading scientists and engineers of the region. *The Frontier Post* was considered a journalistic gem by readers across the nation. Yet all such venerable institutions are now being tested beyond their capacity. A few years ago, I had an opportunity to attend a meeting at Peshawar University to help revise the environmental curriculum for the Higher Education Commission. I fondly remember the faculty who attended the meeting and was so impressed with the quality of their work. The late Professor Hamidullah, who directed the Centre for Excellence in Geology in Peshawar at the time, was among the attendees, and he woefully commented that the Frontier was intellectually losing its assets. Students were afraid to attend the university for fear of being harassed by fanatics and the faculty had to be on guard constantly for fear of offending these guardians of virtue. What was even more astonishing to the good professor was that many of the educated Pathan families were acquiescing in this fanaticism, under the guise of defiant 'tribal pride,' against the West. A strong patriot till his tragic death in a helicopter crash in 2005, Dr Hamidullah, remained in the Frontier despite these terrible odds.

Yet, how many of those who can build the economy of this wonderful region will face the constant fear of being blown up, and remain in physical and intellectual squalor? The story does not end in Peshawar. There was a time when the entire Frontier and the tribal areas was a welcoming place for visitors from all over the world, but they have now become a xenophobic phantom zone. Consider the Swat valley, a place where once city families could enjoy friendly vacations with local villagers and patronise the exquisite artwork of wood carvers, or visit ancient archaeological sites in this idyllic land. The valley was allowed to drift into an insular and arcane theology that scoffs at any mention of art and worldly enjoyment and only after severe military action in the winter of 2007 was this radicalism confronted.

Even further north, there was a time when foreign writers such as Dervla Murphy could hitchhike and bike their way along the Indus with a four year-old child without fear of being harassed. In her book *Where the Indus is Young* Murphy comments that the people of the Frontier were among the most welcoming and hospitable she had ever encountered. The director of the South Asia programme at the Centre for Strategic and International Studies, Teresita Schaeffer, told me that there was a time when Islamabad was the most favoured destination for diplomats living in South Asia. Her own son was so attached to the people, particularly his *ayah,* who cared for him when they were stationed here, that he returned a few years ago to visit her. Alas now, no US diplomats are even allowed to bring their families with them for security reasons.

So what happened to the magnanimity, tolerance and willingness to embrace differences that the Frontier, in particular, was once so well-

EPILOGUE: BEYOND THE RED MOSQUE

known for? The fault clearly lies in our willingness to succumb to the politics of fear and the distortion of theology. Furthermore, during the Afghan war, we were so busy blaming people in the West for this radicalisation that we neglected to address the matter directly. Regardless of who created the problem, we still needed to address these issues as a society. Instead, we allowed a marginal brand of fanatics to bully us into believing that only their interpretation of Islam was acceptable.

Armed with weapons and a suicidal 'freedom from fear', they successfully struck servile fear in the rest of society, particularly in the borderlands. Like the famous Stockholm prisoner, many in the Frontier became so entranced with these intellectual incarcerators that they actually began to like them. The educated class began to believe that somehow the fanatics must be correct—for they had a contorted courage of conviction that made them appear like mythical superheroes. We were all beguiled to some extent by their sincerity towards a greater purpose that we did not dare to understand. We must strive to understand the true message of Islam where the Prophet blessed even his enemies in Makkah and engaged in peace treaties with people of all faiths.

Yet sincerity is in itself not a quality—for one can often be sincerely wrong. As Abraham Lincoln is believed to have warned: 'there is nothing more dangerous than sincere ignorance!' Fortunately, there are enough examples of other models of functional polities that can practise Islam, retain their identity and yet be friends with the world. They are willing to express disdain with the foreign policies of the US and other countries through economic and political means, rather than through the delusion of masochistic self-annihilation. Pakistan's own political crises after the death of Benazir Bhutto have reached a critical pitch. The Islamists are not relenting, even after a relatively peaceful election and the spate of suicide bombings continues to haunt the landscape. Many of these bombers have been identified as youth who have been indoctrinated through incendiary information.

A month after the Lal Masjid incident, a bilingual movie was released in Pakistani cinemas (Urdu and English) titled *Khuda kay liyay* (For God's Sake), that effectively engaged in the debate between tradiationalism and modernity. It was a phenomenal hit across the country as it humanized the discourse between perceived 'terrorists', 'secularists' and 'moderates'. Such expressions of constructive confrontation with intolerant ideologies are now beginning to gain momentum in Pakistan and throughout the Muslim world. Even in remote parts of the country, small civil society groups are continuing to struggle against all odds to establish positive educational institutions. Soon thereafter, I read the award-winning book *Three Cups of Tea* which exemplifies which documents the efforts of American philanthropist Greg Mortenson to establish schools for 25,000 children in Pakistan's northern areas. The International Centre for Religion and Diplomacy continues to hold peace education workshops in Pakistani madrassahs and the United Nations mandated University for Peace is engaged in a multi-country effort to develop lesson plans for peace education in Islamic universities.

Despite the despair that is so frequently felt by many visitors to Islamic schools, there are many glimmers of hope that must not be discounted. As long as we are careful to differentiate between positive and negative learning, progress can be made quite swiftly to move from literacy to true educational achievement. It is high time that we approach the matter with nuance and reject polarized views of the problem. Education in its most integrative and comprehensive sense can only be achieved if we are able to live up to Dr Martin Luther King's famed statement of being able to 'disagree without being violently disagreeable.'

APPENDICES

APPENDICES

Appendix 1

Data from 1994 Study

Table 1: Madrassah Demographics in Ahmedpur, 1994

Police Station	Number of Madrassahs						Receiving Zakat	Total number of Villages	Number of Villages with no Madrassahs
	Total #	% of Total	Sect Wise Detail: Number and Percentage						
			Deobandi	Bareilvi	Ahl-e-Hadith	Shia			
Naushera Jadid	63	24	56 89%	05 08%	00 00%	02 02%	13	41	12
Uch Sharif	93	35	37 40%	50 54%	05 05%	01 01%	03	47	16
Ahmadpur Sadr	46	17	07 15%	35 77%	04 08%	00 00%	05	45	16
Ahmadpur City	31	12	11 35%	10 32%	10 32%	00 00%	04	07	02
Chanigoth	32	12	16 50%	13 41%	00 00%	03 09%	04	47	29
Dera Nawab	01	00	01 100%	00 00%	00 00%	00 00%	00	00	00
TOTAL	266	100	128 48%	113 42%	19 07%	06 02%	29	187	75

Table 2: Results of Madrassah Survey in Ahmedpur, 2004

Police Station	Number of Madrassahs						Number Receiving Zakat	Total number of Villages	Number of Villages without Madrassahs	No. of Registered Madrassahs
	Total #	% of Total	Sect Wise Detail–actual number (%)							
			Deobandi	Bareilvi	Ahl-e-Hadith	Shia				
Naushera Jadid	92	26	62 (68)	26 (28)	01 (01)	03 (03)	15	41	02	01
Uch sharif	113	32	58 (51)	44 (39)	07 (06)	04 (04)	04	47	16	06
Ahmadpur Sadr	77	22	10 (13)	63 (82)	04 (05)	00 (00)	07	45	16	14
Ahmadpur City	40	09	15 (47)	16 (50)	09 (03)	00 (00)	04	07	02	06
Chanigoth	36	10	18 (50)	15 (42)	00 (00)	03 (08)	04	47	29	08
Dera Nawab	05	01	03 (60)	02 (40)	00 (00)	00 (00)	00	00	00	04
TOTAL	363	100	166 (45.8%)	166 (45.8%)	21 (5.7%)	10 (2.75%)	34	187	75	39

Appendix 2
Dars-e-Nizami Curriculum of Madrassahs (books and dates of publication under major categories of curriculum):

GENERAL BOOKS

Title of Book	Author	Publication date (AH)[1]
Am-Mofassal	Jarullah Zamukhshry	538
Al-Kafia	Jamaluddin Hajib	646
Sharh Al Fawaid Al	–	
Ziaeya	Nooruddin Al Jami	898
Al Khulasa	Jamaluddin Al Tafi	67
Al Shfia	Jamaluddin Al Hajib	646

RHETORIC		
Takhes Al Miftah	Shamsuddin Al Qazvini	739
Al Mukhtsar, W,		–
Al Mutawal	Saduddin Taftazani	792

EXEGESIS OF THE QUR'AN		
Jalalain	Jalaluddin Al Mahalli	846
	Jalaluddin Al Syuti	911
Mudarik Al Tanzil	Hafizuddin Al Nasfi	710
Anwar Al Tazil	Umen Al Bazavi	665

PRINCIPLES OF HADITH		
Nukhbat Al Fiqar	Shahabuddin Al Asqlani	852

---

[1] The Hijrah calendar is lunar and hence the conversion from Hijrah to Gregorian calendar requires some nonlinear arithmetic calculations. The following web sites contains an algorithm for date conversion
http://www.islamicfinder.org/dateConversion.php

APPENDICES

HADITH		
Al Mwatta	Imam Malik	197
Al Jame Al Sahih	Imam Ismail Al Bukhari	256
Al Jame Al Sahih	Imam Al Muslim Al Qusheri	61
Sunan Ibn-E-Maja	Muhammad Al Qazvini	273
Sunan Abi Dawood	Sulaiman Al Sajistani	273
Al Jame Al Sahih	Mohammad Esa Al Tirmazi	279
Al Sunan Al Sughra	Shaib Al Sanai	303
Sharh Maanil Aasar	Mohammad Al Tahavi	321
Mishkat Al Masabih	Mohammad Bin Khatib Al Umeri	737

THEOLOGY		
Aquaid Al Nasfi	Najmuddin	837
Sharh Aquaid	Taftazani	892
Al Mwaqif	Qazi Azad Al Din	786
Sharh Al Mawaqif	Ali Al Jurjani	816
Al Hashia Al Zahidia Mirza Mohammad	–	1101

JURISPRUDENCE		
Al Husami	Hassamuddin	644
Al Manar Ul Anwar	Abu Al Barkat Al Nasfi	710
Sharh Noor Ul Anwar	Mulla Jeven	1130
Al Tanqih Ma Sharh Tozih	Ubaiduddin Masood	745
Usul Al Shashi	Nazamuddin Al Shashi	328
Muslim Al Sbut	Muhibbullah Al Baharvi	1190

FIQH (LAW)		
Mukhtasar Al Qadori	Mohammad Al Qadori	428
Al Bidaia Ma'sharh Al Hidaya	Ali Al Marghinani	593
Kanzudquaiq	Abu Al Barqat Al Nasfi	710
Al Wiquaya	Mahboob Al Mahboobi	673
Munya Al Musalli Sariduddin Al Kashghari		7th c.
Tanveer Al Absar	Shamsuddin	1004
Sharh Al Durrul Mukhtar	Alauddin	1088

Noor Ul Izah	Hassan Al Wafai	1069
Al Siraji	Sirajuddin	7th c.

USUL-E-JADAL (DIALECTICS)		
Al Sharifia Ma'sharh Rashidiah	Mustafa Al Jhonfozi	1083
Arabic Prose (Nasar Arbi)	–	–
Mqamat Al Badih	Badi Ul Zaman Al Hamdani	398
Maqamat Al Hariri	Ali Al Hariri	516
Al Nafhatularab	Ahmad Al Sharwani	3rd c.

ARABIC POETRY (ARBI NAZAM)		
Al Mualiqat Alsabh	Jimarurewaya	155
Al Hamasah	Abu Taam Al Tai	231
Dewan Al Mutnabi	Ahmad Hussain Al Kindi	856

LOGIC (MANTIQU)		
Al Shamsia	Najmuddin Al Qazvini	493
Al Qutbia	Qutbuddin Al Razi	766
Al Tahzib	Al Taftazani	892
Sharh Mulla Hassan	Mulla Hassan	1199
Hidaitul Hikmat	Asiruddin	660
Al Hikmat Ul Baigha	–	–

ASTROLOGY (ELMUL HAIAT)		
Al Mulakhas Fil Haiat	Mahmood Al Khwarzami	7th c
Sharh Al Qazi	Moosa Al Mahmood Al Rohi	840
Tashrih Al Aflak	Bhauddin Al Amli	1030
Al Sharh Al Tasrih	Lutfullah Al Muhandi	1145

ARITHMETIC (HISAB AUR HINDSA)		
Khulasa Fil Hisab	Bahauddin Al Aml	1030
Tahreer Aqlidus	Nasiruddin Al Tosi	672

Appendix 3

Administrative Units in Punjab and Rationale for Delineation (particularly of Dera-Nawab/Mehrab Wala)

In Pakistan's administrative set-up, there is a difference between the *sub-divison* and the *tehsil*—a sub-division is an administrative division for purposes of law and order, where as tehsil is an administrative unit for reason of land administration. The sub-units of tehsil is village, where as sub-unit of sub-division is a police station.

It does happen that a sub-division may have two tehsils in it but this is very rare. In more that 90 per cent of cases tehsil and sub-division boundaries are the same. APE being a big sub-division is an anomoly. For example, the area of Police Station Dera Nawab (also written as Mehrab Wala on some maps) caters for Dera Nawab cantonement, and a small town of Dera Nawab, This area used to be the head-quarters of the Bahawalpur princely state (one of over five hundred princely states that existed in the Indian subcontinent at the time of independence in 1947). When the Nawab (Prince) of Bahawalpur was ruling the state of Bahawalpur, the administrative headquarters was in Bahawalpur city but the ruler used to live in Sadiq-garh palace in Dera Nawab.

Even now, most of present day Dera Nawab is either cantt, where a whole army brigade is stationed, and housed in buildings which were living quarters of ministers of Nawab of Bhawalpur. The remaining part of Dera Nawab is the palaces and banglows of former rulers and most of the residents are the former royal family and there staffers.

So it is one of the smallest police station areas in Bhawalpur. Since it was an under utilised police station, later on, 14 adjoining villages which are not part of APE tehsil, but colony villages of neighbouring Yazman tehsil were included in police station Dera Nawab. Meaning—these villages are part of Ahmedpur sub-division and not tehsil (their tehsil is Yazaman).

The administrative consequences of such divisions can occur as follows: the Assistant Commissioner for APE is incharge of crime prevention within this police station area (including these 14 villages) but for all other land matters and municipal and local government issues, they are part of Yazman tehsil, and responsibility of Administration of Yazman.

Since our first survey in 1994 was done by land revenue staff, and most of the data was also from APE, we included only those areas of Dera Nawab that were part of APE tehsil at that time. In the 2004 study we followed the same delineation since it would have created distortions and involvement of another administrative unit (tehsil) if we had included the 14 villages of Yazman falling in Dera Nawab police station.

Most of the area in Dera Nawab is cantonement, and the rest is owned by the Nawab's family—in practicular no village of APE is included in Police Station Dera Nawab.

Compiled by S. Tauqir Hussain Shah for this study.

Appendix 4
Madrassah Reform Strategy and Budget from the Government of Pakistan

(5 YEAR-PLAN)

A project on the subject was prepared at a cost of Rs 6587 million for 5 years w.e.f. 2002-03 onwards. The aim of the project is to facilitate 8000 willing Deeni Madrassahs of Pakistan through teaching of English, Mathematics, Pakistan Studies/Social Studies and General Science from Primary to Secondary levels and English, Economics, Pakistan Studies and Computer Science at Intermediate level to integrate religious education with formal education system in compliance with the President of Pakistan's instructions issued during a meeting held on 2 January 2002 and address to the nation on 12 January 2002.

OBJECTIVES

- To teach formal subjects in 8000 madrassahs to bridge the gulf between madrassahs education and formal education system.
- To open the lines of communication with the Ulama who run the madrassahs to impart formal education in addition to religious education for spreading of Islamic values at national and international levels.
- To improve and update knowledge of their teachers in formal subjects through workshops at different parts of the country.
- To provide incentives as costs of equipments (computers, printers, apparatus etc) for teaching of Computer Science, costs of textbooks, sports and other facilities to madrassahs.
- One-time grant to the madrassahs for improvement of their libraries and equip their buildings.

COMPONENTS

- Grant salaries to 32000 teachers as to 16000 teachers for teaching of the formal subjects at Primary level @ Rs. 3000/- in 4000 madrassahs, to 12000" teachers at Secondary level @ Rs. 4000/- in 3000 madrassahs and to 4000 teachers of 1000 madrassahs at Intermediate level @ Rs. 5000/-for 3 years. The duration of the project is 5 years.
- Costs of: Textbooks, stationary items, sports facilities and one-time grant for library facilities and furniture to all madrassahs. Computer, printers, computer lab. to 1000 madrassahs at Intermediate level and vehicles to 5 *Wafaqs* of madrassahs.

- Training to 32,000 teachers through workshops of 8-day duration each by the respective Education Departments.
- Evaluation of sample madrassahs by Provincial Education Departments and the Federal Government, development of textbooks in the formal subjects for teaching in madrassahs by the Ministry of Education.
- Expenditure on Project Implementation Units at provinces/areas and Federal levels.

ITEM-WISE AND YEAR-WISE DETAILS OF EXPENDITURE

(in millions of Rupees)

ITEMS	I 2002-03	II 2003-04	III 2004-05	IV 2005-06	V 2006-07	Total
1. Salaries						
- Primary	144	432	576	432	144	1728
- Middle + Secondary	192	384	576	384	192	1728
- HSSC	240	240	240	-	-	720
Subtotal	576	1056	1392	816	336	4176
2. Textbooks	150	120	90	-	-	360
3. Sports Facilities	90	90	60	-	-	240
4. Stationery Items	60	60	40	-	-	160
5. Apparatus AVA Computer Lab.	200	-	-	-	-	200
6. Reference Books & Furniture	440	340	240	-	-	1020
7. Computers & Printers	200	-	-	-	-	200
8. Vehicles to Wafaqs	7.5	-	-	-	-	7.5
9. Teacher Training	30	34	80	-	-	144.0
10. Monitoring, Auditing	-	4	5	6	-	15
11. Development of Textbooks etc.	0.8	1.0	1.565	-	-	3.365
12. Operational Staff	2.111	2.111	2.111	2.111	2.111	10.555
13. Honrarium to add. Staff	0.048	0.048	0.048	0.048	0.048	0.24
14. Office Utilities	4.196	1.896	1.896	1.896	1.896	11.78
15. PIU Expenditure	7.712	7.712	7.712	7.712	7.712	38.56
Grand Total	1768.367	1716.767	1920.332	833.767	347.767	6587

IMPLEMENTATION STRATEGY

The project will have a period of 5 years with effect from 2002-03. However, the willing religious institutions will be facilitated for 3 years phase-wise as 3000 and 2000 madrassahs during Ist, IInd and IIIrd year respectively. The 'Ministry of Education will develop textual and instructional material as and when required.

i) OPERATIONAL STAFF: The Ministry of Education (Curriculum Wing) would be the focal place/sole responsible for the implementation of the project. It will recruit operational staff for the implementation of the project as Federal Project Implementation Unit (FPm) comprising Project Director (B-19), 2 Deputy Directors (B-18), 1 Accounts Officer (B.17) with Assisting Staff. Similarly, Project Implementation Unit comprising Project Coordinator, Accounts Officer with Assisting staff to coordinate all the activities in the capital of provinces i.e. Peshawar, Lahore, Quetta and Karachi will be constituted to implement the task in the madrassahs in NWFP, Punjab, Balochistan and Sindh respectively. A project Implementation Unit will be constituted at Islamabad to implement the activities in A.J.K., FANA, FATA and Federal Areas Islamabad. The expenditure on their salaries and allowances as per Federal Government Rules will be paid out of the project.

ii) RECRUITMENT OF TEACHERS AND THEIR TRAINING: Recruitment of teachers will be made by the concerned institutions through a committee comprising representatives of Education Department, Wafaqs and the concerned institution on contract basis as per policy. The qualifications for recruitment of the teachers will be as: SSC + PTC for Primary, FAIFSc + C.T. for Middle, HAIBSc.+ H.Ed. for SSC and MA/MSc. preferably M.Ed. for HSSC classes. The teachers will be trained through 8 day workshops.

iii) RELEASE OF FUNDS: The Curriculum Wing, Ministry of Education will release funds in the following areas to the Education Foundation in each province and Federal Areas, Islamabad for utilization through madrassahs in consultation with the Education Departments:

   a) Salaries to the teachers and their training.
   b) Cost of textbooks, stationery items and sports facilities.
   c) Apparatus, audio- visual aids, computer lab. etc.
   d) Reference books, furniture, computers and printers.

iv) AUDITING OF ACCOUNTS. The Auditor General of Pakistan Revenue (AGPR) would be responsible for the audit of the project accounts on annual basis as well as after the completion of the project.

v) MONITORING AND EVALUATION: The monitoring and evaluation of the project would be done by the Education Departments and Education Foundation. The Federal Ministry of Education will check the activities when needed. For this purpose, a committee comprising representatives of the Ministries of Education, Religious Affairs Finance and P&D will be constituted.

vi) BOARDS AND EOUIVALENCE OF CERTIFICATES: The examination at Secondary and Higher Secondary level will be conducted by the relevant HISEs and certificates will be issued if religious education at *Sanaviya Aama* and *Sanaviya Khasa* respectively is completed by the students. The internal examinations at

Primary and Middle levels will be arranged by the respective organizations/institutions.

vii) THE ROLE OF MADRASSAHS AUTHORITY: The Madrasah Authority will submit an undertaking to the Education Departments/Education Foundation/Ministry of Education for arrangements of teaching formal subjects to. at least 20 students in each class at Primary/Middle/Secondary/Higher Secondary level as the case may be. The madrassahs at different levels in religious education may be considered in the formal subjects for the purpose of providing incentives under this project as mentioned below:
-Hifz/Tajweed-wa-Qiraat/Ibtedayia=Primary
-Mutawassita=Middle
-Sanviya Aama=S.S.C.
-Sanaviya Khassa and above=H.S.S.C.

viii) STEERING COMMITTEE: A. Steering Committee comprising Education Secretary (Chairman), Joint Educational Adviser (Curriculum Wing), Chief Education, P&D Division and Project Director will be constituted to look after and check the over all activities of the project and to solve the problems/policy matters faced during the implementation of the project.

ix) SELECTION OF MADRASSAHS: The selection of madrassahs on NEC formula basis will be made by the Education Departments for onward transmission to the Education Foundation in the Provinces/Areas as the case may be. The Ministry of Education will extend cooperation in the selection of madrassahs as and when required. A questionnaire has been developed for this purpose.

EXPECTED RESULTS:

- The project will establish and strengthen the lines of communication amongst the madrassahs and the government.
- It will educate about 1.5 million students (both male and female) of 8000 madrassahs in formal subjects from Primary to Intermediate level to enable them to continue their studies in colleges and universities.
- It will impart training to 32,000 teachers to improve and update their knowledge in formal subjects and teaching methodology.
- It will provide incentives through books, furnitures, computers, printers and sports facilities to improve their education system.
- It will eradicate sectarianism in the country and will develop friendly atmosphere and national cohesion in the society.

MAINSTREAMING OF DEENI MADRASSAHS OF PAKISTAN

Madrassahs Pakistan are independent institutions and they have organized themselves into five Wafaqs/Tanzeem/Rabitatul-Madrassahs. The government has tried to help these institutions to accelerate implementation of Islamic values, to strengthen the ideological foundation of the country and to bridge the existing gulf between the two parallel streams of education; see details at Annex-1.

In compliance with the Chief Executive/President of Pakistan's instructions regarding teaching of formal subjects and registration of the madrassahs, the following two projects have been prepared and submitted to the P&D Division:

1. MADRASSAHS REFORMS (TEACHING OF FORMAL SUBJECTS IN DEENI MADRASSAHS).

   The project was drafted at a cost of Rs 13691 million for 3 years w.e.f. 2002-03 onwards to facilitate 8000 madrassahs in Pakistan through teaching of English, Maths, Pakistan Studies/Social Studies and General Science from primary to secondary level and English, Economics and Computer Science at Intermediate level for integration of their system with the formal education system.

OBJECTIVES

i) To integrate religious education with formal education system to absorb their graduates in the labour market.
ii) To provide incentives to the madrassahs through supply of equipment, textbooks and grant salaries to their teachers for teaching of the formal subjects.
iii) To improve and update knowledge of their teachers in formal subjects.
iv) One- time grant to the madrassahs for co-curricular activities and reference books for their libraries.

COMPONENTS

i) Grant salaries to teachers for teaching the subjects.
ii) Training to the teachers.
iii) Evaluation of sample madrassahs.
iv) Grant to the madrassahs.

CRITERION

1. The case was discussed with the Ministry of Religious Affairs and criterion was prepared for release of grant to the madrassahs; are main points of the criterion reproduced below:

   i) The grant to madrassahs according to NEC formula leaving 10 per cent for ICT, FATA, FANA & AJK through Education Departments with recommendations of Pakistan MadrasaMadrassah Education Board (PMEB).
   ii) The monitoring and inspection of madrassahs and financial issues will be the responsibility of PMEB in collaboration with Education Departments.
   iii) Appointment of teachers by madrassahs as per rules on the basis of enrolment of students.
   iv) The textbooks will be purchased by madrassahs and the costs will be re-imbursed by Education Departments.
   v) The equipment will be purchased by the Provincial and Federal government.
   The criterion was referred to the Ministry of Religious Affairs for vetting; the response is still awaited. The PC-I will be revised accordingly. A total provision of Rs 500 million (after Rs 300 million cut) has been allocated this year.

2. ONE-TIME GRANT TO MADRASSAHS: The PC-I on the subject at a cost of Rs 12 million has been prepared for 2 years w.e.f. 2002-03 onwards. The aim of the

project is to encourage 10000 madrassahs to register with the government. The project comprises costs of Islamic books and formal subjects books, cost of furniture etc. to equip their libraries. No allocation has been provided for this project.

For effective implementation of the policy of the government for mainstreaming of Madrassah Education System, it is proposed that:

i) 'No Interference Policy' may be adopted in all the fields particularly in the registration of these institutions through an Act to be drafted by Ministry of Religious Affairs in consultation with the Ministries of Education and Interior and the eminent Ulama.
ii) The above programmes for teaching of formal subjects in the curricula of madrassahs may be implemented in consultation with the Ministry of Religious Affairs. The Ministry of Religious Affairs may be requested to vet the criterion and send it immediately to this Ministry.
iii) The strategy for registration of the foreign students and teachers may be simplified by the vetting agencies to encourage them to acquire knowledge in Pakistani institutions in a proper way.

ANNEX-I: STEPS TAKEN BY THE MINISTRY OF EDUCATION REGARDING MAINSTREAMING OF DEENI MADRASSAHS

The Ministry of Education has taken steps to bridge the gulf between Madrassah Education and the Formal Education System. The details are:

i) Collection of particulars of 7000 madrassahs in early 80s. A sketch of particulars (Information collected from 1000 Madrassahs-Questionnaires sent to 7000 madrassahs.)
ii) Preparation and distribution of Directory of madrassahs, Directory of Ulama and Comprehensive Report on madrassahs.
iii) Introduction of some formal school subjects (English, Economics, Pakistan Studies and Maths) at Secondary level in 140 madrassahs.
iv) Supply of books to equip libraries of 70 madrassahs.
v) Distribution of 2000 sets comprising 24 Islamic textbooks amongst 1200 madrassahs.
vi) Release of annual grant-in-aid from Rs. 1.00 to 1.5 million amongst 200 Madrassahs for the last two decades.
vii) Equated Sanad (degree) of madrassahs with M.A. Arabic and M.A. Islamic Studies.

In the context of mainstreaming of Madrasah Education, the New Education Policy (1998-2010) emphasized:

i) To bridge the existing gulf between the formal education and Madrassah Education system.
ii) To equate their certificates/degrees with those of formal education system at Secondary, Higher Secondary and Higher Education levels.

In order to implement the policy, following steps have been/are being taken in consultation with Ulama and Educationists:

APPENDICES

a) Offered English, Economics and Pakistan Studies under two projects at a total cost of Rs 129.95 million for 200 madrassahs during 2000-01 onwards. Under the programme, 75 Madrassahs have been facilitated during 2000-01 to 2001-02 through supply of 5 computers, 2 printers, 20 sets of textbooks, grant of salaries to 3 teachers of each institution and training to their teachers. A profile on the projects.

b) Under an Ordinance 'Pakistan Madrassah Education Board' has been established under the control of the Ministry of Religious Affairs, Government of Pakistan for integration of the Madrassah Education system with the Formal Education System. This Ministry, being a member, has been cooperating since initial stages with the Board.

Appendix 5
List of Qualitative Interviews Conducted (in order of conversation) where interviewee agreed to name being released

Name	Designation
Mr Ijaz Ul Haq	Minister for Religious Affairs
Allama Ghazi Abdul Rashid	Imam, Lal Masjid, Islamabad (d. 2007)
Maulana Akram Kashmiri	Jamia Ashrafia, Lahore
Mr Tariq Mahmud	Federal Secretary Interior
Mr Tasneem Noorani	Former Secretary Interior
Mr Shafquat Ezidi Shah	Secretary Education
Mr Suleah Faruqi	Additional Secretary Education, Sindh
Mr Imran Ahmad	District Coordination Officer Bhawalpur
Dr Farzana Khan	Executive District Officer Bhawalpur
Dr Samina Ahmad	Director International Crisis Group. Islamabad
Mr Taimur Ali Khan	Senior Superintendent of Police, Islamabad
Dr Anis Ahmad	Vice Chancellor, Rafah University
Maulana Khairpuri	General Secretary, ADDM
Mr Tayyab Saeed	Senior Superintendent of Police
Mr Tariq Pervaiz	Additional Inspector General of Police. CID Punjab
General (retd). Moin-uddin Haider	Former Minister of Interior Sindh
Qari Muhammad Hanif Jalandari	Director Khair-ul-Madaaris Multan
Dr Tariq Rahman	Professor of Quaid-e-Azam University
Dr A. H. Nayyer	Senior Fellow SDPI
Mr Shahnaz Wazir Ali	Executive Director PCP
Mr Ghazi Aman Ullah Khan	Magistrate Ahmedpur East
Dr Sarah Wright	USAID Islamabad
Barrister Zafer Ullah Khan	Legal expert and Madrassah Alumnus
Mr Javed Iqbal Awan	Secretary Awqaf Punjab
Mr Malik Kazim Ali	Sessions Judge
Mr Hamid Ali Khan	Distirct Coordination Officer Rawalpindi
Mr Kareem Nawaz	Education researcher
Mr Usman Qazi	Community Development and Rural Sociology expert

Mr Khalid Ahmed	Journalist and researcher
Mr Zafar-ullah-Khan	Friedrich Naumann Stiftung, Islamabad
General (retd.) Hamid Gul	Former Director of Military ISI, Pakistan
Mr Khalid Ahmed	Journalist for *Daily Times*, Lahore
Dr Mehmood Ahmed Ghazi	Vice-rector, Islamic University, Islamabad
Dr Tahir Andrabi	Pomona College, primary author of World Bank study
General (retd.) Jehangir Karamat	Ambassador of Pakistan to the USA (2004-2006)

BIBLIOGRAPHY

Abbas, Hassan (2004). *Pakistan's Drift into Extremism*. London: M.E. Sharpe.
Abbott, Freeland (1968). *Islam and Pakistan*. New York: Cornell University Press.
Abdo, Geneive (2006). *Makkah and Mainstreet*. New York: Oxford University Press.
Abu-Nimer, Mohammed (2003). *Non-violence and peace building in Islam: Theory and Practice*. Gainesville FL: University Press of Florida.
Ahmed, S. c., & Obaid, N. (1970). *Mosque-Madrassah System of Islamic Education*. Karachi: Pakistan Institute of Arts and Design.
Ahmed, Akbar S. (2002). 'Ibn Khaldun's Understanding of Civilizations and the Dilemmas of Islam and the West Today' *The Middle East Journal*, Vol. 56, No. 1.
Ahmed, Akbar S. (1986) *Pakistan Society: Islam, Ethnicity, and Leadership in South Asia*. New York: Oxford University Press.
Ahmed, Akbar S. (1997). *Jinnah, Pakistan and Islamic Identity: The Search for Saladin*.
London; New York: Routledge.
Ahmed, Aijaz (2003). *Madrassahs: A Make-Belief World*. Asia Times Online. http://www.atiimes.com/South_Asia/EA14Df01.html
Ahrari, Mohammed E. (2001). *Jihadi Groups, Nuclear Pakistan, and the New Great Game*.
Carlisle, PA: Strategic Studies Institute, US Army War http://carlisle-www.army.mil/usassi/ssipubs/pubs2001/jih; http://purl.access.gpo.gov/GPO/LPS14542; http://www.carlisle.army.mil/ssi/pubs/2001/jihadi/jihadi.pdf
Aijazz, Ahmed (2003). *Madrassahs: A Make-Belief World*. Asia Times Online. http://www.atiimes.com/South_Asia/EA14Df01.html
Alam, M. M. (2004). *Madrasa and Terrorism: Myth or Reality*. New Delhi: Indian Social Institute.
Al Faruqi, Ismail (1986). *The Cultural Atlas of Islam*. New York NY: Prentice Hall.
Al Qaradawi, Yusuf (1987). *Islamic Awakening: Between Rejection and Extremism*. Abu Dhabi: United Arab Bureau.
Alam, Muhammad Mukhtar (2004). *Madrase Aur Dehshatgardi: Kya Afsana Kya Haqiqat* (Madrasas And Terrorism: Myth versus Reality'). New Delhi: Indian Social Institute.
Alexiev, Alex (2005). 'The Tablighi Jamaat: Jihad's Stealthy Legions.' *The Middle East Quarterly*, vol. 12, No. 1 January.
Ali, Saleem H. (2004). *Mining, the Environment and Indigenous Development Conflicts*. Tucson AZ: University of Arizona Press.
Anderson, C. A. et al. (2003). 'The influence of media violence on youth.' *Psychological Science in the Public Interest*, Vol. 4, No. 3.
Andrabi, Tahir, Asim Khwaja Jishnu Das and Tristan Zajonc (2005). *Religious School Enrollment in Pakistan: A Look at the Data*. World Bank Policy paper, WPS 3521.

Anjum, Ghulam Yahya (2004–in Urdu). *Dini Madaris Aur Ehad-i-Hazir Ke Taqazey* (Islamic Religious Schools and Contemporary Demands). Porbandar, India: Porbandar: Markaz-i-Ahl-i-Sunnat Barkat-i-Raza.

Anwar, Ghazala (1999). 'Reclaiming the religious centre from a Muslim perspective.' In Courtney W. Howland ed. *Religious Fundamentalisms and the Human Rights of Women*. New York: St. Martins Press.

Anzar, Uzma. (2003) *Islamic Education: A Brief History of Madrassahs with Comments on Curricula and Current Pedagogical Practices.*

Arafath, Yasser (2004). *'Indian Census: For A Better Understanding.' Countercurrents*, 18 September.

Archer, Louise, Farzana Shain and Christopher Williams (2006). British Muslims expectations of the government: what schools do British Muslims want for their children? (a review). *British Journal of Sociology of Education*, Vol. 27, No. 5, pp. 659–671.

Armanios, Febe (2003). *Islamic Schools, Madrassahs: Background. CRS Report for Congress*. Congressional Research Service, The Library of Congress. Accessed online http://www.fas.org/irp/crs/RS21654.pdf

Armstrong, Karen (2001). *The Battle for God*. New York NY: Ballantine Books.

Armstrong, Karen (1994). *A History of God: The 4000 year quest of Judaism, Christianity and Islam*. New York: Ballantine Books.

Azra, Azyumardi (2004). *Mainstreaming Islamic Education*. United States Indonesia Society presentation, 31 March available online at www.usindo.org

Bandura, A. (1973). *Aggression—A Social Analysis of Learning*. New Jersey: Prentice Hall.

Benard, Cheryl (2003). *Civil Democratic Islam: Partners, Resources and Strategies*, CA: Rand Corporation. http://www.rand.org/publications/MR/MR1716

Bergen, Peter and Swati Pandey (2006). 'The Madrassah Scapegoat.' *The Washington Quarterly*, Vol. 29, No. 2, pp. 117–125.

Bergen, Peter and Swati Pandey (2005). 'The Madrassa Myth.' *The New York Times*, 14 June 2005.

Betts, Robert (1990). *The Druze*. New Haven CT: Yale University Press.

Blank, Jonah (2001). *Mullahs on the Mainframe: Islam and Modernity among the Daudi Bohras*. Chicago: University of Chicago Press.

Bose, Sumantra (2004). *Kashmir: Roots of Conflict, Prospects for Peace*. Cambridge MA: Harvard University Press.

Boyle, Helen N. (2004). *Qur'anic Schools: Agents of Preservation and Change*. New York: Routledge Falmer.

Brandenburg, D. (1978). *Die madrasa: Ursprung, entwicklung, ausbreitung u. Künstlerische gestaltung d. Islamischen moschee-hochschule*.Graz: Verl. f. Sammler.

Breidlid, Anders (2005). 'Education in the Sudan: The Privileging of an Islamic Discourse'. *Journal of Comparative Education*, v35 n3. pp. 247–263.

Brenner, Louis (2001). *Controlling Knowledge: Religion, Power and Schooling in a West African Muslim Society*. Bloomington IN: Indiana University Press.

Bretherton, Diane et al. (2005). School based peace building in Sierra Leonne. *Theory into Practice*, Vol. 44, no. 4, pp. 355–62.

Brower, Michaelle and Charles Kurzman ed. (2004). *An Islamic Reformation*. Oxford: Lexington Books.

Bunt, Gary R. (2003). *Islam in the Digital Age: E-Jihad, Online fatwas and Cyber Islamic Environments.* London UK: Pluto Press.
Buss, A.H. and M. Perry (1992). 'The Aggression Questionnaire.' *Journal of Personality and Social Psychology.* Vol. 93, No. 3.
Cohen, Stephen (2004). *The Idea of Pakistan.* Washington DC: Brookings Institution Press.
Coulson, Andrew (2004). 'Education and Indoctrination in the Muslim World.' *Policy Analysis* No. 511, 11 March.
Croteau, David et al, eds. (2005). *Rhyming Hope and History : Activist, Academics and Social Movement Scholarship.* Minneapolis: University of Minnesota Press.
Dalrymple, William (2005). 'Inside Islam's "terror" schools' *New Statesman and Society*, 28 March 2005.
Dalrymple, William (2005). 'Inside the Madrassas.' *New York Review of Books*, 1 December.
Danner, Mark (2005). 'Taking stock of the forever war.' *New York Times Sunday Magazine*, 11 September.
Das, Sujit (2006). an Islamic School—the learned ignorance.' *Islam-Watch*, 19 April. Accessible online at: http://www.islamwatch.org
Daunic, Ann P. et al. (2006). 'Classroom-based cognitive-behavioural intervention to prevent aggression: efficacy and social validity.' *Journal of Social Psychology*, Vol. 44, pp. 123–139.
Devji, Faisal (2005). 'Why liberal Islam is not the solution.' *The Financial Times*, 11 November.
Doxiadis, Constantinos (1975). *Anthropoplis: The City for Human Development.* New York: W.W. Norton.
Easterley, William (2001). *The Elusive of Growth.* Cambridge MA: MIT Press.
Eaton, Jana Sackman (2005). The Russian Federation Islamic Republic of Dagestan: Curricular Decentralization, Social Cohesion, and Stability. *Peabody Journal of Education.* v80 n1, pp. 56–80.
Effendy, Bahtiar (2003). *Islam and the State in Indonesia.* Athens OH; Ohio University Press.
Eickelman, Dale F. (1998). 'Inside the Islamic Reformation.' *Wilson Quarterly,* Winter.
El-Gamal, Mahmoud (2006). *Islamic Finance: Lae, Economics and Practice.* Cambridge UK: Cambridge University Press.
Embassy of the Islamic Republic of Pakistan (2004). *Madrassah Reform in Pakistan.* Embassy of the Islamic Republic of Pakistan. http://www.embassyofpakistan.org/pb5php
Epstein, Michael Jay (1989). 'Who Killed Zia?' *Vanity Fair,* September.
Erfan, N., & Valie, Z. A. (1995). *Education and the Muslim World: Challenge & Response; Recommendations of the Four World Conferences on Islamic Education.* Leicester: Islamic Foundation.
Fair, Christine (2008). *The Madrassah Challenge: Militancy and Religious Education in Pakistan.* Washington DC: United States Institute of Peace Press.
Fakhry, Majid (2003). *Islamic Philosophy, Theology and Mysticism: A Short Introduction.* Oxford, England: Oneworld.
Faruqi, Ziaulhasan (1963). *The Deoband School and the Demand for Pakistan.* New York: Asia Pub. House.

Fine, Gary A. V. Campion-Vincent and Chip Heath eds. (2005). *Rumour Mills: The Social Impact of Rumour and Legend.* New Brunswick NJ: Transaction Publishers.

Fortna, B. C. (2000). Islamic morality in late Ottoman 'secular' schools. *International Journal of Middle East Studies, 32*(3), pp. 369–393.

Fukuyama, Francis (2005). 'A year of living dangerous.'

Fuller, Graham E. (1991). *Islamic fundamentalism in the Northern Tier Countries: An Integrated View.* Santa Monica, CA: Rand Corp.

Future Youth Group (2002). *Ideas on Democracy, Freedom and Peace in Textbooks. (Campaign Against Hate Speech)* Islamabad, Pakistan: Liberal Forum Pakistan.

Gerges, Fawaz A. (2006). *The Far Enemy: Why Jihad Went Global.* New York: Cambridge University Press.

Gesink, Indira F. (2006). 'Islamic Reformation: a history of madrassah reform and legal change in Egypt. *Comparative Education Review,* Vol. 50, no. 3, pp. 325–45.

Goldberg, Jeffrey. 'Inside Jihad University: The Education of a Holy Warrior.' *New York Times Magazine,* 25 June 2000.

Gomez, James and Steven Gan (2004). *Asian Cyberactivism: Freedom of Expression and Media Censorship.* Singapore: Friedrich Naumann Stiftung.

Grandin, N., & Gaborieau, M. (1997). *Madrasa: La transmission du savoir dans le monde musulman* (1re éd. ed.). Paris: Arguments.

Guven, Ismail (2004). 'The impact of political Islam on education: the revitalization of Islamic education in the Turkish educational setting.' *International Journal of Educational Development* 25:193–208.

Hallaq, Wael B. (2005). *The Origin and Evolution of Islamic Law.* Cambridge UK: Cambridge University Press.

Halstead, J. M. (2004). 'An Islamic concept of education'. *Comparative Education,* 40(4), pp. 517–29.

Haqani, Husain (2005). *Pakistan Between Mosque and Military.* Washington DC: Carnegie Endowment for International Peace.

Haqani, Husain (2002). 'A History of Madrassah Education', in *Education in the Muslim World: What Next?* Speech delivered at a Symposium at AED, Washington DC 2002. http://aed.org/publications/GLGEducationMuslimWorld.pdf

Haque, M. Shamsul (2003). The role of the state in managing ethnic tensions in Malaysia. *American Behavioural Scientist,* Vol. 47, No.3, pp. 240–66.

Haque, Z. (1972). *Muslim Religious Education in Indo-Pakistan: An Annotated Bibliography.* Chicago IL: University of Chicago, Committee on Southern Asian Studies, Muslim Studies Sub-Committee.

Hassan, Farzana (2006). *Islam, Women and the Challenges of Today.* Toronto, Canada: White Knight Books.

Hassan, Riffat (2000). 'An Open Letter to Chief Executive of Pakistan: General Pervez Musharraf.' *Pakistan Today,* 25 February.

Hefner, Robert W. and Muhammad Qasim Zaman ed. (2007). *Schooling Islam, The Culture and Politics of Modern Muslim Education.* Princeton NJ: Princeton University Press.

Hertz-Lazarowitz, Rachel (2004). Existence and coexistence in Acre: the power of educational activism. *Journal of Social Issues,* Vol. 60, No. 2, pp. 357–71.

Hilgendorf, Eric (2003). Islamic Education: History and Tendency. *Peabody Journal of Education,* v78 n2, pp. 63–75 Aug 2003.

Hoodbhoy, Pervez ed. (1998). *Education and the State: Fifty Years of Pakistan.* Karachi, Pakistan: Oxford University Press.

Hjortdal, O., Arnvig, E., & Holmstrup, U. (2003). Allahs børn [Videorecording (vid); Videocassette (vca); VHS tape (vhs)]. New York: Filmakers Library.

Hussain, Zahid (2007). *Frontline Pakistan: The Struggle with Militant Islam.* New York: Columbia University Press.

IPS Task Force: Rahman, Khalid, Anjum, Adnan & Rahman (2002). *Pakistan: Religious Education Institutions: An Overview.* Lahore, Pakistan: Shirkat Printing Press.

International Crisis Group (2002). *Pakistan: Madrassahs, Extremism and the Military.* ICG Asia Report No. 36. Islamabad/Brussels: International Crisis Group.

International Crisis Group (2004). *Unfulfilled Promises: Pakistan's Failure to Tackle Extremism.* http://www.embindia.org/Artculos/internationsl per cent20crisis.htm

International Crisis Group (2005). *The State of Sectarianism in Pakistan.* ICG Asia Report No. 95. Islamabad/Brussels: International Crisis Group.

Iqbal, Muhammad (1934). *The Reconstruction of Religious Thought in Islam.* Oxford UK: Oxford University Press.

Irfan, Ghazala (2006). 'Reconciling the madrassah with the school: freedom of religion, education and the dilemma of comentemporary Muslims.' *Journal of Dharma,* Vol. 31, No. 1, pp. 117–128.

Jafferelot, Christophe ed. (2002). *Pakistan: Nationalism without a Nation.* London: Zed Books.

Jalal, Ayesha (1994). *The Sole Spokesman: Jinnah, the Muslim League and the Demand for Pakistan.* Cambridge: Cambridge University Press.

Jalal, Ayesha (2000). *Self and Sovereignty: Individual and Community in South Asian Islam since 1850.* London; New York: Routledge.

Jalalzai, Musa Khan (2005). *Islamization and Minorities in Pakistan.* Lahore, Pakistan: Jamhoori Publications.

Jalalzai, Musa Khan (1998). *The Roots of Islamic Fundamentalism in Pakistan.* Lahore: Sham-Kay-Baad Publications.

Jawed, Nasim A. (1999). *Islam's Political Culture: Religion and Politics in Pre-divided Pakistan.* Austin: University of Texas Press.

Jones, Adele (2005). 'Conflict development and community participation: Pakistan and Yemen.' *Internationales Asienform,* Vol. 36, No. 3-4, pp. 289–310.

Kaplan, David (2005). 'Hearts, Minds, and Dollars.' *US News and World Report,* 25 April.

Kaushik, Surendar Nath (1996). *The Ahmadiya Community of Pakistan: Discrimination, Travail and Alienation.* Delhi: Oxford University Press.

Kemper, M. (2000). 'Madrasa. The transmission of learning in the Muslim world'. *Islam-Zeitschrift Fur Geschichte Und Kultur Des Islamischen Orients,* 77(1), 189–190.

Khan, M.A. Muqtedar ed. (2007). *Debating Moderate Islam: The Geopolitics of Islam and the West.* Salt Lake City: University of Utah Press.

Knight, Peter (2002). *Conspiracy Nation: the Politics of Paranoia Postwar America.* New York: New York University Press.

Saeed (now Khan), Marriam (1995). *Comparison of Level of Aggression Between Government School Boys and Madrassa Boys.* Lahore, Pakistan: University of the Punjab, Psychology Department, Masters thesis.

Khalid, Salim Mansur and M. Fayyaz Khan (2006). 'Pakistan: the State of education.' *Muslim World,* Vol. 96, April, pp. 305–322.

Klare, Michael (2002). *Resource Wars: The New Landscape of Global Conflict.* New York: Owl Books.

Kincheloe, Joe L. and Shirley R. Steinberg eds. (2004). *The Miseducation of the West: How schools and the Media Distort our Understanding of the Islamic World.* London: Praeger.

Kronstadt, K. Alan (2004). *Education Reform in Pakistan.* CRS Report to Congress, December.

Kronstadt, K. Alan (2003). *Internal Terrorism in South Asia.* CRS Report for Congress. Congressional Research Service, The Library of Congress. http://www.fas.org/irp/crs/RS21658.pdf

Kuldip, K. (1990). *Madrasa Education in India: A Study of its Past and present.* Chandigarh, India: Centre for Research in Rural & Industrial Development.

Kumar, Nita (2000). *Lessons from Schools: the History of Education in Banaras.* New Delhi: Sage Publications.

Lapidus, Ira (1990). *A Short History of Islam.* Cambridge UK: Cambridge University Press.

Lapidus, Ira (1984). *Muslim Cities in the Later Middle Ages.* Cambridge: Cambridge University Press, 1984.

Lawrence, Bruce ed. (2005). *Messages to the World: The Statements of Osama bin Laden.* New York: Verso.

Leitner, G.W. (1883 and 1971). *History of Indigenous Education in the Punjab since Annexation.* Patiala: Languages Department.

Life Learning magazine (2003). Defining Education (editorial). May/June.

Limaye, Satu P., Robert Wirsing and Mohan Malik eds. *Religious Radicalism and Security in South Asia.* Honolulu Hawaii: Asia Pacific Centre for Security Studies, 2004.

Looney, Robert (2003). Reforming Pakistan's Educational System: The Challenge of the Madrassahs. *The Journal of Social, Political and Economic Studies.* Volume 28, Number 3, Fall 2003, pp. 257–74.

Lukens-Bull, R.A. (2005). *A Peaceful Jihad: Negotiating Identity and Modernity in Muslim Java.* New York: Palgrave Macmillan.

Lukens-Bull, R. A. (2001). Two sides of the same coin: Modernity and tradition in Islamic education in Indonesia. *Anthropology & Education Quarterly, 32*(3), pp. 350–72.

Lynch, Marc (2005). *Voices of the New Arab Public.* New York: Columbia University Press.

Madjid, Nurcholish (2003). *The True Face of Islam—Essays on Islam and Modernity in Indonesia.* Ciputat, Indonesia: Voice Centre.

Mahmood, Sohail (1995). *Islamic fundamentalism in Pakistan, Egypt and Iran.* Lahore, Pakistan: Vanguard Books.

Malik, Jamal (2007). *Madrasas in South Asia: Teaching Terror?* London UK: Routledge.

Malik Jamal (1996). *The Colonialization of Islam: Religious Institutions in Pakistan.* Delhi, India.

Malik, Iftikhar Haider (1999). *Islam, Nationalism, and the West: Issues of Identity in Pakistan* Basingstoke, Hampshire [England]: Macmillan in association with St Anthony's College, Oxford; New York: St. Martin's Press.

Mamdani, Mahmood (2004). *Good Muslim, Bad Muslim: America, the Cold War and the Roots of Terror*. New York: Pantheon.
Marty, Martin and R. Scott Appleby (1994). *Fundamentalisms Observed*. Chicago: University of Chicago Press.
Masud, Enver. (2000) *The War on Islam*. Arlington, VA: Madrassah Books.
Mehdi, Syed Sikander (1992). 'Islam and Nonviolence.' *Gandhi Marg: Journal of the Gandhi Peace Foundation*. Vol. 14, No. 1, April–June 1992.
Mehran, Golnar (2003). The Paradox of Tradition and Modernity in Female Education in the Islamic Republic of Iran. *Comparative Education Review*, Vol. 47, pp. 269–86.
Menocal, Maria Rosa (2002). *Ornament of the World: How Muslims, Christians and Jews Created a Culture of Tolerance in Mediaeval Spain*. Boston MA; Little Brown and Company.
Merry, Michael S. and Geert Driessen (2005). Islamic Schools in Three Western Countries: Policy and Procedure. *Comparative Education*. v41 n4, pp. 411–32.
Merry, Michael S. (2005). Should Educators Accommodate Intolerance? Mark Halstead, Homosexuality, and the Islamic Case. *Journal of Moral Education*, vol. 34 n1, pp. 19–36, Mar.
Metcalf, Barbara Daly (1982). *Islamic revival in British India: Deoband, 1860-1900*, Princeton, N.J.: Princeton University Press.
Metcalf, Barbara (2002). *Traditional Islamic Activism: Deoband, Tablighis and Talibs*. New York NY: Social Science Research Council.
Metzger, Scott Alan (2005). The Kingdom of Heaven: Teaching the Crusades Social Education, v69 n5, p. 256.
Mir, Amir (2006). *The True Face of Jehadis: Inside Pakistan's Network of Terror*. New Delhi, India: Lotus Collection, Roli Books.
Mirza, Younus (2005). 'An American Islamic Education.' *Islamic Horizons*, September/October.
Mitchell, Timothy (1991). *Colonizing Egypt*. Berkeley CA: University of California Press.
Musharraf, Pervez (2006). *In the Line of Fire*. New York: Simon and Schuster.
Musharraf, Pervez (2004). 'A Plea for Enlightened Moderation.' *Washington Post*, 1 June.
Muslim Parliament of Great Britain (2006). *Child Protection in Faith-based Environments*. London UK: The Muslim Institute Trust.
Mustafa, Danish (2002). To each according to his power? Participation, access and vulnerability in irrigation and flood management in Pakistan. *Environment and Planning D: Society and Space*, vol. 20, pp. 737–52.
Muzaffar, Chandra (2003). *Muslims, Dialogue, Terror*. Selangor, Malaysia: International Movement for a Just World.
Nasr, Vali (1995). *The Vanguard of Islamic Revolution: The Jammaat-e-Islami of Pakistan*. London: IB Tauris.
Naylor, R.T. (2006). *Satanic Purses: Money, Myth and Misinformation in the War on Terror*. Montreal: McGill-Queens University Press.
Nayyar, A.H. and Ahmed Salim (2004). Subtle Subversion: The State of Curricula and Textbooks in Pakistan. Islamabad: Sustainable Development Policy Institute (SDPI).

Nelson, Matthew J. (2006). Muslims, Markets and the meaning of a 'good' education in Pakistan. *Asian Survey*, Vol. 46, No. 5, pp. 699–720.

Nizami, Farhan Ahmad. (1983) *Madrassahs, Scholars and Saints: Muslim Response to the British Presence in Delhi and the Upper Doab 1803–57*. Dissertation: Thesis (Ph.D.) Oxford.

Noor, Farish (2006). The difficult path of progressive Islam today. *The Daily Times* (Pakistan), 6 October p. 3.

Noor, Farish (2004). 'Why I Aint No Moderate Muslim.' 30 July posted on http://www.islaminterfaith.org Accessed, 20 April 2005.

Otaky, D. (2006). Reflection 'On' and 'In' Teacher Education in the United Arab Emirates. *International Journal of Educational Development*, v26 n1, pp. 111–122.

Pape, Robert (2005). *Dying to Win: The Strategic Logic of Suicide Terrorism*. New York: Random House.

Pirzada, Sayyid A.S. (2000). *The Politics of the Jamiat Ulama-i-Islam Pakistan 1971–77*. Karachi: Oxford University Press.

Pohl, Florian (2006). Islamic education and civil society: reflections on the Pesantren tradiation in contemporary Indonesia. *Contemporary Education Review*, Vol. 50, no. 3, pp. 389–409.

Rahman, Khalid and Syed Rashad Bukhari (2006). Pakistan: Religious education and institutions. *Muslim World*, Vol. 96, April, pp. 323–339.

Rahman, Tariq (2004). *Denizens of Alien Worlds: A Study of Education Inequality and Polarization in Pakistan*. Karachi: Oxford University Press.

Rahman, Tariq (2004). *The Madrassah and the State of Pakistan. Religion, Poverty and the Potential for Violence in Pakistan*. http://www.himalmag.com/2004/february/essay.htm

Ramadan, Tariq (2007). *In the Footsteps of the Prophet*. New York: Oxford University Press.

Raman, J. Sri (2004). Of Figures And Indian Fascists. *Countercurrents*, 13 September.

Rashid, Ahmed (2000). *The Taliban*. New Haven CT: Yale University Press.

Richardson, Patricia M. (2004). Possible Influences of Arabic-Islamic Culture on the Reflective Practices Proposed for an Education Degree at the Higher Colleges of Technology in the United Arab Emirates. *International Journal of Educational Development*, v24 n4, pp. 429–436 July.

Riaz, Ali (2005). *Global jihad, Sectarianism and the Madrassahs in Pakistan*. Singapore: Institute for Defence and Strategic Studies.

Robinson, Francis (2001). *Spiritual Middlemen: The Ulama of Farangi Mahal and Islamic Culture in South Asia*. New Delhi: Oxford University Press.

Roy, Olivier (2001). *Neo-fundamentalism*. New York: Social Science Research Council.

Rushdie, Salman (2005). The Right Time for an Islamic Reformation. *Washington Post*, 7 August.

Sageman, Marc (2004). *Understanding Terrorist Networks*. Philadelphia: University of Pennsylvania Press.

Sanyal, Usha (1996). *Devotional Islam and Politics in British India: Ahmad Riza Khan Barelwi and His Movement, 1870–1920*. Delhi: Oxford University Press.

Saqib, G. N. (1983). *Modernization of Muslim education in Egypt, Pakistan, and Turkey: A Comparative Study* (1st Pakistan ed.). Lahore: Islamic Book Service.

Schabas, William (2000). 'Hate Speech in Rwanda: The Road to Genocide.' *McGill Law Journal*, November.
Sen, Amartya (2006). *Identity and Violence: The Illusion of Destiny*. New York: Norton.
Shaikh, M. A. (1995). *Sindh Madrassah: A journey through Times*. Karachi: Sindh Madressatul Islam.
Shapiro, Samantha M. (2006). 'Ministering to the upwardly mobile Muslim.' *The New York Times Magazine*, 30 April.
Shehzad, Mohammad (2004). 'The Terrorist Next Door.' *The Hindustan Times*, 24 August.
Sikand, Yoginder (2005). *Bastions of the Believers*. New Delhi: Penguin India.
Sikand, Yoginder (2004). *Sacred Spaces: Traditions of Shared Faith in India*. New Delhi: Penguin Global.
Sikand, Yoginder (2001). *The Origins and Development of the Tablighi Jamat*. New Delhi: Orient Longman.
Singer, Peter, W. (2001) *Pakistan's Madrassahs: Ensuring a System of Education not Jihad*. http://www.brookings.edu/views/papers/singer/20020103.htm
Saeed, Javaid. (1994) *Islam and Modernization: a Comparative Analysis of Pakistan, Egypt, and Turkey*. Westport, Conn.: Praeger.
Shah, Saeeda (2006). Educational Leadership: An Islamic Perspective. *British Educational Research Journal*. v32 n3, pp. 363–385.
Siddiqa, Ayesha (2007). Explaining social schizophrenia. *The Daily Times* (Pakistan), 22 January p. 3.
Sondhi, K. S. (2002). *The Booby Trap: Anthology of Islamic Extremism*. New Delhi: Chanakya.
Stern, Jessica (2004). *Pakistan's Drift into Extremism: Allah, the Army and America's War on Terror*. New York: M.E. Sharpe.
Syed, Anwar Hussain (1982). *Pakistan Islam, Politics, and National Solidarity*. New York: Praeger Publishers.
Tellis, Ashley (2004).'US Strategy: Assisting Pakistan's Transformation.' *The Washington Quarterly*, 28:1, pp. 97–116.
Terzieff, Juliette (2004). 'Pakistan's inner battle for education reform.' *San Francisco Chronicle*, 30 May.
Titus, Murray Thurston (1959). *Islam in India and Pakistan; a Religious History of Islam in India and Pakistan*. Calcutta: YMCA Pub. House.
Tripp, Charles (2006). *Islam and the Moral Economy: The Challenge of Capitalism*. Cambridge UK: Cambridge University Press.
United Nations Educational Scientific and Cultural Organization (UNESCO) (2006). *Volunteerism and Universal Primary Education: The Role of Madrassahs in Education*. Islamabad: UNESCO.
Van den Brink, Rogier et al. (2006). *Consensus, Confusion and Controversy: Selected Land Reform issues in Sub-Saharan Africa*. Washington DC: The World Bank.
Vahab, Fazal. (2001) *Mullah ka Kirdar*. Minglor, Savat.
Verkaaik, Oskar (2004). *Migrants and Militants: Fun and Urban Violence in Pakistan*. Princeton NJ: Princeton University Press.
Wasey, Akhtarul ed. (2005). *Madrassahs in India: Trying to be Relevant*. New Delhi: Global Media Publications.

Weaver, Mary Anne (1995). 'Children of the Jihad.' *The New Yorker*, 12 June, pp. 40–47.

Wright, Robin (1995). 'The Islamist's Theory of Relativity'. *The Los Angeles Times*, 27 January p. 3.

Yakas, Orestes (2001). *Islamabad: The Birth of a Capital.* Karachi: Oxford University Press.

Zahab, Miriam and Olivier Roy (2004). *Islamist Networks: the Afghan-Pakistan Connection.* New York: Columbia University Press.

Zaman, Muhammad Qasim (2002). *The Ulama in Contemporary Islam: Custodians of Change.* Princeton NJ: Princeton University Press.

Zaman, Muhammad Qasim (2007). 'Competing Conceptions of Religious Education.' In Heffner and Zaman eds. Op.cit.

INDEX

A

Aaliya madrassah, 106
Abbas, Mureed, 166
Abdalla, Amr, 171
Abd-ar-Rahman, 4
Abduh, Muhammad, 152-153
Abdullah, Muhammad, 173
Abrahamic faiths, 119
Abu Huraira, 17
Abu-Nimer, Mohammed, 165
Abyssinia, 156
Afghan war, 179
Afghanistan, 17, 20, 26, 31-32, 55, 132, 142
Aga Khan, 38
Aga Khan Examination Board, 39, 65
Aga Khan Foundation, 97
Aga Khan Rural Support Programme, 39
Aga Khan University, 39, 65, 112
agricultural productivity, 58
Ahle Hadith/Salafi, 26, 35, 47, 51
Ahle-Suffa, 17
Ahmad, Akbar S., 13
Ahmad, Mumtaz, 94
Ahmad, Qazi Hussain, 64, 128
Ahmad, Sheikh Rashid, 64
Ahmed, Anis, 41, 70, 89
Ahmed, Khaled, 87
Ahmed, Khurshid, 41
Ahmed, Mumtaz, 154
Ahmed, Samina, 40
Ahmed, Sayyed, 37
Ahmedi, 30, 35
Ahmedpur City, 44-50, 77
AIDS, 145
Aitchison College, x
Akbar (Mughal emperor), 20
Al Muwahhid, 4
Algeria, 159
Alhambra, 5
Alhurra TV, 132
Ali, Shaukat, 41
Ali, Syed Babar, 90
Aligarh Muslim University, 22
Alim, 108
Al-Jama'a Al-Islamiya, 159
Al-Jazeera, 141, 163
Alpetragius (al-Bitruji), 19
al-Qaeda, 70, 136, 146, 158
Al-Rasheed Trust, 85
Al-Sharq al-Awsat, 146
Anwar, Ghazala, 11
Arab-Israeli conflict, 8, 17, 131, 150, 156
Arafat, Yassir, 161
Arif-ul-Husseini, 78
Armenians, 156
Arquilla, John, 143
Arzachel (al-Zarqali), 19
Asia-Pacific Center for Security Studies, 140
Association of Physicians of Pakistani Descent in North America, 162
astronomy, 20
Athna-Ashri, 38
Avenzoar (Ibn Zuhr), 19
Averroes (Ibn Rushd), 18, 152
Avicenna, 162
awqaf, 16, 25, 28
Ayatollah, 9
Azam, Tariq, 63
Aziz, Abdul, 63, 172
Azzam, Abdullah, 40

B

Badawi, Abdullah Ahmad, 119
Baghdad, 4
Bahai, 75, 164
Bahawalpur, 45, 55, 77
Bahr-al-Ulam, Abdul Ali, 92
Balaghat (figure of speech), 20
Balfour declaration, 156
Bali bombings, 121

INDEX

Balochistan, 26, 102, 124, 126
Bangladesh, 16, 29, 98, 106, 132, 165, 177
Bareilvi, 26, 35, 47, 51, 72
Bareilvi organizations, 85
Benard, Cheryl, 134
Bergen, Peter, 13, 132
Bhagwandas, Rana, 80
Bhattarai, Baburam, 88
Bhutto, Benazir, 34, 43, 179
Bhutto, Zulfikar Ali, 29, 78
bidat, 140
Bin Laden, Osama, 40, 100, 134, 138, 146, 156
bin Mawiya, Ali, 84
bin Muawiya, Yazid, 35
Bin Ziad, Tarik, 109
Binori Town madrassah (different from Jamiah Binoria), 85-86, 165
Bohra, 38
Bosnia, 145
Branch Davidians, 176
Brezinski, Zbigniew, 32
Buner valley, 62
Burhanuddin, 38
Bush, George W., 134,138, 150

C

Cairo, 91
Calcutta madrassah, 21
Campus Watch, 9
Canada, 165
castes, 81
Centre for Islamic Pluralism, 151
Centre for Pesantren and Democracy Studies, 122
Centre for Strategic and International Studies, 178
Chanigoth, 48, 56
Chechniya, 139, 143
China, 132, 142, 174
Chomsky, Noam, 150
Christendom, 138
Christianity, 35, 157
Christians, 8, 39, 41, 81, 146
Churchill, Ward, 9, 12
CIA, 142
CILC, 8
Clinton administration, 176

Cold War, 142
Commission on the terrorist attacks of September 11, 2001 (9/11), 13
Congo, 130
conspiracy factor, 141
conspiracy theories, 5-6
Costa Rica, 165
Coulson, Andre, 13
Council of Islamic Ideology, 29-30, 42
Council on Islamic Education, 165
Criminal Investigation Department, xii
Crises Management Cell, xii
critical thinking skills, 7

D

Daily Jasarat, 113
Dalrymple, William, 14
Damascus, 4
Darfour, 147
Darri, 32
Dars-e-Nizami, 20, 23, 36, 109
Dar-ul-Ulum and Deoband, 22
Da'wah Academy, 5
Dawkin, Richard, 151
Deobandi, 26, 35-36, 47, 50, 53, 63, 92, 109
Dera Nawab, 48
Devji, Faisal, 87
Dhaka Aaliya madrassah, 40
Doxiadis, Constantinos, 59
Druze, 35
Dur-ul-Uloom Haqqania, 34

E

Ebadi, Shirin, 162
economic inequality, 158
Effendy, Bahtiar, 11
Egypt, 16, 18, 103, 132-133, 144, 159
Ejaz-ul-Haq, 64
El Fadl, Khaled Abou, 10, 12
Elbaredei, 162

F

fann, 114
Farangi Mahal of Lucknow, 20, 22, 92, 109
Faridiyah, 24

INDEX

fasad, 165
Fascism, 138
FATA, 111
Fatimid, 18
fatwa, 120, 141
FBI, 33
feudal elite, 158
Fiqah, 18
Fiqh (jurisprudence or Islamic law), 19, 108
fitnah, 76, 140
France, 132
The Frontier Post, 177
Fukuyama, Francis,159
Furqania Madrassah, 16

G

Gandhi, Mohandas, 69, 144
Gandhi, Rajiv, 88
Gandhian approach, 7
Garang, John, 147
Geo TV, 141, 163
Georgetown University, 10
Ghazi, Abdul Aziz, 172
Ghazi, Abdul Rashid, 172
Ghazi, Mahmood Ahmed, 41
Ghazi, Mehmood Ali, 105
Ghazni, 19
Ghifari, Abu Zar, 17
Ghosh, Vishvas, 82
Gilgit, 39
Gingrich, Newt, 138, 150
Goldberg, Jeffrey, 13
Gould, Stephen Jay, 148
Granada, 5
Gujranwala, 80
Gul, Hamid, 31, 42, 64

H

Hadith, 18
Haider, Moin-uddin, 105
Haidry Mosque, 126
Haj, 102
Haji, Moulavi Chalilakath Muhammad, 152
Halepota, A.W.J., 31
Halstead, J.M., 3
Hamdard Foundation, 116

Haq, Samiul, 64
Haqqani, Hussain, 172
Haqqania madrassah, 150
Harijans, 81
Harkat-al-Ansar, 47
Harkat-ul-Mujahideen, 85
Harley, A.H., 40
Harmain Islamic Foundation, 37
The Harvard Crimson, 10
Hashmi, Farhat, 118
Hashmi, Naveed Masood, 86
Hassan, Riffat, 126
Hassan-al-Turabi, 146
Hastings, Warren, 21
Hayee, Hakim Sayed Abdul, 19
Hidayat-ul-Muslimin Sangham, 153
Hindu, 65, 82, 86, 103, 115
Hindu-Muslim riots, 137
Hindutva, 143-144
hirabah, 165
Hizb-al-Tahrir, 175
Holland, Samuel, 133
Hoodhbhoy, Pervez, 155
Hudaibiyah, 70
Huffaz-e-Qur'an, 16
Human Development Foundation, 97
Hunza, 39
Hussain, 35
Hussain, Aamer Liaqat, 63
Hussain, Shujaat, 64
Hussein, Saddam, 138, 142

I

Iberia, 4
Idaara Minhaj-ul-Qur'an, 129
Ijaz-ul-Haq, Muhammad, 126, 172
ijtihad, 18, 21, 40, 140, 152
ilm, 114
imams, 16
India, 17, 98, 116, 143
Indian madrassah, 99
Indonesia, 11, 79, 120, 132, 135, 177
Institute for Policy Studies, 27, 41, 71
International Centre for Religion and Diplomacy, 165, 180
International Crisis Group, 14, 29, 68
internet, 89
intifada, 9
Iqbal, Muhammad, 24

210 INDEX

Iran, 88, 136, 152, 154
Iranian Revolution, 79
Iraq, 132, 142, 154
Irfan, Ghazala, 169
irtadad (apostasy), 63
Islamabad, 58, 101-102, 106
Islamabad Capital Territory, 51, 110
Islami Jamiat-e-Talba, 113
Islamic Cultural, Educational, and Scientific Organization, 164
Islamic Relief, 92
Islamic Shariah Court, 167
Islamic State University, 11
Islamic University, 5, 105, 128
Islami-Jamiat-Tulaba, 154
Islamiyat, 31
Islamization, 30
Islamo-fascism, 138
Ismailis, 38
Israel, 17, 131, 140, 150, 157
Istanbul, 91

J

Jaish-e-Mohammad, x, 47, 85
Jalal, Zubaida, 115
Jalandari, Haneef, 113
Jamaat Dawah, 37
Jamaat-e-Islami, 22-23, 28-29, 70, 87, 93, 154, 168
Jamal-al-Din, 92
Jamal-uddin-Afghani, 152
Jami'at ul-Falah, 118, 136
Jami'at-i-'Ulama-i-Islam Pakistan, 129
Jami'at-us-Salihat, 118
Jamia Ashrafia, 94
Jamia Hafsa, 174
Jamia Millia Islamiyah, 136
Jamia Salafia, 93
Jamiaat-e-Ulama-Pakistan, 37
Jamiat-e-Ulama Islam, 93
Jamiya Islamiyah, 128
Jandullah, 87
Japanese, 133, 142
Jerusalem, 91-92
Jews, 4, 8, 9, 18, 41, 65, 86, 115, 122, 139, 146
Jhang, 55, 78
Jhangvi, Haq Nawaz, 78

jihad fi-al-nafs, 69
jihad, 70, 74, 165
jihadi literature, 83
jihadists, 32
Jinnah, Mohammad Ali, 17, 27
Johar, Muhammad Ali, 41, 155
Johnston, Douglas, 171
Judaism, 35, 157
just-war theory, 68

K

Kalam (scholasticism), 19
Kandhlawi, Muhammad Ilyas, 25
Karachi, 106, 126
Karakoram, 39
karkun, 168
Karzai, Hamid, 5, 42
Kashmir, 17, 26, 74, 139, 143
Kayranwai, Rahmat Allah, 99
Kefaya ('Enough'), 144
Kenya, 98, 133
Kerala Aikya Sangham, 153
Kerala Jami'at-ul'Ulama, 153
Kerner Commission, 6
Khadija, 91
Khair-ul-Madaaris, 113
Khaldun, Ibn, 109, 119
Khaled, Amr, 164
khalifa (vicegerent), 120
Khalilzad, Zalmay, 150
Khan, Abdul Ghaffar, 69
Khan, Ahmed Raza, 36
Khan, Ayub, 28
Khan, Badshah, 177
Khan, Sir Syed Ahmed, 22, 152
Khan, Zafar, 38
Khanewal, 55
Kharijite, 4, 12
Khilafat Movement, 22
Khuda kay liyay, 179
Kirman, Ahmed Saeed, 81
Kohistan, 62
Kolkotta Madrassah College, 40
Korea, 142
Kosovo, 145
kufr (heresy), 77
Kyrgyzstan, 132

INDEX

L

Lahore University of Management Sciences, 90, 92
Lajnat-ul-Muhammadiya Sangham, 153
Lashkar-i-Tayyaba, 37, 75, 85, 155
Lawrence, T.E., 14
Lebanon, 16, 164
Leitner, G.W., 21
Libya, 43
Little Mosque on the Prairie, 164
Livelihood Enhancement and Peace, 145
Lucknow, 20, 22-23, 109

M

Madagascar, 132
Madinat-uz-Zehra, 4-5
Madjid, Nurcholish, 122
Madni, Husayn Ahmad, 22
Madrasa-i-A'zam, 22
Madrassah Education Board, 83, 106
Madrassah Firozi, 19
Madrassah Islamia Shams ul-'Ulum, 36
Madrassah Reform Strategy, 104, 107, 124
Mahfouz, Naguib, 162
Mai, Mukhtaran, 166
Maimonides, 4
Majlis-e-Shura, 31
Maktab, 15, 117
Maktab-al-Khidmat, 40
Malabar Muslim Educational Association, 153
Malaysia, 80, 119, 135
Mamdani, Mahmood 32
Manshera, 62
Mansoora, 93
Mantiq (logic), 19-20
Maoists of Nepal, 158
Markaz-al-Dawah-al-Irshad, 37, 75, 165
Markaz-ul-Mar'rif Education and Research Center, 117
Marker, Jamshed, 80
maslak, 35, 39
Mathematics, 20
Maudoodi, Syed Abuala 22-23, 158
Mazahir-ul-Ulum, 25
McVeigh, Timothy, 176
media, role in conflict, 83

Merry, Michael S., 3
Metcalfe, Barbara, 25
Middle East Partnership Initiative, 131
Ministry of Interior, Education, and Religious Affairs, 107
minorities, 79
Mobutu, 142
Mohajir Qaumi Movement (MQM), 39
Mohammad, Mahathir, 119
Moro National Liberation Front (MNLF), 145
Morocco, 4, 16, 164
Mortenson, Greg, 180
Moulavi, Vakkam Muhammad 'Abdul Qadir, 153
Mu'az-ibn Jabal, 17
Muaawiya, 12
Mughals, 20-21
Muhaddis, Shah Waliullah, 20
Muhaddis, Shaikh Abdul Haque, 20
Muhammad, (Prophet), 15, 17, 69, 86, 156
Muhammadiyah, 121
Mullah Nizamuddin (Nizam-al-din Muhammad), 20, 109
Mullah Umar, 34
Multan, 38, 55, 113
munafiq, 140
Murbarak, Hosni, 144
Muridke, 37, 165
Murphy, Dervla, 178
murtad, 76
Musa bin Nusair, 4
Musa, Mohammad Alam, 122
Musharraf, 27-28, 65, 75, 80, 82, 105, 127, 134, 167
Muslim Brotherhood in Egypt, 75, 146
Muslim Mahajana Sabha, 153
Muslims Against Terrorism, 150
Muslim World Outreach strategy, 131
muttafiq, 168
Muttahida Majlis-e-Amal (MMA), 115, 131
Muzaffar, Chandra, 147

N

Nadwat-ul-Ulama, 23, 114
Nadwi, Abu'l-Hassan Ali, 23
Nahdlatul Ulama (NU, Indonesia), 121

Naipaul, VS, 156
Najam, Adil, 96
Nasir, Timotheous, 80
Nation of Islam, 35
National Security Council, 105
Naushera Jadid, 48, 51, 77
Naval Postgraduate School, 130
Nawa-i-Haq, 129
Nepal, 88
New Zealand, 12
NGOs, 83, 153
Nigeria, 132, 145
nizam-i Mustafa, 158
Nizamiyah, 18
Nizam-ul-Mulk, 18
Nobel Prize, 161
Noor, Farish, 135, 147
Northern Ireland, 136
Northwest Frontier Province (NWFP), 62, 102, 108, 124, 131, 150
Numani, Shibli, 23
Nurani Madrassah, 16

O

Obama, Barack, 121
Orientalists, 22
Operation Cyclone, 42
Ottoman caliphate, 156

P

Pakistan Centre for Philanthropy, 96-97
Pakistan Islamic Medical Association, 87
Pakistan Madrassah Education Board, xii
Pakistan Movement, 22
Pakistan Muslim League, 34
Pakistani Masihi League, 81
Palestine, 92, 159
Palestinian territories, 140
Pamuk, Orhan, 162
panchayat, 166
Pandey, Swati, 13
Paramadina University, 122
Parsis (Zoroastrians), 81
Partai Kebangkitan Bangsa (PKB), 120
Pashto, 32
Pathans, 69, 177
peace education, 165
Pearl, Daniel, x, 43, 47

Persian, 108
Peru, 158
Pesantren, 11
Pesantren Lingkungan Giri Ilmu, 121
Peshawar, 33, 136, 177-178
philanthropic donations, 96
Philippines, 145
Pir Karam Shah, 125
Pope, Alexander, 9
pseudo-science, 170
psychological research, 1
Punjab, 107

Q

Qadir, Asghar, 116
Qadiri, Tahirul, 129
Qaris, 16
Qasimi, Isar, 78
Qazi, Javed Ashraf, 112, 114
Qubacha, Nasiruddeen, 19
Quomi madrassahs (Bangladesh), 106
Qur'an, 165, 177
Quraishi, Asifa, 10
Qutb, Syed, 99, 158
Qutbist, 99

R

Rabin, Yitzhak, 143
Rabita, 111
Rabita Aalam-e-Islami (Muslim World League), 99
Rabita Madaaris, 28
Radio Sawa, 132
Rahimi, Sahibzada Babar Farooq, 113
Rahman, Tariq, 109
Raiwind, 25
Ramadan, Tariq, 137
Raman, J. Sri, 144
Rand Corporation, 134
Rasheed, Ghazi Abdul, 63
Razzaq, Maulvi Abdul, 166
Red Army Faction, 158
Red Brigades, 158
Red Mosque, 172
Rehman, Ataur, 87
Rehman, Fazlur, 34, 64
Rehman, S.M., 128

INDEX

Religious Peace Research Organization, 141
rizq, 2
rukn, 168
Rumsfeld, Donald H., 143
Rushdie, Salman, 150
Rwandan genocide, 83, 161

S

Saadat, Anwar, 161
Sadaqa and *Khairat*, 96
Saeed, Hafiz Mohammad, 38, 113, 155
Sagan, Carl, 148
Sageman, Marc, 14
Salafi, 154
Salam, Abdus, 161
Sami-ul-Haq, 34, 42
Sarf and *Nawha* (Arabic grammar), 19
Sargodha, 125
Saudi Arabia, 37, 98, 131, 136, 154, 159
Sawlatiyya, 99
Sayyaf, Abdurrab Rasul, 5
Schaeffer, Teresita, 178
Seerat, 108
Sen, Amartya, xii
Sendero Luminoso, 158
sexual abuse, 67
Shafai, Imam, 71
Shah Waliullah, 21
Shah, Syed Tauqir Hussain, x
shahadat (martyrdom), 115
Shaikh, Ahmed Omar S. x, 43
sharafatnma, 21
Shariati, Ali, 152
Sharif, Nawaz, 34
Sharif, Shahbaz, 105
Shia, 18, 26, 35, 38, 45, 47, 53, 64, 78, 154, 160
Shia-Sunni conflict, 136
Shirazi, Mir Fathullah, 20
Shuja, Hakim Ahmed, 24, 41
Siddiqa, Ayesha, 45
Siddiqui, Muhammad Hassan, 86
Sierra Leone, 8
Sihah-e-Sitta (six most authentic Hadith books), 20
Sihalvi, Mullah Nizam Uddin, 22
Sikand, Yoginder, 116, 127
Sikh, 41, 81
Sindh, 82
Singapore, 122
Sipah-e-Sahaba, x, 45, 50, 78
Siraj, Qazi Minhaj, 19
The SITE Institute (The Search for International Terrorist Entities), 84
The Societies Act of 1860, 106
Somalia, 145
Soroush, Abdol Karim, 155
South Asian Association for Regional Cooperation (SAARC), 82
Spain, 4, 18
Spanish inquisitions, 5
Sprenger, Aloys, 40
Sri Lanka, 88
Students Islamic Movement of India, 155
Sudan, 146
Sudanese Peoples Liberation Movement, 146
suicide bombings, 88
Sukkur, 106
Sulamani Bohras, 38
Sunna, 18
Sunni, 26
Sustainable Development Policy Institute (SDPI), 115
Swat, 62, 178
Syria, 92

T

ta'lim, 2
Tablighi Jama'at, 25, 75
ta-dib, 2
Tafseer of Qu'ran, 19
Taj, Farhat, 67
Tajikistan, 98, 165, 177
Tajvid, 108
Talib, Ali Ibn-e-Abi, 35
Taliban, 42
Tanmiyath-ul- 'Ulum Madrassah, 153
Tanzania, 98, 133, 145
Tanzim Abna-ul-adim, 110
Tanzim al Madaaris-al-Arabiya, 28
taqlid, 152
taqwa, 36
tarbiya, 2
Tariq-bin-Ziad, 4
Tasawwuf (mysticism), 19
Tehrik Jafferia Pakistan, 45

214 INDEX

Tehrik Nifaz-e-Shariah Mohammadi, 34
Tehrik-e-Jaffria, 78
Tehrik-e-Tahuffuz-e-Khatam-e-Nabuwat, 30
Thailand, 139
Three Cups of Tea, 180
Tib (medical science), 20
tribalism, 157
Turkey, 79, 92, 134, 156, 159
Turki-al-Faisal, 100
Turkmenistan, 132

U

Ubada-ibn-Samit, 17
Uch Sharif, 48, 51, 77
Uganda, 98
Ulama, 16, 18, 30, 120, 141
Umayyads, 4, 35
ummah, 29
Unabomber, 88
UNESCO, 155
UNICEF, 7, 44
United Arab Emirates, 151, 164
United Kingdom, 67, 92
United Nations, 1, 86, 120, 177
United States, 134
United States Institute of Peace, xii
University of Dawah, 5
University of Nebraska, 32
University of Punjab, 74
Unocal, 42
Urdu, 16
ur-Rahman, Qari Naseem, 136
USAID, 124, 131-133, 145
Usmani, Muhammad Taqi, 2, 41
Usul-e-Fiqh (principles of Islamic jurisprudence), 19
Uthmani, Shabbir Ahmed, 23

V

Vehari, 55
Venezuela, 132

vocational training, 158
Voluntary Registration and Regulation Ordinance 2002, 107

W

Waco, Texas, 176
Wahabbi, 12, 26, 37, 98
Wahid, Abdulrrahman, 120
waqf, 91, 103
West Bengal, xii
Wiesel, Elie, 149
Wifaq al Madaaris al Arabiya, 28
Wifaq al Madaaris-al-Salafia, 28
Wifaq al Madaaris-al-Shia, 28
wifaqs, 28-29, 31, 111
wifaq-ul-madaaris, 108, 133
Wifaq-ul-Madaaris, 176
World Bank, 14, 40
World Social Forum, 10
World Trade Organization, 128

X

X-Files, 142

Y

Yemen, 103
Yousef, Ramzi, 5
Yousef, Shaikh Hamza, 171
Yunus, Muhammad, 161

Z

Zahid-ul-Rashidi, 127, 129
Zaid-bin-Arqam, 17
Zakat, 31, 43, 49, 100-101
Zawahry, Aimen, 88
Zaytuna Academy, 164
Zewail, Ahmed, 161
Zia-ul-Haq, 3, 30, 33, 62, 101,126